PETER HAINES
& CLIVE BIRCH

YOU THINK
WE'RE ALONE?

Summoned by unseen Energies ...
One Man's Spiritual Journey Challenging
Conventional Views of Our World

First published in the United Kingdom in 2023 by
The Cloister House Press

ISBN 978-1-913460-65-5

Also By Peter Haines

The Clarion Resource
A Matter Of Public Interest
Priory

Dedicated to the memory of Mel Robson
for his selflessness and his final gift.

Contents

Forward

*Clive Birch considers the synchronicity that
brought the two writers together and
the 'rhythm' of the book.*

How 'odd' it was that Pete's path and mine crossed again after so long. 'Odd?' Well, maybe. From a different perspective, though, perhaps it was inevitable.

Peter Haines and I have put so much of our creativity, time, enthusiasm, yes and love, into this book that it has taken on a life of its own. As Pete said at the outset of this writing adventure, it will take on a life of its own. He wasn't wrong.

The writing process could neither be rushed, nor slowed. If we tried to do either the 'book entity' would speed us on our way or apply the brakes in order to re-establish its natural rhythm. It has become a consciousness in its own right. Life has been breathed into it. By 'book entity' I mean the combined energies of all those beings that have been put into the melting pot to create these pages.

The process of reviewing, reflecting and assisting in writing some of the passages of this book has had considerable emotional and internal impact on me personally; me being Clive Birch. It feels as though the adventures and ideas that are being recounted are bringing to fruition or closure the events, contacts, people and that this process must be completed before I can move on with the next phase of my life.

A Shamanic friend recently told me of Carlos Castenada in his book 'Book of Dreaming'. He calls this process of reflecting and review, recapitulation. To do this, the energy body is filled by drawing back the energy given out to people throughout ones life. I don't fully understand this but it resonates with me.

In retrospect, the spiritual and mystical path along which I trod, and on which I sometimes stumbled, has given me the opportunity to work with elements of my being that otherwise would have been left untouched and undeveloped. This process brings to the surface elements which continue to surprise, even amaze. It enables me to unload and leave behind. This has been going on since 1971.

What the book is doing is helping me to speed up the rate at which I have the opportunity to move the process forward.

I had originally given my text for the book a working title of 'footsteps through time... the story so far'. At this point I hoped the reader would yell, "Why?" As the pages are turned and my wanderings and many past lifetimes are explained, all will become clearer. One of my visionary contacts recently had a vision of me leading a camel through the desert. I do like this image of me. After reflection with Pete we decided on the present title. My natural reserve, at first, resisted the apparent egotistical perspective. Pete with his usual practical approach said, "Deal with it!" which is what I am doing. Perhaps hiding ones light under a bushel does not always serve the bigger picture.

Clive Birch
Cheltenham
September 2007

Introduction

Some acknowledgments, some thanks, some apologies and some clarification.

Clive Birch and I have just completed the final proof for this book. What a journey of discovery; and discomfort, and challenge, and frustration, but what fun? It has dawned on me that there are some apologies to make. During my last reading I became aware that I had failed to convey the essence of the real man. The text does little to advise of the true nature of Clive; a man of great warmth and generosity, humour and compassion. He is someone who has little problem challenging conventions, and has so little need to fit in with the rest of us as we happily live our lives in our boxes predetermined by the societies in which we find ourselves. So, Clive for this failure, my apologies.

But my thanks also. I turned to many sources, not least Clive's diaries, unstructured though they are. Without them the daunting task of preparing a biography would have been so much more difficult. And some more thanks. While I pestered and challenged him for months on end, never once did he not respond with information, patience and tolerance. When I said, "Well, yeah, Clive, great, but just what is it that you do? What are you?" In answer, I reproduce his written reply.

My friend and co-writer asked me to sum up my work, as background to this book. What was interesting immediately was that I didn't have a precise definition of what I do. I think this is because I am more interested in what I am and what I am becoming.

This may sound trite and presumptuous but my major interest in this life is working from my soul awareness. Everything else flows from it, mental, emotional and physical consciousnesses are referenced to my soul awareness. So any projects, journeys, work tasks, healing that I start are based in my soul promptings that arise through my intuition which I trust absolutely. Above mental and ego promptings I will follow my intuition even if there doesn't seem a logical progression to the ideas or even if such a prompting would involve a certain amount of courage. The latter is always a challenge as said later in the text, I am not over imbued with intestinal fortitude.

So this is my personal background to what I do. If a particular pattern of activity or thinking no longer serves me then I will drop it. For creating an inner sacred space, when one element is dropped and another is yet to start, allows the opportunity of the soul awareness, or higher self to express itself, to fill the space and lead me to where I need to be.

And while I am doing I have a lot of fun!

So thanks, mate, I've enjoyed my journey with you. And thanks to so many others to whom either Clive or I have turned to help with the preparation for this book. I hold my hand up, not quite unashamedly, and say I must have forgotten somebody, and so for that I take responsibility and apologise. But those I do recall appear now, and it is to you that Clive and I send our thanks.

First thanks go to Kate Strachen, Assistant Archivist, Met Office National Meteorological Archive, Great Moor House, Bittern Road, Sowton, Exeter EX2 7NL UNITED KINGDOM. Who would have believed that she could tell me, in no time at all, what the weather was in France on 10th June 1944. Heavens above, we were at war then, yet the record exists. There is something so very reassuringly English about that.

But it was by no means just Kate who made this book possible. Thanks also go to the French newspaper which reported on Clive's visit to Bordeaux; Alfred Ribi, 'Demons of the Inner World'; Paramahansa Yogananda, 'Autobiography of a Yogi'; Jeff Keller in 'Attitude is Everything'; Dick Sutphen, 'Earthly Purpose'; Niamh Clunes, 'The Coming of the Female Christ'; Thomas Hartrem, 'The Prophets Way'; Dr Yang, Jwing-Ming, 'Qi Gong for Health and Martial Arts'; Ted Andrews, 'Animal Speak'; Mary Carroll Nelson, 'Beyond Fear'; Rupert Sheldrake, 'The Sense of Being Stared At'; Barbara Marciniak; Mel Robson; Salvatore Quosimodo; Stephen Crane; Deepak Chopra; Jacques Rangasamy; Scott Ponting and Alexis Wilkinson Jones; Faye Williams; Audrey Sinclair; Winston Churchill; Joan and Mary Fitzgerald; Star and Willow; 'Lisa Simpson'; Monsieur Normand; Express Newspapers; Martin Kelly; Philip Beck, Oradour, Village of the

Dead. Leo Cooper Ltd; James Watson and Francis Crick; Dr Leonard Horowitz 'DNA Pirates of the Sacred Spiral'; Carl Jung; John Wesley; Beryl Sevior; Ram Dass; Bill Bryson 'The Lost Continent'; Bob Frissell, 'Something in This Book is True'; Pat Cori, 'No More Secrets, No More Lies'; The Daily Mail; and Hazel Barnes.

Finally, and big thanks to everyone at Epic Press. Thanks for all your support and patience.

Pete Haines
Tewkesbury
September 2007

The Father

The story of the tragedy in a small family and its part in another 'war to end all wars'.

Wars, for victors as well as the vanquished, are tragedies for nations; mighty tragedies. Hidden away and all but lost in those mighty tragedies are the countless personal tragedies. Their ingredients include loss, deprivation and hardship, fear, separation and grief.

And while nations bleed, the myriad of tiny, personal, family tragedies are lost. As the nation becomes brutalised and anesthetised to personal loss, those directly involved are shattered.

One, just one, of those long forgotten tragedies was about to play itself out for one small family; a dad, a mum and an infant son less than one year old.

This one small story began on 10th June 1944. A Mk XIII Mosquito sat on a runway in Southern England, its twin Merlin engines warming up.

Just four days before, the D-Day invasion of Continental Europe had started; the Normandy Landings between Cherbourg and Le Havre. The Allies were struggling to establish their bridgeheads. Berlin was still a very long way off.

Only the day before, 9th June, Allied aircraft had started operating from French airstrips. On that same day, Russia began its offensive on the Finnish front. On the following day, 11th June, the Americans would start their bombardment of Marianas and three days after that, the very first B29s would attack mainland Japan. But that was for the near future. Today was still 10th June, a day that will be remembered for generations to come. 10th June was a fateful day for the people of the French village of Oradour-sur-Glane.

This was the Saturday when the Der Führer Regiment of the 2nd Waffen-SS Panzer Division das Reich surrounded the village near Limoges. The SS butchers rounded up the inhabitants of this small, peaceful village. Most of the women and children were herded into the church. There they were burned to death. The men were killed in the streets with a brutality rare even for the SS. In all, 642 civilians lost their lives on this day. Even family pets were shot. By the time the soldiers rolled out that evening, every building, 254 of them, had been put to the torch.

The reasons for massacre are provided by Philip Beck in *Oradour, Village of the dead*.

On this day as they sat on the runway, the young crew, the pilot aged just 23 and navigator aged 28, would have been unaware of this atrocity. Their attention would have been on their de Havilland Mosquito Mk XIII. This is just one of several mysteries and inconsistencies. According to official records, at this time 151 Squadron was operating the Mk VI. Nevertheless, some insist that this was definitely the Mk XIII.

The Mosquito was designed as a fast day bomber, made of plywood of spruce and balsa. Reichsmarschall Hermann Göring had some observations regarding the aircraft. No doubt he wasn't smiling when he said, "The British, who can afford aluminum better than we can, knock together a beautiful wooden aircraft that every piano factory over there (England) is building, and they give it a speed which they have now increased yet again. What do you make of that?" Perhaps with some thoughts of nostalgia Göring also complained, "In 1940 I could at least fly as far as Glasgow in most of my aircraft, but not now! It makes me furious when I see the Mosquito. I turn green and yellow with envy."

Despite the optimism of D-day, Hitler's steel claw still held Continental Europe firmly in its bleak grasp.

By June 1944, 151 Squadron was based at Colerne in the English county of Wiltshire. Yet, this flight in Mosquito HK505, was taking off from Predannack at the tip of Cornwall. It was around midday. According to the Met Office's Archive Department the weather for this part of Cornwall on 10th June 1944 was cloudy with some patches of blue sky visible. The weather in north west France (Brittany) at 1300 GMT, the time at which HK505 was passing over, was "increasing cloud ahead of a small depression approaching from the west. WNW

Force 3-4." As the day wore on, the weather in western France was "cloudy with some rain as the depression crossed the area."

The Ministry of Defence compiled its official account based on the testimonies of those who flew on the same sortie and accounts by French Resistance. The mission was to hamper and harass reinforcements going north to reinforce the Wehrmacht in their efforts to throw the Allies back into the English Channel. HK505's target was near Bordeaux on the Gironde River on the Atlantic coast of southern France. It was close to Bordeaux when HK505 was engaged by the enemy. Locals in the village of Audenge, 40 kilometers (25 miles) west south west of Bordeaux, saw the stricken aircraft. Audenge lies on the inlet Bassin d'Arcahon.

Witnesses tell that they saw the Mosquito circling over the Chateau de Lespinasse. It was obvious that the aircraft was in difficulty. The pilot tried to land in the grounds of the chateau but overran the field, landing upside down in a reservoir. Chateau workers pulled the crew from their cockpit. It was not long before German soldiers arrived and took the injured airmen to the hospital at Salles. From there they were taken to the military hospital in Bordeaux where their injuries were tended. Sadly, both died the following day, 11th June 1944.

Both airmen were buried at Villenave D'Ornoin (St. Brise) Communal Cemetery, in the southern suburbs of Bordeaux. Tended by the Commonwealth War Graves Commission, their graves share a last resting place with six other casualties from the Second World War. The epitaph on the headstone of the dead pilot reads,

1330097 WARRANT OFFICER
T BIRCH
PILOT
ROYAL AIR FORCE
11TH JUNE 1944 AGE 23

Lying next to the grave of the pilot is the navigator, Sergeant Tickle. According to officials in the Audenges Mairie, the Mosquito still lies on its back in the salt water lake. They say that the Rolls Royce Merlin engines appear to be in good condition.

We shall return to the graveside 61 years later. It was during The Great War, 1914 to 1918, that the War Graves Commission became responsible for the maintenance of the cemeteries where British war dead were buried. Prior to their taking control, only officers were buried in individual graves, the other ranks in mass graves. The War Graves Commission changed that by ensuring that all soldiers, regardless of rank, were given individual graves thus aiding the march of democracy.

According to Birch's son, Paul, Terry was a writer with a passion for words. It also seems he was a cheerful character who loved to sing. A favourite was Lili Marlene which he sang often. Neighbours thought this odd since it was based on a German poem of 1915. Terry felt comfortable celebrating what was human about the wartime enemy. In truth the song transcended national boundaries and was sung widely in both English and in the original German by people of all races. Americans particularly liked the song as sung by the German-born actress, Marlene Dietrich.

Paul tells how the grandfather he never met went to Canada in 1941 to learn to fly at night. Back in England he was, for a while, stationed at Staverton near Gloucester. When he flew over his family home he used to waggle his wings to let his family know it was him.

He was a master of understatement and one endearing story demonstrates this. He sent a telegram to Joyce.

POSTED ABROAD. COMING SATURDAY. SHALL WE. TERRY

Shall we meant shall we marry.

Early Life

Clive awakens to his psychic nature at puberty.

England in the 1940's bore little resemblance to England of the early 21st century. 1944 was a time of austerity; of making do. Food rationing had started in January 1940 with bacon, butter and sugar. Meat soon followed in March.

To ensure children maintained their vitamin intake, the Ministry of Health ensured that children had a daily ration of milk, orange juice and cod liver oil. Agriculture Minister, Sir Reginald Dorman-Smith encouraged the nation to 'Dig for Victory'. The lawns and flower beds in private gardens were given over to growing vegetables. Likewise, parks were ploughed and planted with vegetables. It was common to see the gardens of town houses with pens for rabbits, pigs and chickens.

There were many worse places to be than Gloucester in the West of England. The county of Gloucestershire had a rich farming tradition and the people of the towns had access to perhaps a little more than others in less fortunate parts of the country. Many people in the city of Gloucester knew someone from the rural, farming communities. From time-to-time an extra couple of eggs or a few ounces of bacon and meat might arrive on the doorstep. And rabbits were not scarce.

Clothing was in short supply and the nation was urged to 'Make do and Mend.' Blankets were converted into clothes by talented mothers, while parachute silk could be fashioned into underwear. The turn-ups in men's trousers disappeared and women's skirts shortened, all in the cause of saving material. Stockings were simply not available, much to the distress of young women. No problem for the resourceful people of the beleaguered nation. The fashion conscious coloured their legs with gravy browning and eyebrow pencil provided the illusion of a seam. This was fine until it rained.

With their men far from home fighting the Nazis, it was women who laboured in the factories, odd now to think that this had an impact on the status of women. For most this was the first opportunity to earn money for themselves. Hitherto, they relied on their husbands to provide the funds.

The women of Gloucester were no exception. The Gloster Aircraft Company Limited produced Hawker Hurricanes until 1942 when it switched production to the Hawker Typhoon. On 8 April 1941, Sir Frank Whittle's Gloster E.28/39, with its turbo-jet engine, took off from Hucclecote in Gloucester on its first test flight. This formed the basis for the Gloster Meteor, the only jet to be used by the Allied Forces during World War II. The Meteor entered service at around the time Terry Birch lost his life.

The Gloucester Railway Carriage and Wagon Company contributed to the war effort, producing railway wagons to carry Churchill and Sherman tanks, Bailey bridges and Spitfire propellers. The Company maintained the finest stock of timber in Britain during World War II. Queen Mary paid two official visits to the wagon works during the conflict. In July 1941 the company started manufacturing Churchill tanks, producing 764 by 1945. In 1944 it produced the 'Whale' pivoting sections for the Mulberry harbours used after D-Day.

Gloucester factories were in full production throughout the war providing residents with a sense of purpose and employment.

Travel was hard. Petrol had been rationed since September 1939, even supposing people had cars.

To offer protection from Luftwaffe air raids, many homes had Anderson shelters in their back gardens. Made of corrugated iron and issued free to everyone earning less than £250 per annum, over 2 million shelters were installed. Gloucester was bombed on a number of occasions. Often Nazi bombers flew over the city on their flights to the industrial heartlands in the Midlands, an area so crucial to the war effort. Those bombers which had failed to locate their targets would occasionally bomb Gloucester on their return flight.

But there was an upside to this hardship and danger. Today's dieticians suggest that the diets were healthy and balanced. A community spirit grew along with the sense that everyone was in this together. Families, friends and neighbours looked out for each other, sharing their time, rations and care.

This was the England into which the young widow of Warrant Officer Terence Birch and her 11 month old son, Clive, found herself. Joyce Birch was only 25 when she became a single parent.

Joyce cared for the home, her father, Charlie, sick with heart disease and unable to work, and her infant son. In those turbulent times she struggled to create as pleasant a home environment as possible for the three men in her life; husband (until his untimely death), father and son. They lived in a Victorian terraced house in a working class district of Gloucester called Tredworth.

For as long as he can remember, Clive was aware that there were other realities over and above those he shared with his family, friends and society. As a very young child he was thumbing through a comic book. It contained images of the toppling towers of Atlantis. At once he felt a sense of connectedness to these images. This sense of connection was to play a role throughout Clive's life.

On entering puberty the action really started. Household items vanished. Sometimes they would reappear; sometimes they were gone for ever. Many small events, many hundreds of them, all added to the learning, growing and development process.

There was the handkerchief that disappeared from the bedside table only to reappear in the fuse box. The small decorative bell which sat on the mantelshelf of the fireplace would ring when no-one else was in the room. This was a bell that would need to be lifted up and shaken in order for it to ring. From the back garden there was the voice of someone calling "Clive". When investigated, no-one was there. This was particularly frightening to a young, sensitive boy. This voice was heard by several family members. Then there were numerous occasions when the household cat would stare at something or someone moving in the house. With nothing visibly out of place to anyone else, the cat's staring eyes and upraised back fur informed the family of an event in cat reality!

So everyday did these events become, Clive and Joyce personalised the incidents, attributing them to 'Danny'.

One day, they stopped. 'Danny' went quiet. 'Danny' had become such an integral part of the family's life, his antics were missed. Birch describes it now as losing a family member. It was many years later that Birch attributed Danny's activities to poltergeist phenomena. He links them to his progress through puberty.

Birch says, "For me, it seems as though this unique time in a person's life releases energies of which we have little understanding currently. I believe that it was my puberty that was releasing the energies."

The word 'poltergeist' comes from two German words, polter meaning noisy and geist meaning spirit. Poltergeist activity ranges from objects moving, bangs and crashes, voices from nowhere, objects appearing and disappearing, temperature drops and levitation of people. The world of science has a term for what we call poltergeist activity; recurrent spontaneous psychokinesis or RSPK. Poltergeists are not new. They are recorded as far back as the 12th century.

Investigators now link poltergeist activity with adolescents, especially, but by no means exclusively, with girls. Parapsychologists suggest that the sexual drive may create energies which are manifested in poltergeist activity. It may be significant that activities seem to cease when the young person has passed through puberty. However, this alone does not provide the full answer. Poltergeists have been investigated where there has been no apparent connection with pubescent people.

Sexual maladjustment in older people is cited as a cause, as are migraine and temporal lobe epilepsy. 'Cosmic forces' have also been accused. One researcher has suggested that 86% of all poltergeist activity is experienced by families which have recently moved into local authority housing. Whatever the cause, poltergeist activity is not at all uncommon. One is hard pressed to talk to anyone who is unable to recount experiences of their own, or experiences that have happened to close members of their families. But there does seem to be a consistency amongst the confusion. RSPK is associated with those who are experience intense traumatic events like puberty, loss and bereavement, unwelcome changes, house moves, job moves and financial worries.

Birch says, "Perhaps psychic activity, for that's what poltergeist seems to be, is caused by natural laws of which we are as yet unaware. After all, aren't physical laws those for which we have discovered the rules? If we could harness these energies and work with these laws, perhaps psychic phenomena could be brought into the realm of everyday activity, understanding and acceptance. Then they would be described as 'physical laws'."

The Rosicrucians

Training and development of the psychic senses.

The War was over and England had returned to normality, although post War and pre War normality were very different states. The years passed and to the outside world Birch was living a life of respectable conformity, the epitome of middle class conventionality. The 9 to 5 job, 2 sons, mortgage and leisure. But there was more. Underneath and underpinning the conventional reality, Birch was engaged in intense study to develop his internal processes. He believed, as he does to this day, that his apparent psychic experiences and talents were real. As such they could be developed and eventually become useful for the benefit of others and society.

So it was that at 27, Birch joined the Rosicrucian Order. Having struggled with convention, Birch felt the need to develop along a route more appealing. The Rosicrucian Order, AMORC was, and is, a mystical fraternity that teaches development and integration of physical, mental, psychic and spiritual consciousness. It was in the Rosicrucian Order that he felt at home. New friendships were forged which are still active today, more than 20 years after leaving the Order. It was here that Birch found that spiritual companionship can be a very deep, fulfilling and trustworthy form of communion.

Meditation techniques were opening up to him as means of activating and developing the spiritual self. Harmonious rituals demonstrated another path to the spiritual and psychic body, bypassing the objective, intellectual consciousness. While regular study routines balanced the strictly psychic activities.

Quietly at first, Birch pursued these studies. In those times, the 1970s, these techniques were not so readily accepted by society as they are today.

So focussed was Birch that, for the first ten years, he did not attempt to meet other members of the Rosicrucian Order. So profound were the personal experiences and developments, the studies and psychic experiments in his sanctum provided all that he sought.

After ten years Birch joined a local group which met in Bristol. This small group of Rosicrucians was called a Pronaos. Discourses and psychic experiments mixed harmoniously with a relaxed social life. Birch loved these monthly meetings. It was here that long lasting and deep friendships were forged. Here, he felt completely at ease with like minded people. Respect and affection grew.

Birch became a calmer character, less frenzied and distracted by events in the outside world. The Rosicrucian Order thus served as bedrock for principles he was able to develop in a very real sense later in life.

The subtle developments in his psychic nature made some initial small changes. After a while he was able to identify those friends, of a spiritual nature, who were calling him as soon as the phone rang. Other times he would sense an AMORC friend wished to speak to him so Birch would pick up the phone and call the person to be greeted with, "I was just thinking about you."

This developed into conscious psychic connections with others in the Order. There was one experiment where one would attempt to disappear from onlookers while remaining in the same physical space. This yielded some results for Birch. One member was so adept that she would use the technique while shopping in her local town successfully to avoid those people she didn't wish to meet.

Birch's good friend Sylvester recently told him a story concerning the AMORC invisibility exercise. A black friend was in Ghana during race riots between Black and Asian communities. The friend was an AMORC member. One day the friend was driving through an area when he was confronted by an Asian gang who approached his car while displaying threatening behaviour. This was no small problem as people from both communities were being killed.

In desperation the friend called down the invisibility curtain. Immediately the gang stopped, and looked at the driver's position, clearly puzzled and non-plussed. The friend was able to drive away without hindrance.

Birch's good friend Audrey commented that the success of this could have been dependent on the importance of the need. Sometimes we work unsuccessfully with psychic exercises in a practice environment in which success is not vital to our wellbeing and is not a necessity.

Returning to the main story, there was a sense, during these years of work and companionship, that this was Birch's real home; his place where he could be completely his real self. He was 21 years in the Order. Eventually the psychic energy of the Order dissipated for him. The Egregore, as far as Birch was concerned, was withdrawn and Birch left the Rosicrucian Order.

The Egregore was the spiritual meeting place where those in physical life, incarnate and discarnate beings, experienced the special power of the Order, to experience and enjoy it and to continue to build it.

Harvey Spencer Lewis, founder of the Order in its outer manifestation cycle just completed, had said that the Order would last for 108 years in outer manifestation and would then cease outer work. The 108 year cycle was completed with the death of his successor Ralph Lewis. The 108 years had commenced at the birth of founder Harvey Spencer Lewis according to some commentators.

NOTES

These are comments from the official website of AMORC
....AMORC which stands for Ancient Mystical Order Rosae Crucis is not a religion and does not require a specific code of belief or conduct. Rosicrucian students come from a variety of cultural and religious backgrounds. Becoming a Rosicrucian student does not in any way require you to leave your church, join a church, or change your religious beliefs.

The Rosicrucian Order, AMORC is a non-profit educational charitable organisation.

Drawn into Birch's World

Birch finds himself at work in a rural church and the author has his own vision.

So, what is this man like? From a distance, Birch doesn't appear, in any way, extraordinary. To the outside world, to those who don't know him, he appears friendly, relaxed and interested. Modest in manner and speech, it is difficult not to notice his warmth. But for most there is something about Birch which is anything but ordinary.

Most of us have met people with whom we would prefer not to be too close. These are the types who seem to change our feelings about ourselves and the world that surrounds us. They're the ones who seem to sap our strength like they are gaining nourishment from us. They go, leaving us feeling less than in the peak of physical and mental health. They drain our energies. Not good! And we've all met someone like this. Go on, admit it.

On the other hand, there are others who seem to nourish us. I recall meeting the novelist Jilly Cooper. When she entered the room, it lit up. When she talked to people she showed a genuine interest. I watched as people's confidence and stature grew, their self esteem visibly growing. It was as if Cooper was giving part of herself to others for the benefit of others.

Birch is just like this. When we are fortunate enough to find ourselves in a room with him, we seem to become energised and a sensation of wellbeing grows. I am by no means the only person to notice this.

But when challenged on this point, Birch expresses surprise. He denies any knowledge of this strange phenomenon. He says jokingly, "It must be the result of tripling my intake of *Phylosan*". (*Phylosan* is a tonic for the more mature of us.)

During my research for this book I found myself drawn into Birch's world. The experience, while unexpected and inexplicable, was by no means disagreeable. In fact, I confess to finding it all rather fascinating.

Looking back, I felt no sense of the experience being extraordinary. In fact, it felt no more extraordinary than the telephone ringing or watching a bus travel down the road. Yet, extraordinary it was.

The day was only distinguished by the fact that it was a Saturday and winter had just arrived in Gloucestershire. It was a cold, dreary and bleak day. Night was beginning to throw its cloak over the countryside. I was driving through the small village of Stoke Orchard just a few miles from Cheltenham. My wife sat beside me and I think I recall us discussing the merits of getting home for a cup of tea. So tea was on my mind rather than Clive Birch or Stoke Orchard Church.

As we approached the Church of St James the Great, I had a vision of Clive walking towards the church. He was accompanied by a second person. I couldn't determine if his companion was male or female. Let's get this clear. I didn't see Clive walking up the path of the church. What I saw was a vision of the church and the two players.

As we drew level with the church, I heard a voice, just as clear as if someone sitting next to me was speaking.

"Talk to Clive about Stoke Orchard Church."

As we passed the church the vision disappeared. I recall thinking, OK, I'll call him. During the evening I gave this some thought. I concluded absolutely nothing. Here was something I was just going to accept. I waited until Sunday morning before telephoning Clive. From memory the conversation went something like this.

"Why must I talk to you about Stoke Orchard church? What did you do there?"

A moments silence before he replied, "How did you know that?"

"Know what?"

"Know about Stoke Orchard Church."

"Well you did something at Stoke Orchard Church," I said

"Yes, I did."

"And I think you visited the church with someone?"

"It was my partner at the time, Brigid."

"OK. Do you recall ever telling me about it?" I asked.

"No, I'm certain I didn't. There would have been no reason to tell you. I don't think I've ever told anyone about it. In fact, I'd forgotten about it. Thanks for reminding me."

With memory suitably refreshed, Birch explained his presence at the church. This is his story. Years ago, Brigid and he had cycled out into the countryside from Cheltenham. It was a bright summer afternoon. As they pedalled through the country lanes they came across this ancient, rural church. It was quite simple in outward appearance, possibly Romanesque in style, physically low built, and no spire. It nestled in the village of Stoke Orchard. It seemed to say 'I have been here for many centuries. Come on in and explore my secrets?'

So they did. They dismounted from their bikes intrigued by their find. In a garden opposite, they saw a man at work. They asked if he knew anything about the church. Not only did he know but he was a church warden and keyholder. He offered to unlock the church for them to look around.

Birch and Brigid entered into a world of the past. The inside was very simple but had religious texts painted on the walls. These had been identified as no younger than the 12th century. They felt as though they were in a time vault; a real 'Dr Who' experience. This was magic.

Brigid brought out some crystals and laid them on the floor in a pattern that suited the occasion. They settled down into meditation. This felt totally the right thing to do. Although not Christians they respected the centuries of spirituality vibrating from the very stones. They contributed their spiritual energy and the crystals brought their own energy to the mix.

They did not concern themselves with being interrupted by the church warden or any of the faithful. They were there to do the work of the spirit. (Although they had started out in order to have a relaxing bike ride!). They felt that his was God-given work regardless of religious beliefs. During the meditation Birch received the insight that the church had been the starting point for many pilgrims on their journeys to heal their spiritual selves, to experience the divine and to see the religious relics of the time.

Time passed and they lost track. Energies flowed in timeless harmonious patterns. Past centuries and present were meaningless in the communion of souls that was taking place.

Eventually the work was done and they re-emerged into the three dimensional world. Without speaking, crystals were retrieved and they prepared to leave. While retrieving their bicycles from the wall outside the church, the church warden hurtled around the corner at some speed. There was a look on his face which appeared to say,

"Oh, my God, have I given over the church to some evil black magic practice?"

They were innocent of all charges but they thought it best not to disabuse him by telling of their actual activities. They felt the church warden would have been unlikely to have understood their particular work of the spirit. He wouldn't have appreciated that they came from a pure centre as well as he. So they handed the key over promising to attend some regular church services, mounted their bikes and left. True to their word, however, they did return for a service later... much later.

The time came to cycle back towards Birch's flat. It was not be a totally uneventful journey in what had already been something of an eventful day. It was a warm and calm day with no wind at all. Not only was the wind absent, so were people. The country lane back to Cheltenham was deserted. For those who have never visited England, perhaps it might be helpful to point out some facts about the country. Visitors from most parts of the world who arrive in England for the first time immediately notice perhaps three things for which they were not prepared. First, the green, it's everywhere, even in winter, fields, trees, town parks, countryside and road verges, everywhere there is green; a 'green and pleasant land.' Next, there's the weather. Where else can you experience four seasons in one day? Wasn't it Frank Sinatra who so aptly said, "If you don't like the weather in England, wait ten minutes." One thing is for sure, whatever the weather combination, rain will be in amongst it. England is wet, sometimes very, very wet. But wait! Isn't that the reason it's so green? The third thing that visitors notice is the crowds. The word 'notice' hardly does it justice. It's like merely noticing being hit on the forehead with a claw hammer. England is always crowded, day and night, summer and winter, come rain come shine. People are everywhere. Perhaps even more striking (to continue the metaphor) is the traffic. Even the remotest country lanes are, by the standards of most other countries, busy. (Putting this in context, France is four times larger than the UK, yet has a similar population, some 60 million souls.)

I digress to emphasize just how unusual it would have been for Birch and Brigid to cycle back towards Cheltenham on empty roads. Nevertheless, empty the road was. They cycled past a pair of tall, heavy, metal gates that had been closed. Yet, with no possible physical or climate intervention, the gates sprung open with a violent motion and loud clanging noise. They wobbled on their bicycles at this totally unexpected event. Birch couldn't resist the belief that he was being given a message. This message, he was sure, was that the work in the church was complete. The task was done. The explosion of energy and powerful symbolism was almost identical to the one he experienced more than a decade later at the castle of the last white Cathar in France.

The last point to this story is that later, after the gate incident, Birch realised that Brigid and he had helped in the opening, or re-opening, of a channel of energy from this sacred spot in Stoke Orchard. For he sensed that, even before the church had been built, the space had been the centre of true spiritual activity.

Out of the Rat Race

Clive is unshackled from the business world.

This chapter is dedicated to Clive's very good friend, Margaret White, who has been there for him in good times and bad.

At age 48, circumstances and events conspired to fundamentally change Birch's life. Most of us have experienced difficult, uncomfortable and frightening times which require us to take another look at our lives and the way we choose to lead them. So often though, when we look back we realise that the changes we made to cope had improved our lives. Against what we believed at the time, eventually our lives became more enjoyable and rewarding. Nevertheless, at the time, life can be daunting, even scary. It was just such a disagreeable episode Birch now faced.

So typical at the time, Birch had not enjoyed his working day and returned to his home feeling somewhat dejected and drained. The day had been particularly stressful and, he felt, wasted. Fighting through Cheltenham's rush hour, he arrived home feeling tired and de-energised. It was 5.30, early for him to be home. It was a hot humid airless day, typical of Cheltenham in high summer. With that sinking feeling, he threw his suit jacket on a chair and, without thinking, did something out of character. He switched on the television, unusual for this the man who didn't watch TV from one week to the next and never, but never, switched it on unless there was something specific to be watched. But tonight was different and it was to start a series of events which Birch could not possibly have foreseen.

As the TV lit into life he paid little attention. His mind was on this wretched day, and there was food to consider. Bit by bit, his eyes and brain migrated to the set. The image on the screen was an enormous pyramid. He immediately recognised it as the Pyramid of the Moon at Teotihuacán, not far from Mexico City. Odd that he should turn the TV on. Odder still that only weeks before, he had been reading a book about none other than this vast, mysterious pyramid and temple complex.

As he watched the TV a remarkable thing happened. His mind leapt back to Clive as a young child, flicking the pages of the comic book. He suddenly felt the same sense of connectedness as he had all those years before when he looked in awe at the illustrations of Atlantis. He shuddered with excitement, all memories of the grinding, disappointing day swept aside.

The programme finished, but Birch hadn't. He sat wondering about the significance, if any, of Teotihuacán, Atlantis, early home, turning on the TV and this sensation of connectedness, Imagination? Co-incidence? Fantasy? Maybe all of these? Birch was stuck with the notion that it was strange for these events and images to have been presented to him. After a few moments of consideration he arrived at the conclusion that there must be, there had to be, yes, there was a link. This Jungian concept tells that events in our lives are linked as a result of our conscious intervention. This is parallel to the Rosicrucian teachings that we attract the events we need for ourselves that we need for our growth. (This concept is beautifully explained by Jeff Keller in 'Attitude is Everything'.)

Then came the Road to Damascus moment. Without seriously considering the implications and practicalities, Birch knew he had to visit this enormous and mysterious place. With his coy smile he recalls the words, "For fools rush in where angels fear to tread." I omitted to reply with the line a little later in Alexander Pope's Essays on Criticism, "and short Excursions makes". Not really fitting. Birch wasn't considering any short excursions. No sir!

And what did this Englishman know of this place? And while I mean no disrespect, with the best will in the world, Birch was no Marco Polo, Robert Falcon Scott or Ernest Shackleton. When the Aztec marched into this part of Mexico they discovered Teotihuacán abandoned; no people, no written records, no clues to identify its builders or inhabitants. Teotihuacán means 'place where people become gods'. A mystery indeed.

But, for the present it was back to those irritating and inconvenient practicalities. For some while work had been difficult. Much of this disagreeable experience was caused by changing government agendas, relevant since his employer had been acquired from the private sector and dragged kicking and screaming into the public sector. This was an irony when the flow tended to be from public to private.

Balancing the needs of the stakeholders, both private and public, had been fraught with difficulties. Each had their different agendas and cultures. Policies changed and the staff members were restless. Budgets were being cut by government and yet expectations of increased productivity never abated. In addition, as budgets and profitability fell, the training centres that Birch managed, were sold three times to different training companies. The management of these companies varied from the charlatan to the incompetent to the uncaring. Birch was finding the stress difficult and he had become ill. Within days of his decision to go to Mexico, circumstances intervened. His state of health, which had been in decline for many months, took a sudden and dramatic turn for the worse. Just a few days after watching those evocative TV images, Birch was struck down by a mystery virus. His doctor diagnosed it as such and he was signed off work. This infection, on top of his already shaky health, was debilitating. Being confined to his home would normally have been a wretched experience, but now Birch viewed it as an opportunity. Ill though he was, he wasn't too sick to think and plan his trip, for planning it did require. There was not regular bus service from Gloucestershire to Mexico. (Nor, indeed, was there an irregular service.)

Birch considered the convenience of the mystery bug. Could it be that an unseen energy was lending a helping hand?

The weeks marched on with little improvement in his health. His staff members who visited from time to time were struck by how ill he appeared. Maybe worse, he seemed so uncharacteristically low. He lacked the vitality and cheerfulness that so characterised the man.

For ten years Birch had worked in government funded training initiatives. Lowly paid at the beginning, nevertheless he was fired with enthusiasm in contributing to the development of individuals seeking positive employment experiences in those times of high unemployment. Initially he was fortunate to work for a caring, charitable organisation. He was content then. He felt that he was making a real difference. This was a time of high idealism in his life. 'Poor but happy' is how he describes it. There were many successes in developing confidence and work related skills. And as time passed, promotions and increased responsibilities presented themselves.

Then the axe fell. While still on sick leave and still feeling distinctly unwell, Birch was visited by members of his employer's senior management team. They arrived at his home, friendly and sympathetic, full of courtesy and concern for his health and wellbeing. Instead of the traditional basket of fruit and appropriate reading material, they brought a very different gift; a redundancy notice. All in the cause of strategic downsizing, you understand? Well, no not really, he didn't understand.

Birch had been a senior manager with considerable responsibility for the success of his division and the care and performance of his staff team. Members of his staff have explained that they were always mindful of Birch's concern for them. But there was also the salary. He had been fairly well paid and now, with minimum notice, he was unemployed. This was a shock and, at the moment of impact, a disappointment.

Odd that the surprise wore off and the disappointment evaporated as the hatchet men left. Negativity lasted as long as it took for the suits to walk down the driveway and get to the road. It's amazing how resilient, flexible and adaptable we humans are. Birch realized that the moment had just passed that would change his life for ever. Finally the burden of responsibility, the stress, the worry of the last few years had been removed. Any misgivings he might have had about his trip to Mexico had been taken away. In fact, he describes the moment as being set free of a debilitating encumbrance.

And wait! Why had he, just minutes before, been worrying about money? Wouldn't money always look after itself providing he was careful? Just in case that theory was rubbish, Birch had remembered that his lifestyle and not inconsiderable salary had enabled him to save a modest nest egg. Three years had seen the accumulation of several thousand pounds. So what was the problem? Whatever the future, he would be comfortable for a while with the ability to make choices. He had long since realised that being poor was no shame, just an inconvenience which deprived people of the ability to make choices. Funny thing was, in the past he had often wondered why he had been saving this money. He had no need for it; furthermore he had no plans for it. Maybe now he had his answer. He describes this fund as the 'material enabler' for his fantastic trip; the trip of a lifetime to exotic and exciting places.

When he awoke the following morning he felt better than he had for many weeks. By the end of that day he felt better than he had for months. As the days and weeks passed, his health got better and better.

It wasn't long before psychic changes started to manifest in preparation.

Birch relates a story he loves which seems apposite. He heard it on a Ram Dass tape many years ago. Dass tells the story of a very successful businessman in the finance industry. He quit his corporate life in the 1970s, threw his business suit aside and joined an Ashram. He grew a beard, wore flower power clothes, played the guitar, meditated and grew vegetables. He lived this life for eight years.

One day he was walking down a street in Los Angeles and bumped into his old employer who was very pleased to see him.

"We have missed you, you were the best we ever had at what you did. Would you like to come back?"

The ex-businessman hippie thought for a while and then replied, "OK, why not?"

He discarded his hippie clothes, shaved off his beard, bought business clothes and went back to business. Ram Dass asked him if anything had changed.

"Everything has changed. Before, I was a stressed out executive. Now I hang out with a bunch of other guys and we happen to be dealing with business. The thing that has changed is my attitude. Now I am living."

So for Birch he threw away his business suit and has considerable sympathy with at least the first part of this story.

Getting Ready for the Trip

Psychic and physical events push Birch forward.

So it was that the weeks of incapacity had confined Birch to his home enabling him to plan his trip. He had decided to acclimatise himself with a visit to the USA before going south to Mexico. He saw the US as having a similar culture and the same language; well, more or less the same language. This idea was a comfort to Birch. He felt wary about Mexico which he perceived as being a country and culture far removed from his experience; an alien land.

A friend had advised starting his tour with a visit to an ashram near San Diego, California. These ancient hermitages have their beginning in India where they provided a tranquil refuge. Hindu in origin, they often had a mystic leader. Located far from the hubbub of everyday life, ashrams encouraged spiritual and physical exercises. Some provided learning and education, even training in the art and science of warfare. Far from being consigned to the history books, ashrams are becoming more popular with new locations are opening, even today. This may well be a reflection of the way in which so many of us in the West live our frenetic lives.

This particular ashram had been founded by Paramahansa Yogananda, of whom, more later. The helpful friend had told him that the ashram would ground him in the vibration of the Americas. Birch didn't have a clue what he was talking about, but it sounded like good sense. The friend, Bryan, (he will also reappear in later pages) also suggested that Birch read 'Autobiography of a Yogi' to add to the preparation of the trip.

Buying the book, Birch learned that Yogananda had been an Eastern mystic who had gone to the USA in the early years of the 20th century. He sought to bring together the materialism of the United States and the spiritualism of the East, not the religion, but most definitely the spiritualism. Birch found the biography fascinating. It described the life and adventures of the mystic, but Birch was particularly taken by the humour. He describes it as a joy to read. When he finished the last page and closed the cover, he thought he had done with Yogananda.

During his time of forced inactivity due to miserable health, Birch had slipped into the habit of waking early each morning. Maybe this was due to his condition and the fact that he was no longer tiring during frantic days at the office. In any event, there was no pressure to get his eight hours sleep in. He took to meditating between 2 and 4 a.m.

Not long after finishing the autobiography, he woke in the early hours as had become usual. What was not usual was that he wasn't alone. On this dark and cold winter's morning, it would be hours before most opened their eyes. Birch had a visitor for there, sitting towards the foot of the bed, was Paramahansa Yogananda. Clad in orange robes and appearing just as solid and real as a living person, sat a man who had died in the 1950s. Now, most people might consider this not to be what they would most want going on in the early hours of the morning, or any other time for that matter. Birch claims he is not blessed with intestinal fortitude. When faced with physical or other threats, his instinct is to take to his heels, discretion being the better part of valour. High-tailing it as fast as his big feet could take him would be his normal reaction. Yet on this occasion, being alone and in the company of a dead mystic, he felt only calm. Yogananda turned his smiling face towards Birch and he spoke.

"When you are in America, I will be there for you." Time would show this to be true, as we shall see in later pages.

The vision or entity as Birch believes it was, disappeared. Birch pinched himself. He felt no stress, no fear, nor even excitement. He just lay back and returned to sleep. In the morning he ran the events over in his mind. When analysing the appearance of a man who had been dead for over half a century, it presented a few problems. He was unsure what had really happened a few hours earlier. Even though he had worked for years on his psychic awareness, his visionary experiences had hitherto been slight, even tenuous. This was the first time a person from a different reality had appeared to him. It had looked at him, smiled at him and, even more remarkably, spoken to him. Rational thought and logic suggested it hadn't happened, but happen it had. In that knowledge Birch was certain. He had been blessed and privileged. It was an amazing experience and now he felt sure his trip would be something out of the ordinary.

Another event was soon to take place which was unexpected and, for a while, unbalancing, but it was not completely out of his experience.

Around the world in many cultures it is recognised that each human being possesses an envelope of energy surrounding the body. This envelope is commonly called the aura. The science community has recognised this aura and is able to photograph it by the process known as Kirlian photography. This photographic process has captured images of the aura around humans, animals and plants. Birch had long been aware of this energy field around his own body when he had been in a sensitive state.

One day during daylight hours, he became aware that a third of his energy envelope, on the right side of his body, had disappeared. It was as if someone had sliced it away with a knife. It felt extremely odd and Birch says, unbalancing. It felt as if he had lost part of his physical body and it made him most uncomfortable. He was walking around lopsided. This persisted for several hours. That evening, replacement energy arrived to fill the gap. He describes this as though part of his ancient past had represented itself. Whatever the truth and the reason, he now felt in balance once more.

The appearance of the yogi and the temporary loss of his energy envelope seemed to Birch to be fantastic. He kept the events to himself apart from certain trusted friends who were themselves on a similar path. He had long worked with other realities but never experienced such impressive, or some might say bizarre, experiences. He was reticent about sharing this with others. He knew that most would brand him a maniac, egomaniac or deluded. While understandable, it is not hard to see this from Birch's point of view. He began to view the events as part of his unfolding consciousness in preparation for what he was to encounter on his journey. Time would suggest he was right in this belief.

During the preparation for the trip he experienced another amazing psychic appearance. He believed it happened as a result of him making a request to his higher self or soul. We all, he says, have a connection to a higher soul. Each higher soul or higher self has a number of souls attached to it from which it learns the lessons of life, wherever they may occur in the universe. Thus there is a 'family' of souls, for want of a better word, connected to the higher soul. One day in meditation, Birch mused on the physical reality of other beings in 'his' family.

Instantly on the screen of consciousness, two images appeared. One was the head of a lizard-like being with a crocodilian headed. As it turned to look in his direction he saw that this being had incredibly intelligent eyes. The vision quickly faded to be replaced by another. Now he saw a 'group' being which looked like a clump of tulip flowers. Each individual head possessed an eye in the centre of the tulip-shaped bloom. Each eye, Birch felt, possessed its own intelligence but was also part of a group intelligence. Perhaps this group intelligence worked similarly to birds when they wheel very fast together. This vision also quickly faded leaving him, once again, to attempt to make sense of the baffling images. To date he hasn't fathomed their meaning nor has he had repeat, similar visions.

Birch was still suffering, from the virus that had assailed him; that mystery virus which had removed him from his negative employment situation. He took a trip to visit friend Bryan. He was looking forward to a social event at Bryan's home in a leafy Oxfordshire village. Pleasant discourse and a gentle walk were followed by a visit to a café along the river bank near to Bryan's home. As they sat sipping their coffee their conversation was broken by a woman who Bryan knew vaguely.

"I am sorry to interrupt you both, but I am a healer and I have just had an inner prompting to offer some healing," she said while looking at Birch. The two men sat absorbing this offer for a while before Birch felt prompted to accept. So there, in the middle of the café surrounded by others eating and drinking, this lady started her hands-on healing, there and then. Birch sat passively, absorbing the powerful vibrations. At the same time Bryan went into meditation to assist in the process, or so Birch assumed. The odd thing about Bryan's meditation was that it was performed open-eyed with the pupils orbiting the whites. This apparently bizarre ritual went on for some minutes at the end of which Birch felt that something had moved in his body. All the while the other very English people got on with their talking and eating in the café, so typically ignoring the bizarre threesome. The healer woman took her leave after profuse thanks from Birch.

The next morning when Birch woke up he felt so much better. The virus had almost completely gone. He was delighted. Birch mused on the apparent coincidence of his visit to Bryan and of being in the exact location at the exact time that they met the healer. She had said that she had never been in that café before, neither had Bryan. Birch knew that this was no coincidence. He was indeed being looked after.

One interesting series of experiences came as opportunities, for Birch at this time. A friend offered Birch the chance of posing as a life model. Before the trip to the USA the opportunity to earn a little more money, albeit small amounts, was appealing. He was nervous about the process before the first session.

Arriving at the first art class, he was confronted by a group of some 15 would-be artists; mainly women. Off came the clothes and he was required to arrange his body in an appropriate pose. The first couple of minutes were full of activity. As the tutor withdrew and the silence took over, the realisation swept over Birch that here he was totally exposed physically. This was the start of the inner battle for Birch to confirm his self worth, with no clothes on! His background in meditation and *tai chi* now came into its own. He was able to take himself away from his nakedness, re-affirm his self worth and return to the room mentally. Now he felt comfortable for the 2 hour session. It worked on this first occasion, just as it did for subsequent sittings.

After each session he was invited to examine the results of his poses on the canvasses that circled him. The way a certain component of his anatomy was portrayed was particularly interesting from the middle aged women. One wonders what is going on in people's heads.

Eventually the time came; the big moment of departure. All the months of planning, research and preparation would soon be put to the test. Birch felt trepidation and excitement. It was his first flight in a Jumbo jet. He also remembers awkwardness. 747 travel was mundane for millions, but not for him. He had yet to experience the boredom of a long haul flight.

Two hours after take-off, he closed his eyes as the newness and novelty of intercontinental flight wore off. Immediately his eyes shut he felt himself enter another area of reality. He was relaxed, savouring the experience. Suddenly without warning, a small clay or metal figurine landed with a crack onto the meal tray in front of him. He quickly saw it to be in the form of a Mayan priest. He was shaken by the appearance of this image and its dramatic appearance. He was startled and immediately drawn back from his altered conscious state. He was clear he was in his normal three dimensional reality, sitting in his seat in the airliner. But now the meal tray was in the up position and there was no sign of the Mayan priest figure. At least it took some of the boredom out of the long, tedious flight.

Eventually he landed in San Francisco International Airport. Tired though he was, or maybe because of his fatigue, he was struck by the toughness and barely suppressed aggression of the police in the airport; it was scary. He found their faces hard and the conspicuous display of their firearms was disconcerting. He was used to the more relaxed and unarmed presence of British bobbies in public places. And this was well before 9.11; that terrible day when the world changed forever, the change being most evident to the general public at international airports.

As he approached the window at passport control he was nothing short of shocked by the rudeness of an immigration officer. He had made the fatal error of standing in front of the green line painted on the floor. He had incurred the wrath of an officer who combined a hard shout with a hard glare. He hadn't even entered the country and he was already missing the politeness of British civil servants. Welcome to the States, Birchy!

What to do now? He had a two hour wait before his onward flight to San Diego would be called. He felt slightly wrong footed by the confrontation with the noisy and ill humoured official. He really didn't feel like getting it wrong again. Only one thing for it; find the departure lounge and sit quietly, not much excitement to be had there and not much opportunity to get into any mischief, might even have the chance to grab some shut-eye. But what a revelation; Birch was enrapt. He was fascinated by what he now saw to be a different culture. He spent this time watching the people; amazing people, their talk, their accents, some of which he couldn't place, and their clothes. This was a wonderful and educational experience. Two great nations separated by a common language. He could now see the wisdom in Churchill's words. The reality was now dawning on him that some of the differences were not just skin deep. They might go much deeper, but just how deep were the differences between the USA and dear Old Blighty? He was soon to find out.

Now he could see why his thoughtful friend had suggested acclimatising at the ashram; good advice indeed. He was feeling alien in this country but, to counter this, he was sensing something that grew in importance as the trip progressed. What he now felt were the vibrations of this land. Through all the concrete, glass and plastic, hubbub, noise and movement, he found the energy of the Americas to be overwhelming.

The flight from San Francisco to San Diego passed off uneventfully apart from slight withdrawal symptoms from coffee and tea, the voluntary denial of which had become a minor feature of the trip. The first sight of a desert terrain through the window of the aircraft was different enough to be fun.

Finally, after what seemed like a week of airports, aircraft, waiting, sitting, queuing, being questioned, it was a relief to leave the terminal and board a minibus. Some fellow passengers were dropped off at various airports around the city. One couple thanked the driver as they alighted. The poor man seemed almost nonplussed that anyone should appreciate the service.

"Hey, it's what I do," he replied as if thanks were superfluous. It transpired he was from New York. OK, thought Birch, perhaps an expression of gratitude in this culture is rare?

As they left the city he settled back in his seat to enjoy the rest of his journey. How different all this was from the elegance of Cheltenham, the predominantly grey skies and regular rain, the green parks, roads in constant gridlock and crowds.

There's that name again; Cheltenham, Cheltenham Spa, home to the prosperous and well connected. The visitor would immediately recognise the architecture as Regency; tall, elegant, spacious and grand. The mineral springs were discovered there in the early years of the 18th century and since then the town hasn't looked back. The Duke of Wellington was an early visitor attracted by the waters and respectability. Echoes of his visits remain today. The homes of the prosperous bordering Wellington Square wouldn't look out of place in the most upmarket streets and squares of West London.

The Promenade is a shopping street, a place to do lunch, and a place to be seen that might, at a push, rank among the top streets in the world. And a smart walk away is the world famous horseracing course, the home of National Hunt racing.

Cheltenham even has a place in national and international industry and commerce. Few of the workers building their aircraft in Seattle will not have heard of Smiths Aerospace. And it's not just Smiths that places Cheltenham on the world aviation map. There are other well known brands and companies nearby which are accepted and respected names in aviation and defence industries.

Mention a financial services company and the chances are its head office or UK national office will be within a few minutes of the town. Then there's the Government Communications Headquarters, known to all as GCHQ, employing thousands as it goes about its business of... of, well, whatever it does.

And the list of sons and daughters of Cheltenham reads like a mini Who's Who. Some of the best known are actors Sir Ralph Richardson, Robert Hardy and Martin Jarvis. Edward Adrian Wilson died with Scott on the ill-fated Antarctic Expedition of 1912. The world owes a great debt to Edward Jenner who invented vaccination, and music lovers with recognise the name of Gustav Holst of Planets fame.

Arthur 'Bomber' Harris who only died in 1984, was head of Bomber Command in WWII. So unjustly, he has been subject to criticism as the unthinking and politically correct apply standards of today to those that they feel should have applied in the first half of the 1940s. Knights George Dowty, founder of Dowty Rotol, and Douglas Dodds-Parker, MP and member of the Special Operations Executive (SOE) in WWII appear in this august list. Before names take over the entire book we'll finish here except for one more who deserves mention, Eddie 'the Eagle' Edwards, Olympic ski jumper.

So, that's Cheltenham, extraordinary in many ways but all is not quite what it seems. Based on the real thing, Bath which traces its history back to Roman times, Cheltenham is a bit of a sham. It was thrown together cheaply and quickly, a sort of freeze dried instant coffee, totally acceptable but not Italian espresso.

Back now to the minibus in California's sun. As they drove into the hills the aridity of the desert terrain and the unfamiliar vegetation was almost shocking to Birch. The two things that compounded this 'culture shock' was the absence of animals and the utter silence. Silence is a rare state in overcrowded England. Birch was to come to love this environment later.

Now the driver couldn't find the ashram. Eventually they saw another human being. Stopping to ask directions was fruitless. The guy they selected didn't speak English. On they drove, Birch with that sinking feeling. He had been travelling for 24 hours when the bus drove into a lush valley surrounded by low hills. It was a great sight to the travellers. The driver was absolutely entranced by the lush greenery nestling in the severity and drama of the desert. They debussed and wandered for a while, drinking in the sights and atmosphere. Birch described how he thought it looked like the Garden of Eden. The more cynical might feel that, after such a journey, the average landfill site might have appeared appealing.

"We must be here?" said the driver, more to himself than to Birch.

The driver was so nonplussed that he didn't seem to know how much to charge for the journey. Birch offered $20 as an opening to negotiations. Much to Birch's surprise the driver pocketed the first offer, got back in the van and drove off. Birch felt a little mean by underpaying, however he comforted himself by feeling that it had been his task to bring the driver to this valley.

Beneath a tree, which offered some sort of shade, sat a man relaxing in his chair.

"Oh," said he, "you have returned to us."

"Uh, no," Birch replied. "I've never been here before."

"Yes, you have."

"No, I haven't." Not wishing this encounter to degenerate in pantomime, Birch wandered towards the ashram's office.

This bizarre exchange could easily have been put down to mistaken identity had it not been for another encounter the following morning. Another person Birch had never seen welcomed him back to the ashram. Two cases of mistaken identity were not so easy to dismiss. The visit had started with an interesting twist.

Ashram

*Spiritual support from physical
and non-physical sources.*

The office directed Birch to his accommodation, a wooden chalet, set back up a slope overlooking the valley. Throwing his baggage onto the bed, he sat on the veranda watching the sun go down. The cicadas chirped away and the wild dogs howled in the distance as the sky darkened. For the first time in many hours he stretched his aching body. A warm glow of satisfaction and anticipation washed over him. He was here. What would the next few days hold?

He sat absorbing the sights, sounds and smells of this desert so far from his home. Just as he was stirring to take himself off to the beckoning bed, his vision blanked. It was replaced by a brilliant blue light before returning to the dark night sky. This happened on two more occasions. He was reminded that prior to leaving the familiarity of home he had been working with a potent energy which manifested itself as a brilliant blue light. He staggered to bed and was asleep almost instantly.

The next three weeks were a total departure from the life Birch had known. It was with increasing ease he immersed himself into the life of the ashram. Morning, lunchtime, and evening meditations and chanting, punctuated the day. Monk-like, mealtimes were spent in silence. Birch chose to work in the gardens. He wanted to build up his strength and, in any event, he enjoyed the fresh air, such a welcome change from much of his life to date. Far too much of that been spent in an office, in meetings and doing battle with the alien contrived world of computers. And it tickled him to think of being where he was, weeding under a brilliant blue sky and palm trees, temperature in the 80s, while dear old England was moving inexorably into autumn. The season of mellow fruitfulness might be appealing for some, but Birch knew where he preferred to be.

The lush and exotic greenery of the gardens contrasted strongly with the dry surrounding hills and desert beyond. Much of the time the gardens were very quiet. Very few of the residents seemed to visit here. In one corner was a wooden Japanese style building used for meditation. Birch would meditate here at lunchtimes instead of his room. Again it seemed to be scarcely used by the residents. It became something of a personal refuge.

Life quickly and effortlessly moulded into the routine of the ashram. There was something protecting, nurturing and positive about the environment in which he now found himself. What was more; he loved it. He soon began to grasp why it was that so many people chose to give up the material trappings of the Western World, give up the jobs they had struggled so hard and long to attain. Instead they chose this relatively trouble free, single sex, temple and workplace which provided such an appealing alternative. For Birch this was a pleasant, rejuvenating, revivifying experience to begin his monumental journey to... well that was just it, where indeed?

In so many ways this was a haven of peace, tranquillity and escape, although Birch never viewed it as escape. For him it was preparation and acclimatisation; an oasis of peace in a busy, noisy and stressful world. But even this extraordinary place was not entirely insulated from the outside world. It sustained itself by the sale of hothouse flowers and vegetables. One day the senior person in the ashram, a monk, complained about the necessity of having to learn to type. The thought occurred to Birch that the 20th century will leave no stone unturned to instil itself in every corner of activity.

There were development opportunities also. After a lunchtime talk given by a monk on the subject of 'being in the silence', Birch discovered his negativity rose to the surface. Doubts of his future financial position floated up. As he rested after work he allowed these thoughts to melt away. He felt very clear during meditation after that. Clearly there is no security in materiality alone.

Birch had taken a crystalline stone to the USA. He had stumbled over it when walking at Hawkwood, Stroud, England at a Temple Study Group meeting retreat the previous July. As the weeks rolled by in the ashram, one surface of the stone transformed, becoming clearer and lighter. Before he left, Birch placed the crystal in the gardens as a marker of his presence. A short prayer completed the process.

One evening Birch watched a baseball game on TV. After three quarters of an hour nothing seemed to be happening, although those around him seemed enthusiastic enough. He thought that maybe cricket, with its arcane appeal to the English and the nations of the former empire, would have a similar appeal to them as baseball had for him.

The days sped by and Birch became more and more comfortable at the ashram. His meditations stretched out until one Thursday he had been able to complete the recommended full three hour weekly meditation. He had become fitter, stronger and more relaxed. Sleep patterns stretched to ten hours a night. Physical exercise and the process of personal recovery continued apace. The initial two week stay had been extended to three weeks. Despite the extension he didn't feel quite ready to leave. One wonders if he was becoming institutionalised.

One day Carlos, Birch's work supervisor, told him not to work too hard today as he needed to be fresh for the three hour meditation that evening. It certainly gave another focus to the true place of work in the pantheon of activity. It was also apparent that this haven of peace and tranquillity could become a prison, given Birch's enquiring nature and increasing discomfort with unchanging routine. He had seen a few things that were warning signs; people shutting themselves away from the sometimes hard lessons outside.

One time he came across one of the residents sitting in a car which had been driven to the ashram by a woman. Both the resident and the woman were clearly distressed, both staring ahead, set faces, tearful eyes. What painful experience or tragedy had caused this man to separate from the outside world and enter the monkish environment of the ashram? Birch would never know.

On another occasion he saw the resident who looked after the office, clearly in some mental distress. The man excused himself saying he had to go to his room, and left the office to tend itself. Whatever mental trouble besieged this man, it had not been removed by residency in the ashram.

How many others in this idyll were carrying scars and wounds that were so difficult to heal? Something else Birch would never find out.

One mealtime during the announcements that followed the silent repast, the presiding monk told the assembled that there would be a visit to Lakeside, another Yogananda ashram situated at Los Angeles. He also said that priority for the trip would be given to residents before visitors to the ashram. As the company filed out from the food hall one of the residents encouraged Birch to try to get on the visit.

The following Friday Birch duly presented himself at the gathering point, the only visitor to do so. The five coaches filled up, at the end of which there was one seat left for non-residents. Birch triumphantly entered the coach. It seemed that Yogananda was not only looking after Birch but making extra opportunities available.

On the journey to Lakeside, Birch fell into conversation with another of the residents. This young man was of a spiritual disposition and clearly intelligent. Almost casually Birch raised the subject of reincarnation if only to engage this pleasant, articulate young man in open, honest debate.

"Master (meaning Yogananda) wouldn't wish us to discuss this." The young man quickly quashed all further conversation on this matter.

Birch was taken aback by this. He had assumed that the ashram was open to all subjects of a spiritual nature. Whether the young man was discomfited by Birch's particular slant on this, or perhaps the teachings of the Self Realisation Fellowship forbade teachings 'outside the box'. Whatever the reason for his reticence, Birch doesn't believe that Yogananda himself would ever have had a closed mind.

These three incidents suggested to Birch that it was time to leave the comfortable nest and refuge of the ashram. It was not to become his home.

The drive to Lakeside along the six lane highway was his first experience of the US interstate highways; so different from British motorways as these great conduits drive right through the hearts of the cities. This tide of traffic was starting to turn him off buying a car once he left the ashram. It had seemed a good idea to provide convenience and freedom. Now, Birch wasn't so sure.

Birch had a great time at Lakeside, Hidden Valley. Lakeside was set in a very tight bowl with a peaceful lake at the bottom. It was surrounded by many different varieties of trees and shrubs. At the top of the bowl overlooking the ocean was a beautiful white walled temple seating 400. It was claimed that it was packed out every Sunday for worship. Birch spent the day relaxing, exercising, meditating, swimming and boating on the lake.

The residents of the ashram always referred to Yogananda as 'Master'. Birch never did. For him he was Paramahansa Yogananda, one of the great mystics of the 20th century. Birch didn't believe that his relationship with him was any the less respectful. It was just different.

There was one other surprise for him. When he told residents of his personal contact with Yogananda, he expected them to relate similar incidents, as they were living in the ashram founded by him. Much to his surprise, none did. In fact they were all surprised by Birch's early morning contact with him, possibly especially so since Birch was an outsider. It was at this moment that he realised that he had been especially blessed.

On the last Sunday, the day before Birch left, he went for a walk in the countryside with two other English visitors to the ashram. As the three walked and chatted they were surprised by a coyote that crossed their path. This was a pleasant and perhaps unusual event. It was possibly more relevant than Birch realised at the time for, as he discovered later, the coyote is a member of the same family as the wolf, larger than a fox, grey in colour. The wolf was to become Birch's 'power' animal. That was the animal to which he would be most likely to connect to achieve a measure of its abilities and strengths. The manipulation of these energies is central to the work of many shamans. This symbol of animal power was to have significance for Birch later.

On the walk Ian and John, the two English chaps, told Birch that a human's normal vibration is 65 MHz. If you hold a cup of coffee it will take it down to 58 MHz. A cold will take it down again to 50 MHz.

Birch never joined the Self Realisation Fellowship, the organisation that was running the ashrams and propagating the wisdom of this great man, Yogananda. To its credit it honours the saints of all religions in its prayers, including venerating Jesus, Krishna, Sri Yukteswar (Yogananda's teacher) and Yogananda himself.

At this time Birch was a member of the Temple Study Group as well as following his own path. Membership of another body was not necessary for him.

Having said this, he didn't feel negative towards the San Diego Ashram, SRF, or indeed Yogananda himself. The whole experience for him was to ensure that he did not become too comfortable and that he should continue with his journey. Yogananda had kept his promise. He did look after Birch through the good offices of the ashram and its people.

He had become too comfortable. Perhaps he was using this as an excuse not to continue his journey. He forced himself to leave. It was high time he made progress. As the third week drew to a close, he arranged for a microbus to collect him. Time to see the wider USA, it was beckoning.

As an initial and temporary resting place, Birch had booked into the Banana Bungalow; cheap surfer accommodation on the seafront at San Diego. It sounded like Club 18-30 as described by Peter, another English guy in the ashram. Still it was only a temporary jumping off spot, besides he didn't have any other contacts at the time.

California and Beyond

Into the heart of 'Mammon'.

This next phase of the travels became pure vacation for Birch. The spiritual energies were put behind him until a small adventure with Clive's friend. Bryan was due to meet him at LAX, Los Angeles Airport, three weeks later.

A chatty microbus driver, typically Californian in his openness, made the journey to Banana Bungalow pass quickly.

The bungalow was a rip off at $20 per night, and a dive, to boot. One night's stay there was more than enough. Fortunately a couple of English girls who also had the misfortune to have booked into Banana Bungalow advised moving to Hostel International in downtown San Diego.

The latter was more like it being conveniently placed to town, and all together better quality accommodation. Fortune smiled on Birch, he had a bunk bed room to himself. It was quiet with only his energies and space for meditation. Great stuff!

One fun evening was spent learning poker in the company of three young Japanese and one American. Birch won. 'Beginners luck', he said, almost embarrassed as his fellow players looked at him as if he were a hustler.

Birch made friends, as much as one can in the shifting backpackers and travellers world, with two Japanese guys. Hero was planning to live in Europe but he couldn't, or maybe wouldn't, tell Birch why. Jun wanted to be a primary school teacher at home. Young, enthusiastic and full of energy, they typified the positive spirit of so many young people. One of them was a great fan of Elvis Presley. A fact that Birch found surprising given that Presley had died before the young Japanese had been born. When asked why he liked Elvis songs so much, the young man rustled in his English-Japanese dictionary, looked up and smiled.

"Because his music makes me feel beloved," he said without a trace of self-consciousness. Birch was taken aback. So much for the inscrutable, machine-like, Oriental mind so ingrained into the attitudes of Westerners.

One perspective that came to Birch during his stay concerned the wealth of this nation and its conspicuous consumption. He was starting to feel less negative, albeit temporarily. It would be very comfortable and pleasant to live here. General affluence and fine weather helped this idea as did the apparent personal safety of the downtown area. The only police that he saw were riding bicycles and wearing shorts. This was a far cry from the screaming sirens in many locations.

On the last evening of his five day stay, Birch was working meditively, re-connecting more strongly with his heart. He became more relaxed when he knew the rules of his environment and was able to function normally. When one doesn't know the rules, external boundaries are more rigid and behaviour patterns circumscribed. That evening, as he worked quietly and internally, Halloween was in full swing outside. People enjoyed creating a noisily party atmosphere. Birch was content in his own space and with his own company.

Five days in San Diego was quite long enough for him. Staying longer would be merely experiencing; consuming more tourism. Birch had called Doug Cox, brother of Jan, a friend from Cheltenham. Doug was happy for Birch to stay with him in Palm Springs/ Cathedral City. The two are extensions of each other. Travelling up by Greyhound bus, Birch found a desert environment turned into a suburban garden. The valley floor had been the seabed, several times over the eons. More recently it had been a desert until 20 or 30 years before.

This area had three tremendous advantages. First, there was a wonderful winter climate with temperatures over 80° F (27° C) in November. This was the result of the mountains on three sides that trap warm air in while keeping out humid air and wet weather from Los Angeles and the coast. Second, the shape of the topography and some of the mountains, akin to the neck of a bottle, funnelled in beneficial winds. These rotated the blades of enormous wind farms which supplied the area's electricity needs. Third, a subterranean lake supplied all the water the valley required.

The rich, famous and well-heeled live there in condominiums protected in walled-off estates. Doug pointed out Bob Hope's mansion.

It was set on a mountain bluff overlooking the neighbours huddled together on the valley floor.

Birch visited a graveyard which was well laid-out and tended. Each grave was marked by a single, simple, uniform commemorative stone set into the well tended lawns. Sprinkled among the graves of ordinary folk, (ordinary rich folks, that is,) were simple headstones marking the last resting places of Frank Sinatra and Sony Bono, he of Sonny and Cher fame, and latterly Governor of California before losing his life in a skiing accident. The State of California is an amazing place unlike any other that Birch had visited. Sony Bono, Ronald Reagan, Arnold Schwarzenegger all came from the world of entertainment to reach the heights of state governor. The electorate there have a never-ending love affair with celebrity, and yet this is a state of almost unparalleled riches. If it was a country it would have the sixth highest GDP in the world.

Birch stayed in Doug's beautiful house. Doug was enormously generous with his time and support, just like so many Americans. He was a comparatively relaxed, mild mannered man. Doug's military, clipped manner occasionally came to the fore. There was warmth about him that Birch wouldn't have associated with a military person.

One afternoon, as Doug was out running errands, Birch was relaxing, resting in and beside the small pool in front of the house. He realised that the date was November 5th. Guy Fawkes night meant darkness and fireworks in Britain. But there he was in California, relaxing in the sunlight and warmth. It all seemed so surreal.

Before departing for Santa Monica, (close to Los Angeles,) Birch took a cable car trip into the spectacular mountains. The temperature dropped to 50° F (10° C), but it felt warmer in the bright sunshine and clear, dry air. There was snow in the crevices. Looking across the valley floor, Doug pointed out a scar in the far distant landscape. It marked the join between the two tectonic plates that are the source of earthquakes throughout California. Such tremendous locked in energy, Birch thought to himself. If only it could be harnessed in the way that the wind energy was there.

It was time to leave. Doug's golf competitions were looming and his wife was due to return from visiting a sick relative. Birch felt that he had been a reasonable companion during this break in Doug's routine. Birch liked Doug enormously. He had been a colonel in the U.S. army and greatly enjoyed, it seems, listening to Birch's stories concerning World War II from a British perspective.

Birch returned to a hostel, this time in Santa Monica. It was time to enjoy a few more days by the sea. The hostel was crammed with people. He was back in the accommodation maelstrom.

It was while he was there that realisation dawned. The energy of California was such that new ventures had a head start. Birch found the energy he felt was extraordinary and invigorating. He wondered and worried how he could put this into words. Troublesome though the words might be he was able to draw parallels with the successes of the fruit business, wine production and, of course, more recently Silicon Valley. This open and creative energy is felt in the very air and the earth. Not that Birch found much earth in Santa Monica. Most of it was covered in concrete. However a walk on the seashore sand sufficed.

A trip to the Getty Museum in Los Angeles was a must for the traveller. The hugely impressive series of buildings, more like a small city, was dedicated to the display of art objects from all over the world. As he stood on the hilltop overlooking Los Angeles, it struck Birch that the U.S.A. is the new Rome. It dominates the world economically and politically, just as Rome had two millennia before. The U.S.A. has done this with the aid of its multiplex communication systems. The roads and sea routes for the Romans were the information and communication technologies (ICT) of today's U.S.A. Perhaps the U.S. role at the centre of its Western empire is more subtle than was Rome with its plethora of military conquests. Rome was very adept however, at attaching itself to client states which it dominated and, to all intents and purposes, controlled. There are certain modern states that would accuse the U.S. of doing the same thing.

The U.S. has a superabundance of self-confidence and self-belief. It views its own ways as being superior to those of other cultures. There is much positivity and extroversion among those U.S. citizens that Birch met and observed. He felt sure that Romans at the height of their power were similar.

Recently there was an interesting comparison made on British radio between the now defunct British Empire and the U.S. Empire, for that is what the latter is. The claim was made that the British Empire was long lasting for a number of reasons. First, it was enormously successful financially being a net lender to rest of the world. Second, the British people went to colonise and engage in the cultures. This facilitated the transfer of British culture, social networks, legal processes, attitudes, commitment to common goals, almost by a process of gradual osmosis. Third, they saw this and carried it out over a very long time period; centuries in some cases. Patience and long term commitments were the key.

It was argued on the other hand, that the U.S. Empire was most likely to be of much shorter duration, also for three reasons. First, the U.S. is not a balanced financial organism. It has enormous debts and borrows massively on the world money markets. Second, the people of the U.S. are not interested in spending their lives in the far flung corners of the Earth. Therefore, those U.S. citizens that are seconded to other countries - Iraq, Afghanistan to mention a couple - live in ghettos separated from the local communities. They create small pockets of little U.S.A. There is no subtle drawing in of other countries' communities into the philosophy or lifestyle in a subtle way. It is a 'take it or leave it' approach. Mostly they leave it. And thirdly, the U.S. psyche is very short term. There is little long term commitment to the societies with which they interact and control. The concentration span of many Americans is short, and not helped by the dreadful dross served up on TV.

Birch makes no value judgement here. These were the comments of a British historian.

Back to the trip, on 11 November Birch caught a bus to San Francisco from Santa Monica through the Los Angeles Bus terminal. The terminal was a scary place, right in the heart of the ghetto. The very air and buildings exuded anger and depression. Birch was relieved to leave it. Someone that he spoke to in the terminal said that everyone gets locked in after dark because of the fear and reality of local crime.

Soon the scenery turned into scrub covered hills, again with no animals visible. But of course there wouldn't be many animals, he mused. There was insufficient rainfall to produce much plant growth. Ironically it rained heavily on this journey but then, life is like that. The rain gave way to a heavy, overcast sky as the bus drove into flat agricultural plains. Birch found the openness of this terrain exhilarating. It was such a far cry from the constricted, constrained atmosphere of the hostel he had just left.

It felt good to be away from Santa Monica and the heavy energies of people in the hostel. He was surprised at his reaction. Being in those energies had been acceptable at the time. Being free of them was better. It also felt fine travelling by bus. There was enough for Birch to absorb without the added pressure of driving in an alien environment. As the bus sped northward Birch had the strong intuition that this had been the northern outpost of the Atlantean empire in the very distant past.

The miles sped by, hundreds and hundreds of them. Now, this concept is not so easy for the average, untravelled Brit. Living on a small island with an uncomfortably dense population brings insularity and a restricted view of geography and distance. At home, while journeys may take a long time because of road congestion, it is rare indeed, to drive for hundreds of miles. Most locations are not hundreds of miles away from any other location. I am reminded of some members of my own family who accompanied my wife and me on a holiday to Orlando, Florida. It was their first trip to the States. One morning they announced they were going to drive up to Gracelands for the day. Responding to my surprise they showed me a map to demonstrate that Gracelands was only a few of inches from Orlando. They never did get to Memphis, Tennessee.

At last the bus reached San Francisco the outskirts of which were a highlight for Birch. As the bus drove over the Golden Gate Bridge at 7 in the evening, the lights in the downtown area were like a fairytale display. Birch felt like a child again, confronted with his first candle lit Christmas tree. The skyscrapers huddled together appearing as castles of light. At this point Birch wasn't thinking of the environmental strains as a consequence of this display.

A night in Hostel International was followed by an enormous breakfast in a 1950s diner, which Birch could not finish, much to his chagrin. Music by Fats Domino and Chuck Berry brought memories flooding back of innocent, young, teenage days. Birch had to drag himself away.

Onto the Alcatraz tour. Set on an island, it was reached through the clearing mists by ferry; very atmospheric. He walked round on the well executed tour wondering about the generations of prisoners who had been incarcerated within those walls. He could almost feel the longing and aching hearts that would have desperately thought about freedom, home, families and the world outside.

On his return to the city it was fun riding the streetcars up the very steep streets. As Birch described all this I could see his thoughts in his eyes and hear them in his voice. Boy, was this a good holiday or what!

But there was one negative note there as Birch strolled around downtown San Francisco during his second evening. The sudden noise of a police siren accentuated by the towering walls of the skyscrapers set so close together, brought Birch back from a relaxed reverie. Tyres screeched in protest at sudden braking and male and female police officers leapt out of a patrol car. They raced over near to where Birch was walking and manhandled some street people. They were easy to spot with their down-at-heel, raggedy appearance, and they pushed shopping trolleys containing their worldly possessions. The officers handled the 'bums', as the Americans pejoratively call them, very roughly. Twisting arms behind backs and clamping on wrist constraints they tossed them into the police car. These 'bums' weren't doing anything wrong on the street that he could see. Indeed, Birch hadn't even noticed them until the police car screeched to a halt.

There was one further negative image. Birch and some other hostel guests returned from the Alcatraz trip. They came across an unfortunate 'down and out'. Birch dislikes the word 'bum'. He was sitting on the sidewalk, begging with a cardboard sign around his neck. It read, 'Prozac did this to me'.

Birch only stayed two days. There were many more places to go and people to see. The pleasure of this journey was intoxicating to a man who had never before strayed from Europe.

Birch had already called Bob, an American he had met in the ashram and who had generously invited him to stay in his home at Lake Tahoe. Bob seemed pleased to hear from Birch so arrangements were made for him to travel to Lake Tahoe, again by bus.

The lake shore at Tahoe was entrancing, indeed one of the most beautiful locations Birch had ever seen. The lake shore was completely unspoiled. Mountains and fir trees came down to the shore. As Birch walked along the shoreline there was total silence apart from the call of birds. The air was pristine, clear and cool.

The surface of the water was calm and would have been millpond still except for very small movements. The placid water stretched into the distance and a light haze made more atmospheric by looming mountains in the distance. Birch felt like pinching himself for this wonderful opportunity to experience this beauty. It was difficult to drag himself away. He felt as though transported to one of the more positive scenes in 'The Lord of the Rings'.

Bob said on Birch's arrival, "Our home is your home". The generosity of Americans as hosts continued. Bob presented his guest with a Hopi Indian silver bangle. This gift partially recompensed for a silver ankh which had been given to him by good friends, and then lost. This was a feature of many of Birch's journeys to sacred places. It was as though some part of his unconscious left a token of his passing, or even an object which contained his vibration. He hasn't yet discovered why this is so.

On the second day of Birch's visit, it snowed heavily. Icicles hung from the roof tiles. It looked so beautiful. Amorah Quan Yin, a writer on spiritual matters, says that such weather can bring to material manifestation the strongest spiritual vibrations due to the perfect geometrical construction of snow. Another spiritual writer has said, 'in the beginning God geometrised'.

Birch felt joy in that perfect location. He felt so well at 7,000 feet (2134 metres), away from pollution and what was more, he was sleeping like a log!

Bob and his wife, Mary, took Birch to a self realisation ceremony in, bizarrely, the nearby city of Reno, down on the valley floor. A spiritual ceremony in the gambling city of Mammon! Birch felt comfortable back in spiritual mode with Bob and Mary meditating and performing simple kriya yoga - the yoga form so valued by Yogananda - before the start of each day. It was great for Birch to feel so spiritually and physically energised.

When the time came to leave, to save a 13 hour plus bus journey back to Santa Monica, Birch flew. He thought the ticket price of $111 was dirt cheap. He met Bryan at LAX.

Bryan is a man of shorter than medium height, straight-walking, straight-talking and to the point. He moved with a lightness and fluidity that befits an ex-dancer. He hadn't done any exercise for years and yet kept a youthful figure into his forties. When Bryan and Birch climbed Cathedral Rock in Arizona, Birch struggled to keep up with him as Bryan bounded lightly upwards. This was despite the fact that Birch had a marathon running background. Bryan had an open-eyed way of looking at one, pulling others into his extrovert personality. He was a man of great charm. Birch most certainly wouldn't choose to race Bryan up Cathedral Rock. He had absolutely no doubt he would come off second best.

It seemed to Birch that Bryan lived a life of total self-confidence. He worked as a photographer in order to earn enough money for his healing work and travel. He attended spiritually based lectures and courses to further his knowledge. It was typical of the man that he wouldn't hesitate to stand up in the middle of a lecture, and confront the presenter if he believed them to be making false or misleading claims. This would not be to enhance his own ego, but to get closer to the truth, never mind if there were six or seven hundred people present.

On one occasion he ran out of money in the middle of a trip. Without fear, he went into meditation until the name of a potential contact came into consciousness. He made contact and, lo and behold, help in the form of funds was forthcoming, enabling him to complete his trip. He was one of the few people that Birch knew who lived his truth and trusted totally in the ability of the cosmic forces to help him out of tight situations.

A night's stay in Santa Monica was followed by breakfast. Looking at each other as they ate, the question arose as at the end of Spike Milligan sketches, "What do we do now?" No thought had been given to their time together, except that they would spend time together. The silence was broken by Bryan.

"Let's go to Las Vegas." Quite why two mad mystics should want to go to this central den of iniquity was beyond Birch. Yet he found himself agreeing to the slightly disagreeable proposition. The reason for their visit became clear once they were there. Cheap flight tickets of $85 dollars were duly purchased, flights taken, and a stretched limo taxi whisked them to a hotel recommended by the driver. The hotels in Las Vegas are generally cheap in order to allure the visitor and to get them to part with their hard earned at the tables or the fruit machines.

On the first morning, the twosome sat in the hotel café for coffee. Birch saw the young female manager deal very effectively with a subordinate over a disciplinary matter. Birch's business background made him appreciate the work that this woman had just done. He told her so, and she thanked him for saying it. For long Birch had felt unappreciated by his superiors in the business environment. In fact it was all still a recent memory and he remained grateful for his release. He was pleased to be able to give this young manager some positive feedback.

The next two days were spent lounging by the hotel pool, walking around the various visitor attractions and having a few beers. Birch particularly liked the historical Egyptian stele, the spectacular glass pyramid hotel and the nightly pirate display. This was great fun, but what had it to do with their journeys? All was revealed on the second night of their stay.

During that evening Birch began to receive promptings that they should go into meditation. They did this and once in the meditative state Birch received information intuitively concerning a visualisation that unseen benign cosmic forces wished the twosome to complete. As Birch received each element, he shared them with Bryan. In this way they worked to create the visualization and turn it from a cosmic impulse into a human consciousness reality. The visualisation was thus grounded in three dimensional reality.

In this visualization, the two men were called on to mentally create two vortices around Las Vegas. The first, internal vortex rotated clockwise. The second external vortex rotated anti-clockwise. The rotational movement of the two was such that they held each other in balance. The internal vortex allowed the negative vibrations of the city to escape into the cosmic, enabling the spiritual forces to nullify them. The purpose of the outer vortex was to allow light energies; positive energies to enter.

The whole structure could then separate the city from other centres of light, preventing contamination and stabilising this work. The two men stayed in meditation until they felt that the work was done. Wrapping up the process, Birch called on spiritual forces to continue to hold the structure together. With that, Bryan and Birch left it in their capable hands.

This was the reason the two men were 'encouraged' to go to Las Vegas. The next day they left. As they flew out, Birch and Bryan believed that their work in that place was done.

Perhaps some words of explanation are appropriate here. Visualisation, for Birch, is to mentally create and build coherent images as an extension of the meditative process. The aim is to create thought forms - mental images - of desired outcomes. These coherent images, powerfully visualised, are released from the mind to be subsequently 'worked on' by the higher consciousness. The latter will create realities, in this third dimension (the current reality in which we live today), from these thought forms provided they are coherent and powerful enough. This process must be balanced with a positive intent. This process is the basis of much so-called magic.

A vortex is a powerful moving form of rotating energy which will 'suck in' more energy, distribute it, or exclude it, depending on the intention of the meditator and his success in creating a particular thought form.

Upon review, Birch felt that Las Vegas was Sodom and Gomorrah on a bad day. And yet he felt that there was also so much positivity among the ordinary workers he'd met. Birch sensed that a number of taxi drivers, bell hops and others were holding the matrices of light which helped prevent the city disintegrating in its own mental energy filth. Birch also remembered that when the decision was taken to go to Las Vegas, there was an inrush of energy into his body. Was this latter coincidence or confirmation?

Birch met someone he viewed as an enlightened person. She worked for the Sahara Hotel as a 'taxi caller'. She made a very wise statement as he and Bryan left, saying. "The only thing wrong is not doing what I really want to do."

In that place of grasping materialism a prey to the dark forces if there was ever one, the dark energies were offset by the people that served this particular 'machine', the bell hops, hotel receptionist, taxi driver, taxi caller.

As the two travelled on Birch felt that it was ironic that he had travelled to so many places of material wealth in the U.S.A. to experience, to absorb and to heal; Palm Springs, Beverley Hills (when staying in Santa Monica), Lake Tahoe, Las Vegas.

Looking at Birch, he didn't fit the archetypal visitor to these places with his backpack, dusty shoes and baggy trousers.

Bryan had been invited to Thanksgiving in Crestone in south west Colorado. Air tickets to Colorado Springs were just $85 each. On the plane, Birch quietly went into meditation, tuning into Christ conscious energy. As he looked out of the window he felt a tremendous energy from the mountains. He had never been to Tibet, but these mountains exuded a remote master energy similar, he guessed, to that of the Himalaya. Tibet is the perceived home of beings of the highest consciousness.

At Colorado Springs airport, practical matters came to the fore. Bryan, using his considerable charm, persuaded Amber, the Avis representative, to rent a car for a knock down price. Maybe Amber hadn't exactly eaten out of Bryan's hand, but it wasn't far from it, as Birch recalls. She even laughed at his jokes. Birch stood back to watch a master at work. He knew it was time to take a back seat as far as this negotiation was concerned.

Two tough days were experienced by the dynamic duo with Mark and Alice, Bryan's contacts there. The guests were invited to stay. First, a trip to the local shop was required for food. The host had no food in the house and no money! "Mmmm," thought Birch, "this might be an interesting stay."

Mark, he, and Alice, she, claimed to be working with masters to bring twin flames (those that have a close soul linkage) together. Birch felt that a major part of their time right now might be better spent working on their own relationship. He reproached himself for being judgemental.

In his late twenties, yoga teacher Mark was tall, lithe and a graceful mover. He was hawk-nosed and sported hair in a top knot. He was second in the pecking order to his embittered, late forties, tired-faced partner. Her body was starting to bend forward with age. He was dependent on her emotionally, while she was wrapped up in her internal hell and anger. Birch liked him, but kept her at bay energetically.

"What a lovely couple of days in prospect," Birch thought. It was mystery why this man, with such great potential, was linked to such a disagreeable, unlikeable and unlikely partner. It came as no surprise when it emerged in conversation later, that she messed up his yoga groups by upsetting his students. She claimed that she would be in her body for 500 years. Somehow Birch doubted it. He had difficulty in suppressing a snort of disbelief at this announcement. She appeared not to be interested in life at all.

Bryan was looking to build a house on their land. This idea was abandoned after a violent argument erupted between Bryan and Alice. The other two stood quietly by as the storm raged. Birch tried to mediate with little success. There was another reason for abandoning the building project. It transpired that the odd couple didn't own the land after all!

There was one magical happening for Birch. On the second evening of the visit, Mark took the travelling duo to an open air swimming pool. The water was pumped straight from ground retaining a steamy hot temperature; just comfortable enough to swim in. The outside evening temperature was dropping in the high plateau, yet the swimmers relaxed in the hot water suffused with beneficial chemicals. As Birch swam he could see the snow capped mountains in the distance. The air was wonderfully fresh. A magical hour this was.

A two days stay was enough for the visitors. They said their goodbyes and left. There was a strange happening as they drove round and round the valley, unable to find their way out, despite the fact that their arrival had presented not the least problem. This navigational challenge led Birch to muse on the issue of 'tiling'. This is a mystical, or even magical, principle where participants in a ceremony will circle the space to be used at least three times to create an internal, beneficial environment.

Birch wondered if maybe they were tiling the valley in their car. It was some time and several miles before they located the exit and made good their escape.

There is a story in certain circles, that the walls of Jericho were destroyed by the Israelites using this principle in a destructive manner. The story says that the Israelites walked around the city for days. As they did so they generated a standing wave of energy which eventually shook the walls down. Unfortunately for this story, modern archaeologists claim that Jericho had no walls. Ah well, you can't win 'em all! It was a good story, anyway.

There is another story that tells of the imprisonment of a Native American in a fort in the old West. The medicine man of his tribe came and sat outside the fort where he drew circles in the dirt with his finger. After three days a wave of energy built up so strongly that the prison walls were shaken down, and the prisoner casually walked away to freedom.

Bryan and Birch drove for over a day from Crestone to Sedona, Arizona. All day they drove through high plains, 5 - 8,000 feet high (1524 – 2438 metres); thousands of square miles of it. As he sat quietly staring out of the window Birch imagined being Clint Eastwood in the film 'High Plains Drifter'. Perhaps it was just as well that Bryan was driving. Birch dropped out of this reverie as he realised that, in his Eastwood role, he didn't possess the horse, the cigar and, most definitely not the rugged good looks. The only comparison possible was that by this time Birch did have the stubble!

Driving into Sedona, Birch dropped Bryan off at a new age shop that they passed. Bryan wanted to try to sell his spiritual cards that were his business interest. Research failed to discover if this endeavour was successful. They found their motel but discovered it had no record of the booking. Birch was surprised because he had thus far been impressed by the service and efficiency of the Americans. However, no booking and no spare rooms! On the evidence of past incidents, this failure suggested to him that they were meant to stay elsewhere.

In the event they stayed the night in a geodesic dome. No other insights came to the dynamic duo to explain this change of plan although, due to the space, Birch was able to stretch in his *tai chi* exercise the following morning. That was the morning both men went to the Church of the Golden Age. Sananda, the chap running the service, channelled an Egyptian priest around Birch. In his own words this channelling brought the Egyptian who was guiding Birch. Birch thought that maybe he had picked up Yogananda's vibration putting his own spin on the Indian mystic's presence. The whole service was filmed by a Belgian film crew for that nation's TV service.

The two met Maria, an American, who had moved to work in Washington in order to work spiritually with politics. Both were charmed by her open nature. She was a great fan of Al Gore who was Vice President of the U.S. at the time. Maria had worked on Gore's election campaign. Interestingly, in later years Gore became a great advocate of working harmoniously with the planet. Birch wondered if Maria had, indeed, had a subtle influence.

The two travellers drove to Cathedral Rock, a large monolith with a spiritual reputation among Native Americans. They met Maria there. The two men climbed up. Maria passed on the opportunity. She was vastly overweight and wisely stayed at the bottom.

At the top of the climb, Birch had an intuitive insight. There were two enormous spires rising skyward. They were separated by a flat saddle of rock. He sensed that one of the spires had an amazing vibration which represented the spiritual future for humanity and the planet. The other spire was more passive and symbolised the lower vibrational present time. It was an emotionally moving experience. He felt that he was playing a part, small though it may have been, in bringing these two elements into reality. He also sensed that being in this place was assisting him to increase the power of his spiritual work. All this while, Bryan meditated.

Birch returned down the rock to rejoin Maria. Bryan continued his internal work. As Birch descended, he passed two people climbing. Pretty soon afterward Bryan joined the other two. When he reached his companions he told them that the newcomers had started to smoke pot. Birch felt relieved that he had left the spot while the energies were still high.

Later, Bryan and Birch had an insight simultaneously. Maria's future would include the possibility of her taking a political role. She would also have the opportunity to appear on TV in order to promulgate her ideas and beliefs concerning spiritual politics. The three separated after Cathedral Rock, the two men to drive to Tucson, Maria to return to Washington.

Tucson, surrounded by desert, was home to another of Bryan's contacts. Crystal had started the self styled University of Melchizadek in her desert suburb home. Bryan seemed to have a propensity for 'collecting' these slightly eccentric, mystically oriented people. Perhaps

Birch was another one of those? Crystal was a small, thin woman, very energetic, around seventy years of age. She lived in a beautiful Spanish-Mexican style house with a female companion who seemed to be carer-cum-housekeeper-cum-bottlewasher.

All participated in a meditation. This was powerful for Birch and made him feel light headed. The two men recovered by eating large amounts of pizza back at their motel and by sunbathing next to the pool until the sun went down. Birch thought, "Ain't life a bitch!"

The third and last day in Tucson was a tourist day for them. They went to the to a magnificent mission church, Francis Xavier. Birch was drawn to a nearby hillock which had a cross on the top and a Lourdes-type healing reputation. Stone lions sat guarding two entrance portals to the circular walk up the hill. This was curious and not Christian symbolism as far as Birch knew. In ancient Egypt, lions were placed as protection outside temples. Years later, in meditation, Birch was given the image of a lion to use as protection when attempting to secure good vibrations for a friend's living space.

He lit a candle in the church for a wheelchair-bound girl that the two had met in the motel. Bryan had done some healing with her.

In the afternoon they went to Tombstone, from the sublime to the ridiculous, literally. They discovered it had been kept more or less as it was in the old West days. The people and the place were rooted in the past. The energy dynamic was like a sink and the two came away feeling drained. A stop for a drink in a saloon bar enabled the travellers to overhear some of the locals discussing another local who was not present. One of the party threatened to shoot the missing person the next time they met. Time to leave!

Leaving Tucson, off they drove to Encenitas, California to visit the Self Realization Fellowship Gardens; a trip of over 300 miles (483 kilometres) to the ocean. They relaxed in the flower garden overlooking the Pacific Ocean discussing their journey together, for soon they would part company. Each now had different agendas and objectives. They still had a little while longer together, and continued up the coast so Bryan could practice his negotiating techniques in order to sell his cards. They called at St Louis Obispo and Carmel, the latter being where the aforementioned Clint Eastwood had performed his civic duties as mayor. On to Belen, New Mexico, out in the 'boondocks' was their last place to visit together. Bryan still had it in mind to build a house in the U.S. This seemed the last possibility. A realtor (estate agent in English) directed the guys to a mountainous area approximately 10 miles (16 kilometres) away. Across flat scrubland and close to the mountains some people were building their own homes.

"Is this the sticks, or what?" Birch didn't share this thought with the still enthusiastic Bryan. They saw a couple of self-built houses of rough, and not so rough, construction. The third place was being built out of old tyres (tires in American) filled with sand.

"Yes indeedee, this is the sticks," mused Birch. "So this is eco-culture?"

The owners of the tyre house were very welcoming as were the three dogs that nearly licked the two visitors to death. Birch could see that even Bryan's enthusiasm was starting to wane. The cap was put on the whole episode as, when asked about the area, the male house builder talked of the endemic corruption and violence. He claimed that the valley was a through route for the cocaine trade to the cities of the north. The final nail went into this particular coffin when he flipped up his sweater to reveal a large handgun strapped to his waist. He claimed that the police were powerless against the crime wave.

"Um, right, ah, yes, well, it, uh, we must be getting along," Birch thought. "Let's get my sorry ass out of here." Birch was beginning to think in the vernacular. Bryan seemed to pick up his thoughts and they bade the 'homesteaders' goodbye, and beat a hasty retreat to the apparent safety of nearby Albuquerque.

In retrospect Birch thought that the 'homesteader' idea was for people who would re-create the 1850's frontier mentality in the new millennium. The lawlessness around was all part of the scenario created by the populace. If you want to stare into the pit, you will see the darkness.

Bryan and Birch had worked well together. Now it was time for them to go their separate ways. Bryan dropped Birch off at a hotel in Albuquerque then drove north to Taos. From there he was going to Colorado Springs to return the car. Birch wanted a few days without driving around the country. A stay in the capital of New Mexico was appealing.

On his first morning without his travelling companion, Birch caught a bus into the old town. On the way in, a young guy handed out cookies and candy clearly revelling in the giving spirit. He seemed to be pretty well accepted by the fellow bus travellers.

Birch wondered if this would happen in England. Probably not, he concluded. He also thought of the oft quoted phrase that the U.S. and the U.K. were countries separated by a common language. To him, over the weeks of his visit, he was starting to realise that the differences in culture between the two were vast, never mind the language.

A long talk with a shopkeeper confirmed that there was still an old 'backwoods' attitude. Birch thought that perhaps some people saw this as an antidote to the stress of modern living. There was also the point that, with more physical space in this country and with less interference from government, the individualist spirit is stronger in the U.S. than in the U.K.

As Birch stood and chatted to the shopkeeper, a Navajo artist came in to ask permission to display a couple of his beautiful paintings. Around the old town square surrounded by traditional adobe buildings, proud, fine looking Navajo Native Americans displayed beautifully worked jewellery and colourful shawls and loose clothing for sale presumably for the benefit of tourists. In a central grassed area two cannon from Spanish colonial times, carefully restored, evoked the atmosphere of the past.

Native American Spirit

*First experiences of the psychic
power of indigenous peoples.*

A couple of days in Albuquerque was enough to recharge Birch's batteries. And the roaming spirit was beginning to give him itchy feet again. He met a group of three people, two Americans and one Brit, spiritual travellers like himself. The four of them decided to go to Chaco Canyon together. The timing of the visit was fortuitous. It was the time of the winter solstice, and this would increase the energies further.

Historically Chaco Canyon was a place of great significance and power to the Pueblo Indians as well as latter-day spiritual workers. It remains a cultural centre for them along with the Hopi and Navajo Indians to this day.

The site comprises around thirty buildings, each huge with over 100 rooms apiece. It is said that some were constructed as astronomical observatories. Chaco Canyon is the hub of a network of ancient roadways. It is not easy to dismiss this site as insignificant.

Chaco is harsh; blazing hot and dry in summer, bitterly cold and dry in winter. And while archaeological evidence of farming has been found, it is questionable if 1,000 years ago, local farming methods in this hostile environment had the capability to support the community. Maybe it imported food from outside? However intuitive insights tell us something different.

According to the New York Times of 29th September 2006...

The great Chaco civilization, trading partner of the Maya, established a far-reaching sphere of influence in the North American desert a millennium ago. Among the most remote and mysterious of their outposts was Chimney Rock, in what is now the very southwest corner of Colorado, 90 miles (145 kilometres) from Chaco Canyon in New Mexico, the center of the culture.

Why did the Chaco people – the Anasazi, or 'ancestral Puebloans,' as their descendants prefer – build an enormous ceremonial Great House at Chimney Rock, so far from home, 1,000 feet (305 metres)above the nearest water supply and at the base of immense sandstone spires?

It was not until two decades ago that archaeologists arrived at an explanation that most now accept: the Chaco people built the Great House as a lunar observatory precisely aligned to a celestial event that occurs just once in a generation.

The collection of artefacts at the Chaco Museum comprises a staggering 1 million items. This resource is hugely valued by the scientific community not least for the quality of the supporting material.

There was a mound there that had particular spiritual significance, according to Birch's new companions. Getting lost, they didn't arrive at the main entrance until late afternoon. As the party drove into the Canyon a bird swooped low in front of the vehicle. Instead of flying off, the bird followed the curving road. It appeared as though it was leading them in. It seemed to the group that this was a positive symbol. Now the delay in finding the entrance also seemed significant. As the party poured from their car, a shaft of sunlight shone directly on top of the mound. If the arrival had been a few minutes before or after, the symbolic moment would have been lost. The party walked to the mound upon which the sun still shone.

A simple meditation was performed. The energies resonated in Birch's being. He experienced emotions from the past, sensing that those present had lived in that place when it had been a thriving community. The valley was filled with life, colour and energy, but the climate was different back then. Crops were grown, turkeys bred for their meat, and ceremonies were performed. This was a place strikingly teeming with life. Now the valley was silent except for the movement of the few visitors and the caw, caw, caw of the birds. Time stood still for a precious few minutes. Eventually the spell was broken and the little party returned to the present.

They were interrupted by a valley guard who accused them of digging in the mound looking for artefacts. Clearly this had been a problem in the past. He was not exactly threatening, but clearly he was not a happy bunny. His attitude changed completely when he learned the true work and intentions of the foursome. In fact he was delighted that a spiritual ceremony had been performed here. As the group chatted amicably, without warning a tremendous animal wail erupted from beyond the canyon rim. The park ranger looked up and said, "That's strange the coyotes never call out at this time of day."

Birch recalled his encounter with the coyote on the ashram walk. Was this place honouring their ceremony with this communication from the animal kingdom?

As the party started their drive out of the canyon in the gathering darkness, Birch looked up to the canyon rim and saw two coyotes looking down at them. It was as though they were communicating. He wanted to shout out, "We know why you were here. We salute you. Goodbye."

That night the party found a bed and breakfast between Chaco and Bernalillo, their next port of call. Bed and breakfasts in the U.S.A. tend to be very different from those in the U.K. Those in the States are more upmarket and thus more expensive. But they are something to be enjoyed from time to time, by the intrepid traveller.

This particular B&B was famous, according to the owner, for having its own ghost. Always a good selling point for customers is a ghost; good for business. The story behind this particular ghost was that the old building was formerly used by the Spanish military when the land had been part of New Spain. The owner said that the ghost of a Spanish soldier guarded the building by walking up and down. Apparently, the apparition was seen regularly. On this occasion he must have had a night off. Everyone slept soundly with no interruptions, ghostly or otherwise.

The next day, the four were joined by two other Americans staying in the B&B, and together they drove to Bernalillo to experience a sound chamber. This chamber was used for chanting by those of a spiritual interest. The idea was that the circular shape of the building, and the use of certain building materials, enhanced the sounds uttered by humans. Great fun was had by all, and the six were joined by local people to create some great sounds.

Then it struck him. Birch realised with a shock that this was Christmas Eve. What a different life he was leading now? He had to pinch himself. All the experiences he was having, and all the amazing people with whom he was sharing these experiences, made his mind boggle. He recalled Christmas Day the previous year. He had spent it in his flat in Cheltenham, on his own. He discovered how happy he felt with this new Yuletide experience. How pleased he was to be able to break with the mundanity of the life he had led so recently. There he was, thousands of miles from home, the cold, the wet, and able to meditate and perform visualisations in that rich land so full of promise, energy and mystery. He was having the most amazing time of his 56 years. One experience tumbled into the next. It was so exhilarating.

After the chanting the group engaged in a casual conversation. Birch spoke briefly of his plans to be in Teotihuacán at the spring equinox and of the connection with the Maya priests.

"That's interesting," one of the locals said. "There is a lady named Cynthia who you will find having lunch in a restaurant downtown. She's training to be a Mayan priest."

"Oh, oh," thought Birch. Undoubtedly he felt another adventure coming on.

The sound chamber party broke up. Birch and a couple of others hightailed down to the aforementioned restaurant. A few enquiries brought Birch to the table of Cynthia. He found a warm, welcoming lady with the direct, down-to-earth approach. Birch loved this trait so common with Americans. Birch took to her partner, Gale, immediately.

Gale was very tall with a long pigtail in the Native American tradition. He had dropped out from a big government job to live the tradition of the Arapahoe tribe in their reservation. A deep, resonant voice was complemented by a pair of humorous eyes that looked at Birch with an open, unblinking gaze, but in a very friendly manner. He was struck by Gale's apparent strength of body and expression. Birch took to him immediately.

As the party ate their meal together, Cynthia explained the apparently strange occurrence of a white woman learning the Mayan tradition.

"I am working with a Mayan priest called Don Alejandro in Guatemala," she explained.

"With all due respect, why should this shaman teach a Western person his ancient practices?" asked Birch.

"Don Alejandro has been guided to spread the ancient knowledge to a wider public," she replied.

Birch explained his interests, enthusiasm and past experiences. This was enough to gain Cynthia's attention and his words seemed to encourage her.

"We're going to Guatemala in early January, to work and travel with Don Alejandro. Would you like to come?"

"Does the Pope go to church? Are apple pie and motherhood good things? Are frogs waterproof?" he answered.

It was at this point that Birch found it necessary to explain his English humour. After some extensive paraphrasing, Cynthia was able to understand that, yes, he really wanted to go. There was only the administrative issue of extracting the $1800 from his account in England to pay for the trip. This was duly accomplished and things were set up. However, the time was not yet right. There was more adventure to be had before Guatemala for Cheltenham's traveller.

Lena, one of the party of three with which Birch was still travelling, did a tarot spread for him that evening. He was struggling with all the events and opportunities opening up for him. She spoke of Birch 'being turned inside out,' of much karmic debt to be repaid, of much energy being made available, of initiation, of dropping things from the ego. This was serious stuff. Birch listened and understood intellectually what he was being told. But it was over the following months and years that much of what Lena said, came to pass in his life and adventures. It was then that he understood in a deeper sense.

The party travelled to Taos to spend Christmas Day in a hotel in this old Spanish settlement. All of the party were free of family commitments. It was remarkable how they had come together and how they shared these experiences with harmony and companionship. Once settled in the hotel, Ben, one of the party, discovered that there was a Native American ceremony on Christmas Day, the next day, on the local reservation. Outsiders were allowed to witness the event. They agreed to make this the highlight of a very different Christmas Day.

The ceremony at the reservation of the Puebla people was attended by a very large crowd of mostly white watchers. Before it all began the attendees were told that no photographs were to be taken, that this was a sacred ceremony, and that it was a privilege for them to be there to share it. This announcement certainly set the scene. What followed was an amazing experience. If Birch had to create a list of the top ten moments on the journey, this experience would have featured.

There was a long wait after the scheduled start time, but it was worth it. Eventually a line of male Native American figures appeared, sparsely dressed with shells attached to their ankles, and fronds of plant material tied to their bodies. The line remained stationary and silent for a while. The older men stood in the middle, mature men either side of them, younger men and boys on the outside. In the quietness the expectation was almost palpable. Had someone been clumsy enough to drop a pin, it would have created a stir. It was as though time stood still. The atmosphere was such that Birch found himself holding his breath. He describes it rather like watching those underwater shows on TV. As we watch we can't help holding our breath while Jacques Cousteau goes deeper.

Silence reigned for what seemed an age, or maybe it was only a couple of seconds. Time had no meaning in this sacred time and place. Suddenly, at an unnoticed signal, the line of men started the most hypnotic dance. First to the left then to the right, their legs moved in unison. The whole moved as one in this ancient dance to the sacred Earth Mother, the protector and nurturer of their sacred way of life. There was no separation between the individual and the group. The dance danced itself.

Only the older men in the middle of the group chanted as the dance fulfilled itself. The chanting increased in power and energy to almost unbearable levels. Did the dance last for a minute or an hour? Birch had no way of judging. This experience was beyond judgement. The sacred dance was performed in three places on the reservation. The dancers moved silently from one location to the next. Watchers followed, numbed and quietened by the experience. No-one spoke. At the end, the dancers moved back to their homes and the audience dispersed quietly. As the group drove away, Birch realised that this was the most profound Christmas experience he had ever had.

Back at the hotel, Birch and Mike, another of the party, had a dip in a hot spring, re-living and recovering from their breathtaking experience.

A friend of Birch's, Richard, tells a story. One day he was walking in the desert in Arizona when he came across a Native American squatting on the desert sand. Miles from anywhere, the two men were isolated.

"Ah, you have come," said the Native American.

Richard was so dumbfounded by this bizarre meeting and communication that he dutifully followed the other man. Personal safety issues never crossed his mind. This man took Richard to his nearby village and led him to a rooftop vantage point. There he left him. This was in Hopi country at second mesa. The Hopi mostly live on three flat topped mountains which are called 'mesas'.

Richard was then witness to three days and nights of ritual dancing, chanting and ceremony. At the end of three days, Richard left. To this day, he has no idea how the other man knew he would be walking where he was, or why he was selected to see the incredible spectacle. In another story that appears in later pages, we will see a glimmer of the alternative reality of Native Americans. At that time we might choose to consider that it wasn't so long ago that these people were referred to as 'savages'.

It was time for this party to break up. Birch travelled south and picked up a rental car to move around quietly for a while before the sojourn to Guatemala. Relaxing, enjoying hot springs, catching up on sleep, and all the while he tried to make some sense of the experiences of the past weeks. But it was still too early to make sense of the whole. He concluded that 'going with the flow' was perhaps the best way of coping for the time being.

Guatemala

Fantastic adventures in Central America.

It is possible that some British readers might find it a challenge to point to Guatemala on a map. (It can be found on the North Pacific Ocean, surrounded by Mexico, Belize, Honduras and El Salvador.) It is a country that rarely seems to feature in the media in the UK. So this might be a good place to take a brief look at this tumultuous land.

Mayan in origin, the region flourished in the first millennium AD. Conquistador Pedro do Alvarado invaded in 1524. Winning independence from Spain in 1821, it became a republic in 1839 with the collapse of the United Provinces of Central America. In 1944 the left wing governments instituted social and political reforms much to the advantage of workers and farmers, but to the disadvantage of landowners and the military. Covertly backed by the US, the country was taken by Col. Carlos Castillo Armas in 1954. From then it was subject to a series of violent, repressive dictatorships and gained an unenviable reputation for its death squads. The Civil War lasted some 36 years during which time the indigenous Maya were the target of extreme abuse. Eventually the US cut off its military aid by which time it is reckoned that some 200,000 people had lost their lives. Some observers claim that over 1 million refugees were created.

A degree of peace finally came in 1996, but in a climate of blame and recrimination. US President Clinton apologised for the support his country had given to the preceding military governments. Unfortunately, all was not to remain calm. When the government took steps to stimulate the economy, tax increases triggered violent protests.

Now a constitutional democratic republic, Guatemala's chief of state and head of government is President Oscar Jose Rafael Berger Perdomo.

This hot and humid country is peppered with volcanoes and is no stranger to violent earthquakes. It is also battered by hurricanes and suffers from water pollution and soil erosion. Its population of 13 million is primarily Christian but we also see indigenous Mayan beliefs. Over 50% of the inhabitants are still below the poverty line.

Drug trafficking remains a problem, and Guatemala is considered a major transit country for cocaine and heroin. Corruption and money laundering persist. Although it is becoming a destination for foreign tourists from the US and Europe, visitors are subject to high levels of violent crime. Vehicles are hijacked regularly and it is best to remain in the cities after dark. Unfortunately, visitors are mistrusted as some Guatemalans believe they are there to kidnap their children.

It was into this discomforting environment that Birch was bound.

But the time for the next adventure had arrived, and it was with some trepidation that Birch caught a flight from Albuquerque to Houston to meet with other members of the party. Despite all the recent adventures, Birch was sick with concern. This was his first time in a third world country, first time in Central America. He consoled himself with the thought that he was with a party of others, some of whom had made the trip before.

The party was met at Guatemala airport by the van that was to be their transport for the next two weeks. Exhausted, they fell into bed after a drive to the city of Antigua. Birch was too tired to make sense of his surroundings in what was now the early hours of the morning. The only images that caught his eye as they left the airport was of a burnt-out car, and the low wattage of the street lights. To the eyes of a Westerner used to big city bright lights, they created a dim, slightly depressing environment.

Welcome to Central America!

The next morning brought an entirely different series of images. Antigua was a charming old Spanish colonial city, well laid out with low buildings in the old style. This city had been the capital of Guatemala until an earthquake had almost demolished it. The Spanish masters wisely decided to build their new capital away from this particular earthquake area, surrounded by three potential volcanoes.

This was so much the better for Antigua which had reinvented itself as a tourist centre, and one where many schools teaching English flourished. Guatemala City on the other hand, was typical of a third world metropolis of 3 million people, traffic polluted and endemically poor.

That day, the travellers enjoyed some retail therapy, relaxed in the town square, ate the local culinary specialities and caught up on a little sun. Indigenous people from the countryside trying to sell their wares besieged them wherever they went. Ponchos, cowboy style hats, tee shirts in local vibrant colours were hawked alongside obsidian knives and trinkets. Hard bargains were struck, mostly to the advantage of the vendors, Birch suspected. He didn't mind about this. He was sure that they had a lot less money than he. They were excellent sales men and women, never giving up on a potential sale if they saw the slightest crack in the resolve of the potential purchaser.

Before meeting Don Alejandro the party was offered a trip to a nearby small town where a shrine to local deity attracted many from across Guatemala. An effigy of the deity, Monximon, was housed in a building with enough space for his believers to sit and present offerings of tobacco and food. The party of gringos led by a local from Antigua treated the visit with respect, giving their own offerings and prayers.

As the party drove back to Antigua, local men were returning from their labours in the fields. They wore curiously coloured shorts. Birch later discovered that the colours changed from village to village to denote where they belonged. They all wore cowboy style straw hats and carried their fearsome looking machetes. It was on this drive that Birch and the other gringos saw vast quantities of rubbish strewn across the countryside. This particular care for the environment did not seem part of their social consciousness. Even the Mayan priests they came across later in their trip dropped litter with no apparent sense of caring. This troubled all the gringos.

Birch was reminded of one thing that now bothered him about his stay at the ashram. Despite the wonderful climate, without exception the residents used the electric driers for their clothes. Birch had done the same. Perhaps he might have found a place to hang his clothes. He pondered on his inability to have thought this through and worked out a more personally acceptable solution.

Next day they returned to Guatemala City to meet Don Alejandro and the three Mayan priests who were his helpers and supporters on the journey. Don Alejandro had a small office in the city. Their host was a very small man in stature, not unlike the rest of the indigenous population. But Birch was struck by his amazing, deep brown eyes.

When he looked into them it was as though those eyes had experienced hundreds of lifetimes; had seen the experiences of the ages, and was looking out in the latest lifetime merely as the extension of millennia. Birch was impressed.

Don Alejandro Oxlaj's own website gives a helpful description of the man.

Don Alejandro is charged as the primary keeper of the teachings, visions and prophecies of the Mayan people. He is head of the National Mayan Council of Elders of Guatemala, Day Keeper of the Mayan Calendar, a 13th generation Quiche Mayan High Priest and a Grand Elder of the Continental Council of Elders and Spiritual Guides of the Americas. He is also an international lecturer on Mayan Culture.

A second Mayan did not look like a priest at all. He had what Birch describes as a very strong face, and a powerful body with muscles in places that Birch didn't even have places, (or so he claimed). This was accompanied by a deep, gruff voice that seemed to say, "Hear and obey."

It transpired that this man was Don Alejandro's 'minder'. This minding was not only in a physical sense but in a psychic one also. Thus, if Don Alejandro was psychically attacked, then it was the job of this man to deal with it. Birch decided that he would prefer not to meet this chap on a dark night in a narrow alley. In fact, Birch was happy to be on the same side as this 'minder'. The other two Mayans appeared to be amiable men; very much the subordinates. Behind Don Alejandro's back they called him 'The General'.

The party was now fifteen strong and consisted of ten gringos (a slightly derogatory word for white people), one El Salvadorian who translated and was also a trainee Mayan priestess, and the four Mayans. The whole party crammed in to the van which had been fitted out with seats, not very comfortable seats. The tyres were bald to the extent that the canvas showed. They wouldn't have passed muster in the U.S. or U.K.

"Calm yourself, Birchy. Courage!" he thought as he considered the possible disagreeable consequences of an accident in that deathtrap. "Welcome to Central America!"

Then the driving into the heartland started. The late afternoon saw the cramped party arrive at a fairly pleasant, modern hotel. Birch and his newly designated roommate, Jeff, took the opportunity to swim in the outside pool, relax and chat on the harsh grass while they enjoyed the air and sun. That evening both of them started to itch. They had been invaded by tiny insects called 'jiggers' by other gringos. These insects jumped onto the skin from the grass and bored a hole into the skin keeping an air hole free to breathe. Birch in particular was assailed by these very uncomfortable, unwelcome visitors. The infestation continued for the next week until one of the others in the party, Charlie, came to the rescue. He claimed a psychic connection with the insect kingdom, and performed a healing. Lo and behold, the insects and the itching disappeared. Birch's relief and gratitude were boundless. Nevertheless, Central American insects seemed to greatly enjoy dining on gringo blood. One of the Americans who had been to the country a couple of times said that over time a person's resistance would be built up.

Charlie told Birch a story concerning his connection with the insect kingdom. Two insects landed, one on each of his wrists. Before they could sting him, he sent them love and they flew off without the sacrifice of biting him. To do so would have meant their certain death.

Next stop Honduras, another Central American country to the south of Guatemala. Much of the journey was over dirt roads and through jungle. At one point, the narrow road was blocked by a bullock. Totally unconcerned, it just sat chewing the cud contentedly. No amount of blowing the horn had any impact. The driver got out and waved his arms and shouted to get the animal to move. Eventually, as the beast ambled off he looked round as if to say, "I live here. Who are you?"

The miles rolled by. After what seemed like a week, the party reached a small open space that was the border between Guatemala and Honduras. It was just a clearing in the forest, no border posts there. The van was besieged by men bearing massive wads of notes. They were there to change Guatemalan quetzals into Honduran lempiras. The rate was two quetzals to one lempira? Not exactly high finance and a far cry from banks and ATMs!

That evening, safely settled in a modest hotel in the jungle, Don Alejandro gave his first talk to the group. He spoke of the background of the Mayan struggle against imperialist Spain, of the continuing fight for the rights of the indigenous people, and the journey the party was taking would last one Mayan week of 13 days. Don Alejandro spoke in Spanish but threw in words and phrases from his native language, Quiche. This gave Rosemary, the translator, a great challenge. While she spoke English and Spanish well, she didn't know Quiche.

"I interpret from the sense of the overall commentary," she said when asked how she coped.

Gradually Birch tried to acclimatise himself to the local 'bugs' by cleaning his teeth in local water. But wisely he continued to drink bottled water and only ate cooked food. He avoided milk and fruit juices. They had a particularly bad reputation in promoting the Central American version of 'Delhi belly.' In Mexico it is commonly called 'Montezuma's revenge' by Western sufferers.

The first temple stop was Queruga, the site of fascinating stelae. Each one had representations of each of the races on the Earth. There was Native American, white, black, oriental, all portrayed clearly.

"How did the ancients, in the middle of Central America, know of oriental or black people, Native Americans of the north?" thought Birch. This was, and remains, a great mystery to him.

The party moved on to the incredible ruined city and ritual centre of Copan, where the buildings are cyclopean in scale. They impress as historical monuments, but some are powerful energetically. Don Alejandro introduced the group to the place, but slowly to allow gradual acclimatisation to the energies. The weather was cloudy; a blessed relief for Birch. Blazing heat had been anticipated.

One of the party, Paula, had a cathartic experience at the 13 step temple. She collapsed in an emotional state having seen herself in a vision, as though coming home. She could not place this experience into a logical framework.

At the end of the day, the party squashed into the van to return to Copan town. Apart from the hotel the town was down at heel and very poor, but Birch felt safe. He strolled alone through the crumbling town square after dark. There were no local people to be seen. Perhaps they were resting at the end of the day's labours. The dim local lighting gave an air of gloom as Birch perambulated in the evening peace.

Later, Don Alejandro spoke powerfully of the Earth changes at the end of the Mayan calendar. The Mayan calendar is a complex system of interlocking elements. Understanding requires years of study. It is 26,000 years in length and ends on 21st December 2012. By this date, great changes to the Earth are forecast by many commentators, including the Mayans. The 'General' also spoke of an illness that would strike white people in 2008. This would be genetically attracted to the race. (Well, we will soon find out if he was right or wrong!)

Grimly, Birch thought of the terrible suffering perpetrated on the Mayans by white people over the centuries, even up to the year before his visit. He wondered if this prophesied disease were to come to pass, would it be a repayment for all the pain and suffering perpetrated on the indigenous peoples around the world.

Until arriving in Guatemala Birch hadn't realised that there had been a terrible civil war perpetrated on the Mayans and other indigenous people. The aggressors were the largely white elite who occupied the cities, owned the wealth, and dominated politics. The army had been the perpetrators of much suffering. However there had been no overall 'victory' and the army had been withdrawn to barracks. Until the previous year Don Alejandro and the Mayans had not been allowed to visit or perform ceremonies in their sacred places. Birch felt doubly honoured to be able to be there.

One frustration for him was his inability to speak Spanish. He could not communicate directly with the Mayans. There was so much knowledge and wisdom to be learned from them. Don Alejandro had an interesting way of dealing with questions that he deemed to be inappropriate, at least inappropriate for him. Jim, one of the Americans, had a powerful intellect. He knew very detailed facts concerning the Mayan calendar while Birch only had little more than a rudimentary knowledge. However, while Jim's intellectual understanding was impressive, his diplomacy was something less than well developed. He would ask Don Alejandro detailed questions concerning the calendar or the Mayan philosophy. Don Alejandro would sometimes answer when all were gathered in group session. If Don Alejandro didn't wish to answer, he would merely stay silent. The whole group would sit there, sometimes for minutes on end. Birch wondered if Jim gained any other benefit from this trip other than to broaden his knowledge.

At the start of the second day, Birch had breakfasted in a lean-to in the local market with the Mayans plus Jan and Lothar (two of the gringos in the party). He thought back to a meal he had with Bob and Mary in a luxury hotel in Tahoe, not so many weeks before. He compared it with the very simple fare being served by the local ladies cooking over open vats and fires. Today, he and his friends were sitting at rough tables with simple food in front of them. Birch felt both of the meals had been a blessing.

The second Copan visit started with fire ritual. Birch didn't sense that the energies had been very powerful on this occasion. By the evening however, he felt that energies had moved within him.

There were times when Birch, especially those times on his own, when he felt a sense of isolation. This isolation generated nervousness and fear. One of those occurrences was about to happen. After Copan, Birch walked on his own back to the hotel in the town. He became lost and the only human contact he had for a while was a small boy. Needless to say the language difficulties were immediately apparent. In fact, this lad didn't even sound Spanish. Fortuitously, Birch stumbled into the Mayan priests who were walking this road; lost became found!

From time to time Birch's thoughts strayed to his forthcoming visit to Mexico. Those around him didn't exactly fill him with confidence. A woman he'd met in Copan spoke of being robbed there. Gale told him that it was a real bad place to be and that the police were worse than the bandits at robbing people. Fortunately Birch did not find that to be true when he reached Mexico.

The travelling continued in the gruelling heat. Birch was working hard to cope with the temperature. (We Brits must have some sympathy for him. We're more accustomed to chill and rain. At the time of writing this it is summer in the UK. We have every reason to expect it to be warm and dry. We might even expect to be planning barbeques and weekend trips to the beach. Instead, we have endured weeks of rain. The sun hasn't been seen at all in southern England. In fact, we have been subject to unprecedented, catastrophic floods. Grim times, indeed.) Birch was also faced with the language, bugs, culture, and other members of the group as well as the exhausting travelling. Someone once said that to endure was enough. This could have been Birch's theme for this part of the journey.

Interest was kept alive during the driving hours with the telling of stories. Gale told how the Arapahoe would butcher their meat. They maintained their own herds of cattle. When they needed to eat meat the elders of the tribe would go to the herd, put their blankets and sacred objects on the floor and chant to the herd. Without fail, after a time the herd would move away leaving one beast on its own. This was the animal that the herd had selected to sacrifice. One of the tribe, who had gone through a special ceremony of preparation, would shoot the lone animal. What a different way of looking at animal slaughter, thought Birch.

One day the party arrived at a cave that was bigger than a cathedral. It took some time and effort to climb down into it. Once inside, the travellers saw that the place was lit by many candles. Obviously Mayan faithful had been there earlier. This place was called Moncaun or

Chichoy. The first impressions were of power and presence. The Mayans prepared the fire ceremony. Candles were lit around the fire and the group settled around in preparation for meditation. Without warning, the flames of the candles changed from the usual flickerings to the shape of perfect vortices; not an every day phenomenon. Birch's jaw dropped open as did those of several gringos around him.

"It's OK," said Don Alejandro through Rosemary, the interpreter. "This is a sign that the spirits are here."

As the group drove away after the ceremony, Birch had the thought that maybe psychic phenomena were easier to manifest and experience in a society that wasn't totally committed to logic and linear cause and effect.

The party moved on to El Socaro which was in the middle of an agricultural co-operative. The homes were little more than shacks yet the vibrancy and contentment of the people was palpable. No stressed and strained faces. The sacred site here was on top of a hill and the venue for another fire ceremony; very powerful for some. Charlie, Birch's insect healer, collapsed with the power of the energy released from within him as the ceremony progressed.

The group was now down to eleven members. Jan, Lothar and Jeff, Birch's room mate, had flown back to the U.S.A. Ruffino, one of the Mayans had returned home. So it was a depleted party that went onto the next sacred site, Iximce, a Mayan pyramid. It was a place of tremendous power. Inside it was a round, raised baptismal plinth. Baptisms were accompanied by fire in the ancient times. Birch stood alone, visualising the past; this time in his intellectual awareness.

On to Panatachel on beautiful Lake Atitlan; a fresh water lake high in the Guatemalan sierra. The place was a holiday resort. The group arrived after refusing to stay at the first choice town. The energies were sink-like, and the hotel more drain-like. After they drove away, the Mayan told how the town had been almost destroyed in the recent civil war. The pain and suffering were sadly still very apparent.

Once in the Panatachel hotel, Birch went to bed, diarrhoea, exhaustion, or perhaps the energies of the war-torn town having taken their toll. It was necessary to rest. The next day he felt much better. This town was to play a big part in one of Birch's later journeys. That story will be told later. In the meantime, at some point the party had crossed back from Honduras to Guatemala. Birch had no idea when that was except that it happened before Lake Atitlan. All the travelling merged into the background.

One morning Don Alejandro announced that today was the day of the dog in the Mayan calendar. This was virtually meaningless to Birch who was a Mayan calendar free zone! During the travelling that day Birch saw numerous dogs on the road! Perhaps he was looking for them, perhaps not. Others in the party also commented on this 'doggy day'.

It was time for another sacred site visit, this time to an ancient archaeological site called Abaj Takalik, Don Alejandro said that it was 12,000 years old. The conventional archaeological paradigm claimed it was much younger than that. 12,000 years old would contradict the assumptions and conventions concerning such sites. This was a sacred place of the Olmec people; a mysterious race who, in their statues, showed the facial characteristics of Negros. There was no trace of Negros in present day Central American racial characteristics. The low stepped pyramid and adjacent buildings were totally different in style and construction to the others they had visited.

Don Alejandro showed a deep square hole dug by archaeologists to expose remains at the bottom. Above the remains there was a grey ridge of lighter soil that was volcanic ash. Thus the Olmec remains at the bottom were older than the volcanic activity. It is accepted by authorities that the volcano erupted 12,000 years ago. Ah, the problems scientists have to deal with!

One time the party was visiting a museum the central floor area of which was completely filled by a pyramid. It was painted in the most vibrant colours with magnificent carvings of fabulous beasts on the sides. Don Alejandro told the group that this magnificent work of art had been moved from the original site and repainted by local artists. This pyramid had been discovered inside an outer pyramid. On a later trip to Mexico, Birch discovered that this was not an uncommon practice of the ancients. As the group was absorbing this vast undertaking of the past, Don Alejandro talked more of those ancient times. Every ten years the soothsayers would gather and perform their magical ceremonies, their purpose to decide if the people of the city should leave or remain. If the messages that they received was for the society to leave, then that is what it would do. Buildings would be filled with rubble, covered over with earth, and the society would move away lock, stock, and barrel. What a different way of looking at social reality?

The last day of ceremony was carried out near Don Alejandro's house. The venue was owned by the Mayan elder council. It was spectacularly perched on a ledge far above the valley floor. Birch felt it awe inspiring. For the first time he connected with the actual ritual process. Perhaps his improving health played a part in this? Previously the rituals that he had previously seen and taken part in had gone over his head.

There were other groups at the ceremonial site, some with more backward looking ways of worshipping the deity, according to Birch. One group, not Quiche Maya, sacrificed a cockerel in front of everybody. Birch was sickened by this, thinking that this was a throwback to times long gone. Or was it?

The 13 day journey, one Mayan week, was over. A kaleidoscope of images passed across Birch's consciousness; spectacular scenery, different rural cultures, exhausting journeys, struggling to maintain health. All merge into Birch's picture of 'walking the journey'. He reckoned he'd fulfilled the debt to the Mayans by honouring them in the journey and in the ceremonies.

Bliss! The day after the Mayan journey, Birch woke up in Cynthia's house in Antigua. He had been invited to stay; more generosity and hospitality given by an American. It was wonderful not to be rushing around, jumping into the van to go to another sacred site after a long exhausting drive. A lie-in until 9am was like sleeping half the morning away compared to the last 13 mornings. There was no more squeezing into the van at 'minder's' command of "Vamonos". (Let's go!)

The previous evening, Don Alejandro conducted a ceremony to cleanse Cynthia's new house. Birch had already done a simple walking ceremony as his contribution. He wondered how much good the ceremonies had done because there was an immediate problem getting into the property. The door key failed to turn in the lock without considerable effort and patience.

"Perhaps," Birch thought, "the spirits are resistant to new energies entering?"

As Don Alejandro's ceremony started, one of the women shut the door leaving the key inside; problem number two. After the ceremony Gale wrestled to dismantle the lock. As Birch watched it seemed to him that it had become a real initiation for Gale. He struggled to enter without violence and without violating the energies of the place. The fact that he was able to enter through prayer and intelligence was a real test for him. That night, Birch invoked protection energies and asked that the old energies of the house move away.

Now there was time for rest and reflection in the days spent an Antigua. Cynthia looked into Birch's chart, Mayan style. She reminding him of his propensity to either freeze or trample on the situations life threw at him. This insight came at that time to provide Birch with the opportunity to break the mould.

One day Birch was collecting his laundry in Antigua; another blessing, clean clothes!

One of the assistants said to him in good English, "I expect that you have many girlfriends?"

"No," replied Birch. "Why do you say that?"

"Because your clothes are so clean!" she answered finally. Presumably she meant before they were washed.

Charlie had been staying with Cynthia as well. He thanked Birch for the help that he had provided during the 13 days. Birch was surprised at this comment.

"I did nothing," said Birch.

"You listened; a true friend."

Cynthia had also proved to be a true friend during the travelling. One evening, while all were squashed in the van, Birch was feeling particularly negative. He had insect bites on his body and swollen arm from a particularly voracious insect; 'Montezuma's revenge', and he felt sorry for himself. This was not a good time. Birch must have been complaining, for Cynthia's voice suddenly cut in, upbraiding him for being negative and encouraged him to be more positive. Birch took the advice and, guess what? The difference in his attitude made him feel much better. Sometimes a true friend is someone who sees a bigger picture around us and then lets the rest of us in on the secret.

One day Birch was lounging in the doorway of the hardware shop near the centre of Antigua. Cynthia and Gale were shopping inside. He was idly watching the world go by, Latinos and Westerners crossing the square in front of him. The thing that most struck him was the difference between the Latino women and the Western females. The Latinos were all feminine, as was expected of them in this society. In dress, movement, hairstyle and the very vibration that they were exuding they were saying, "Look at me. I am female."

The Western women on the other hand, were projecting an entirely different energy. It was as though they were unconsciously saying, "I am integrating both female and male into my being and psyche. I am becoming a balanced being in terms of my energy pattern." This would be in harmony, Birch thought, with the way Western society was developing. Women now play an equal role in the home, society and at work. They have to be all things to all people. Birch realised how difficult this must be.

"Mmmm," he thought, "I wonder if Western men are doing the same by integrating the female energy into their psyche and being."

Gentle walking and *tai chi* assisted in bringing Birch back to a situation where he was ready to move on again. He realised with some surprise, that this was the first time that he had done *tai chi* for some while. Perhaps he hadn't previously had the space and time? He could have done some in the ashram, but that would have been at the expense of honouring the Yogananda practices. It had been important for Birch to integrate into the whole life in that place.

Jim, one of the travelling party, had been staying in Antigua. Gale, Cynthia, Rosemary and Birch had been gathering together with him during these days, reflecting and reviewing on aspects of their adventures. At dinner on one occasion, Birch questioned the cockerel sacrifice at the last sacred site. He found this act revolting. Rosemary's friend, Elizabeth, said that the group doing this were from Iximche. It was, she said, a normal part of their rituals. They were not Mayan. Birch said that Christians could seize on this as an illustration of barbaric practice of the indigenous people, notwithstanding our own personal distaste. Elizabeth became defensive to an extent that Birch considered it wise to let the subject drop. Yet this exchange left him wondered why it was that she had felt the need to defend this practice, so abhorrent to most Westerners.

That night Birch had a confusing dream in which he travelled to a hotel with someone named Diane or Diana. At first the pair could not get into the hotel. The way was barred for their car. Birch went to reception followed by the car which miraculously appeared in the hotel. There were two items on the back seat of the car, a suede jacket with brown woollen sleeves and a light coloured raincoat. In the next scene Birch walked through a long, low shed filled with dust which covered his clothes. He knocked into an obstacle along the way. He was concerned that his appearance would be strange at the business meeting that he was to attend.

In the next scene he was walking along a road with the Diane/Diana character. They came to a bungalow. At the nearby roadside there were two women dressed in Mayan-like headgear. Birch asked them if Peggy was inside the bungalow. Peggy was recognised as someone who had, in reality, been helpful to Birch in the past. Birch attempted to introduce the Diane/Diana figure to the Mayans but couldn't remember her name. The Diane figure then fell to the ground against a yellow metal bar fence. This fall damaged her knee.

Despite the bizarre nature of the dream, Birch felt that there were messages inside it for him. In some contexts Diana is the goddess of protection and of the hunter; her animal is the stag. Birch had certainly been hunting on his travels. His quarry had been experiences rather than creatures, but now he wondered if he needed the protection of the Mayans, and possibly also the group, in the alien environment of the travels. The goddess Diana used the bow as the symbol of journey.

Gale told Birch that he, Birch, had selected a bunk in Cynthia's house that was oriented east-west. This orientation would facilitate dreams.

Birch was speaking with Gale on the subject of democracy. He asked the American why it was in the so-called free world that there was so much corruption in its institutions. It was Birch's view that the sudden inrush of power was too much to handle for many egos. He added, "Not everyone can be a Ghandi. In fact, very few can; maybe only one."

Gale's view was that those that most wanted this power were the very ones who should be excluded from it. He talked of giving power by lottery and of making the job so difficult that, at the end of their tenure, the office holders were only too willing to give the job back. In addition, if the idea of service to the community was paramount, then it could be viewed, by the office holders, as a gift to the society.

"Ah well," thought Birch, "nice idea but pie in the sky unfortunately."

Birch read a commentary from 'Earthly Purpose' by Dick Sutphen which had set him off on this track. He recalled a quote,

"We have to act. When we stop questioning and speaking out against the things we feel strongly about, we give permission for our rights to be taken away. Indifference and apathy will bury us. People may not be indifferent or apathetic, but ignoring a threat will lead to the same end."

Nobel prize winner, Salvatore Quasimodo said, *"Indifference and apathy have one name – betrayal."*

American novelist, Stephen Crane said, *"Philosophy should always know that indifference is a militant thing. It batters down the walls of cities and murders the women and children amid the flames and the purloining of alter vessels. When it goes away, it leaves smoking ruins, where lie citizens bayoneted through the throat. It is not a children's pastime like highway robbery."*

On another occasion Birch, Cynthia and Gale considered the Toltec way and their approach to living in the 'Now'. In this philosophy, the Angel of Death teaches us to forgive ourselves, forgive our past errors, for we are the greatest judges of ourselves. No-one judges us as harshly as we ourselves. Over and over again we punish and torture ourselves about past misdemeanours. The Angel helps us forgive ourselves, to live in the moment with clarity and intensity, and to dream our future without the hang-ups of the past. The Toltec way also reminds us that we are dreaming objective consciousness and when we are in what is called the 'dream state', we are really removing barriers to our consciousness. This links with Yogananda's teaching in which he also says we are dreaming objective consciousness and when we dream we are dreaming inside a dream.

Gale and Birch had watched a 'Merlin' movie. It was relaxing, knockabout fun. It served to remind Birch of the deficiencies of those who are our leaders as exemplified by the weaknesses of the kings, however well intentioned they start out. The old saying that power corrupts, can be amended by saying that power unbalances and weakens moral resolve however well intentioned at the outset. In the movie, Merlin was half-human and deployed human strengths and human weaknesses as well as the magical superhuman traits of the divine. It could be viewed that the film exemplified the struggle of a mystic person walking his path.

As Birch moved towards the end of his stay in Guatemala and would soon be taking his flight back to the U.S.A, he thought of his journey as establishing and maintaining power. He hoped that this was without ego but with focus, unobtrusively and with discretion and love in his heart.

The last night that Birch was lying in bed in Cynthia's house, energy came into his consciousness in the form of a parasitic black cloud. Birch set up a barrier and it disappeared. He then asked his higher self, from whence came that energy? He was given the names of two people well known to him in the U.K. He was also told that one of the two was a trickster. A 'protective source' was immediately made available to him in the form of 'grandmother energy'. This was typically Mayan, and was blue-grey in colour. The shape of the grandmother was very clear, a small dumpy lady with smiling face and clear bright light around her.

Thereafter, Birch received two warnings concerning personal protection. One was a vision of a fireman completely encased in protective clothing against the flames. The second was of a wine bottle with a very tight lid of a complicated type. Birch asked why he had been psychically attacked. A one word answer came back, 'jealousy'.

Birch was finished with Guatemala, or perhaps Guatemala was finished with him. Next stop Austin, Texas.

Austin, Texas through Mexico

*From 'chill out' to the heat and
power of pyramid power.*

Birch uses the phrase, 'Austin, Texas through Mexico' in the commonly accepted sense in the U.S.A. In the U.K. the title would be 'from Austin, Texas to Mexico'. However, when in Rome...

Birch flew into Houston from Guatemala after paying a 'get out' fee of $50 from that country. It seemed that it was a gringo tax which Birch resented. That local people would receive that money was, most probably, a forlorn hope in that corruption ridden country. Birch was starting to become a little blasé concerning his travelling and the safety issues to which he might be exposed. This became especially apparent now that he was back in an English speaking country and in a culture with which he could feel comfortable.

He rang a hostel to arrange a bed for the night, then caught a shuttle bus that he thought would take him to the hostel. Accompanying him were two businessmen with suits and briefcases. During the journey, it transpired that the shuttle did not go all the way to the hostel. The two businessmen looked concerned. It started to dawn on Birch that he could be in real danger when one of the two made an unsettling comment. He said that for a white man to be dropped in the middle of the black ghetto (which was the planned end point of this journey) was a recipe for disaster. It was then that the white knight stepped forward in the shape of the shuttle driver.

"Look," he said, "I cannot drop you off at the normal end point. I will take you all the way to the hostel." Birch was relieved. It was then that he remembered Yogananda's words all those months before. "When you are in America, I will be there for you."

The driver did as he promised, taking Birch to the door of the hostel. That which followed was one of the strangest nights that Birch experienced on this trip. Shouting and banging of doors disturbed his slumbers. The following morning Birch discovered that someone had been thrown out for non-payment of his overnight fee. In the light of day Birch sensed that the energies in this place were uncomfortable. As soon as he could he packed his bags and trotted off to the Greyhound bus station. It seems fortunately that this was within walking distance. Birch saw no-one and felt well protected.

Jeff, Birch's erstwhile room-mate from Guatemala, had invited him to stay in his home. True to his word Jeff was waiting to greet and collect the dusty traveller from Austin bus station. Jeff soon set about introducing Birch to the seductive pleasures of Austin. Unbeknown to many people there is more live music in Austin than in New Orleans at its peak. Jazz, blues, classical, rock music played live in most of the university city's many restaurants. Austin has a population of over 700,000, ten per cent of which are students at the University of Texas.

It is the capital of Texas and one of the country's fastest growing cities. In 2006 it was voted the second best city in which to live. Its nickname 'Silicon Hills' gives a clue to a large part of its employment base.

Home to the Tonkawa, Comanche and Lipan Apaches, white settlers established the village of Waterloo in the 1830s. It was chosen to be the capital of the Republic of Texas in 1839 which assured its rapid growth. It was rechristened Austin in honour of Stephen F. Austin. Austin, known as the 'Father of Texas', played a major part in the state's colonisation and in politics.

Admired today for its university, high tech and scientific excellence and its active political scene, music remains a major part of the city's culture.

Small wonder Birch came to like the city so much.

On the first evening the two men went for a meal and then to a club for live music. They met a couple of American women and chatted pleasantly. One of them had been married for three years and was saving to buy a house. She exhibited some traits that Birch particularly likes in American women; enthusiasm, exuberance and energy.

Yep, there was no doubt about it, Birch was looking forward to staying in Austin for a while to hang out, relax, have fun, and enjoy whatever came his way. And so it was to be; relaxing, fun and enjoyable. Now that Birch had temporarily set aside travelling, he really felt comfortable in this culture with Jeff and his friends.

The fun was interspersed with visits to the Friends Meeting House. Birch enjoyed classes and the Quaker quiet meeting time and listening to members discuss their spirituality. Many of the Quakers were members of the University faculty. Listening to intelligent clear speakers was an inspiration. Birch became so relaxed that he allowed a small beard to grow and had an earring in one ear. Hippiedom had come to the traveller. Birch felt that this time in Austin was good preparation for Mexico and it allowed the 'internal dust' to settle after so many adventures and insights in Guatemala.

He did some healing work with one of Jeff's friends who suffered from an eating disorder. He utilised sacred geometry in the healing. Birch was soon to leave to go to Mexico so he regretted that it would be unlikely he would ever learn if the healing had been successful.

Nearly a month was spent in Austin. The seductive nature of the good life almost sucked Birch in. It was the prompting of Birch's soon-to-be companion in Mexico that stirred him into action and to take the flight to Mexico City.

In Mexico City Airport he met his friend John who had flown in from U.K. From there it was a short journey to his hotel. Disaster struck when Birch could not find his Visa card, the conduit through which his funds from his U.K. bank had been channelled. Between the two of them there was just enough money for one night in the rather classy hotel. John was a tall imposing figure, physically strong and a martial arts expert. Besides being a companion, Birch felt that John's presence was as a potential minder. Not in the psychic sense as had been Don Alejandro's, but in an altogether different sense. John was there for his own spiritual reasons. He had felt the pull of Teotihuacán, just as Birch had.

The next morning the pair walked to the British Consulate which, thankfully, was not too far away. The staff members were extremely helpful. Birch was able to make a call to the U.K. to cancel the old Visa card and arrange for a new card to be sent to the consulate in Mexico City. The pair was also advised to stay at a hotel near the Alameda Park on the grounds of economy. A night's sleep and the two awoke to a nearly money less day. It was not a comfortable position in which to find themselves; a strange land, no friends, no friendly bank manager. By and large this was not the happiest of waking moments. Then Birch remembered that he did have his debit card, part of his survival kit which he had not yet used on the trip. Joy of joys!

With a certain amount of trepidation Birch walked to a nearby ATM. With shaky hand he fed the last chance card into the gaping mouth, entered his U.K. PIN and, glory be! Mexican pesos spewed out. Birch almost fainted with relief. The duo was delivered from a potentially inconvenient, embarrassing and awkward situation. As it was, it took nearly two weeks for the replacement Visa card to arrive.

Birch and John could now relax and start to plan their time in Teotihuacán. In order to safeguard themselves, the men bought staple fare from the local market and ate the same things each day. They employed this tactic during the early days of their stay. Packets of ham, cheese, plain biscuits, fruit, orange juice and water were the staple diet for some time. They survived surprisingly well on this unchanging fare. Both men felt well.

The one amazing synchronous event that happened in Austin became a great help to the 'dynamic duo.' Birch had been advised from the U.K. to buy a book, 'Beyond Fear' by Mary Carroll Nelson about the teachings of Miguel Ruiz. This explained ritual meditations that Miguel, he of the Toltec spiritual following, had performed for years in the incredible pyramid city. Birch had attempted to buy a copy of this book in Austin by visiting the massive bookstores in the university city. In this huge, book-oriented environment, Birch found precisely one copy of the book that he needed. Here was a sign, he believed, that the resources he needed would be provided; no more and no less. On the night before the first visit to Teotihuacán, or 'Teo' as it became known to the twosome, Birch had a dream. He saw the dichotomy of the light (Teo) and the dark (Mexico City) and the subtle influences that the powerful influence of Teotihuacán brings to the troubled Mexico City. It is perhaps helpful to remember that Teotihuacán is just 40 kilometres (25 miles) northeast of Mexico City.

On the first occasion the Aztec entered the valley they were absolutely amazed to find Teotihuacán in all its magnificence. The site was absolutely empty, no-one was there. The Mayans had gone.

The Mayans were a racial group that inhabited Central America. It ceased to be an advanced civilisation in the 12th century. Succeeded by the Aztec, the Mayans lived in amazing cities, cyclopean in scope as explained elsewhere, and yet this advanced and talented people had not invented the wheel. At the core was a priesthood whose advanced knowledge, they claimed, had originated in the Pleiades region of space. The Mayans are still an important indigenous race in Central America. Members claim to hold secret knowledge relating to man's true history, rather than the biased archaeological theories thrust upon us by the West. Don Alejandro calls the Mayans 'the keepers of time'.

The first attempt to reach Teotihuacán was thwarted when the pair went to the wrong bus terminal in this massive city. The lesson taught them to be more thorough with their planning. To this end, when the two returned to the hotel, they read and discussed ways to manage the day and the trip to Teotihuacán on the next day. This planning included returning to the Hotel Toledo before dark, late each afternoon, to the secure protection from the imagined violence that lurked outside. Whether this threat was real or imagined, the pair had no idea, but better to be safe than sorry. Despite John's martial arts prowess the pair was here for spiritual reasons. They had no intention of looking for trouble.

At last the reason for the whole trip could begin for Birch. He could relax inside. It was as though his inner being opened up and said to itself, "Ah, here at last. You've made it, old son."

After the difficulties of the previous day the journey to Teotihuacán was surprisingly easy. Two legs of the very impressive underground, (built using oil revenues in the 1970s and superior to the London system,) were followed by an hour's bus trip from Terminal Norte. At this point I had to take issue with Birch. I had an overwhelming desire to defend the London Underground. I reminded him that the London mass transit system is the oldest in the world with the Metropolitan Line opening in 1863. To this day, the system is one of the world's busiest railway systems.

To continue, the pair managed to catch their bus on the second attempt. As the bus approached its destination Birch peered through the window and saw a mountain. It was with mounting excitement, even awe that Birch saw that what they were moving towards was not a natural part of the topography. No mountain this, but a massive human construction, the huge Pyramid of the Moon.

Birch felt ecstasy. He was coming home. Why he felt this way could not be seen as logical. Yet he was convinced that 'this corner of a foreign field' was where he had been before, and where he should be now. A possible explanation comes later in the reincarnation chapter.

The pair immediately went to Tetitla which is set a little away from the main complex. There were two reasons for a gradual approach to the main site. The first reason, Birch was so full of emotion, a rising energy, and he felt it appropriate that his entry should be gradual. Secondly, Tetitla was a very special place and merited an approach in its own right. Tetitla is the ruins of a temple complex. Miguel Ruiz says that it is the source of black light for healing our wounds, from childhood to the present day. The two men wandered the complex separately, lost in their own personal worlds. Birch discovered a magical place. This was a narrow corridor following high walls. He placed his hands and forehead on the wall from which he received tremendous vibrations. He was transported, in consciousness, to other realms. He travelled to the stars, navigating the cosmos in a freedom of movement and experiencing an ecstatic high. With a real effort he pulled himself back into three dimensional reality.

As he wandered around the complex of small rooms and corridors the feeling of coming home again engulfed him. The pair meditated in a central room. In his enhanced conscious state Birch saw a concentric spiral of energy rising upward from the temple. This spiral was almost identical to one he had perceived in a meditation some years before at the Rollright Stones, a sacred stone circle near Oxford. As the pair left the complex they were assailed by an almost ravenous hunger. "This spiritual work takes a lot of energy," Birch said to John. They ate their food underneath a tree which offered protection from the sun. An interested local mongrel was rewarded by scraps thrown in its direction. Birch felt totally at peace as he munched; more at peace than at any time he could remember. The energies were subtle, but overt and strong for the other man. Birch also sensed that for them both, the affects of these energies would continue for some time.

They moved on to the main site. The size of the ground plan was truly staggering. How people from a bygone age, and considered by some to be primitive, could conceive of such an undertaking and then build it, was not easy to grasp. This place must be visited to be fully appreciated. Other visitors walked around as though visiting a historic monument. The two gringos felt hypnotically connected to the temple complex, feeling pulled in by its magic.

Teotihuacán translated, means the 'place where men become gods'. Birch was beginning to understand why it was so called. Not that the pair felt very godlike, more like children in an energy sweet shop. They walked towards the citadel complex which included the Pyramid of The Feathered Serpent the feather plumed serpent god. Here they conducted the meditation of the seven material claims on each human, and the seven emotional releases as outlined in 'Beyond Fear'. The pyramid was the lowest of the three in the complex, but was the one with most outer adornments.

Next the pair filed in to the narrow defile between the pyramid and stone steps opposite. This was a place of staggering vibrational impact for. Birch looked up towards the dragons' heads flanking the steps of the pyramid. The scale of the place and the vibration held Birch transfixed in their grip. Again it was some time before he felt able to leave. Sadly, on subsequent trips, Birch discovered that this place was closed to visitors.

Birch and John moved to a massive platform on the edge of the citadel area. Looking towards the Pyramids of the Moon and the Sun in their immensity, this platform was sited for maximum visual effect. As they stood on the platform and gazed at the pyramids they realised that it was those pyramids that represented the end of this particular initiatory journey.

By this time, Birch was filled with the vibrations of Tetitla and the Pyramid of The Feathered Serpent and was incapable of functioning on a psychic level. It was time to return to Mexico City and the Hotel Toledo. Ah, Mexico City with its wall-to-wall people, 20 million plus of them, and its smelly drains. The pair toyed with the idea of staying in a hotel close to the site but decided to stay remote from it between visits. They did start to walk to the hotel close to Teo, but Birch felt heavier and heavier as they approached it to the extent that his feet were dragging. This wasn't right or comfortable.

That evening Birch worked on the Tetitla inspiration of releasing old wounds and negative thought patterns allowing them to return to the earth and be dealt with there. During this process he had a vision of the original lemniscate, a sacred geometry energetic flow shape that he received in meditation before the whole journey began. The lemniscate is in the shape of a figure of eight that, led on its side, facilitates energy flow around its perimeter. In mathematics it is the symbol of infinity.

Mary Carroll Nelson wrote the following concerning Tetitla in 'Beyond Fear'.

In Teotehuican there is a residential compound one and a half kilometres from the pyramid of the sun close to the River San Juan called Tetitla. Tetitla means 'place of stones'. Many murals have been found there.

Tetitla is a place of pure black light. This is a healing energy which goes into the wounds we carry around with us and clears away the poison from them. The black light is pure love or the love that purifies, even the wounds you don't know that you have, based on childhood fears, will be released in this light. False images will break down. Anger may change to sadness, which is just a symptom of the cleansing you will experience as you allow yourself to express an emotion for the first time after many years of repressing it under a mental image.

The second day at Teotihuacán saw the duo buying their food at the market and changing from shorts into long trousers to comply with local practice. Each day they left the hotel Birch would nod in greeting to a guard outside the bank. He had a warm feeling towards it since the successful transaction with the debit card. The guard would nod back. As the days went by, the nods would turn into smiles between the two. The guard carried the most enormous gun. It looked like a shotgun, was almost as big as the guard and would be capable of creating all kinds of unpleasantness if it was ever discharged. There were quite a few robberies in the city.

Back at the site the pair revisited the Pyramid of the Feathered Serpent and the surrounding citadel. Birch did not feel the same power as he had the previous day. The gift of this place to the two gringos was complete. Birch spoke with a couple of English girls who had been travelling for eighteen months. They were delighted to hear an English accent. Well, they would be, wouldn't they?

Birch and John walked up the Avenue of the Dead, and meditated under a tree before crossing the River of Death. This was a very dramatic name for a smelly trickle of water and gloop. The purpose of this meditation was to leave old thinking patterns behind. Birch's meditation gave him a surprising insight. He received a message that he would benefit from being married. Whow! To say that he was surprised at this message would be an understatement. This was not the reason for his visit, or so he thought. He had come, in his objective consciousness, to experience, to travel and maybe have some insightful visions. Looking for a marriage partner was not on the agenda. At the end of the meditation he went through the short list of potential candidates. He dismissed each on the list for one reason or another. It was a very short list. He moved on.

A few days later, while meditating in the same place, he received the information that he ought to eat bacon. The two seekers ate under a shady tree and while they were there, met two ladies from New Mexico. They wore their traditional long pleated dresses. Birch talked enthusiastically of New Mexico after which the two ladies suggested meditating and fasting before scaling the pyramids.

The next ceremony in the 'Beyond Fear' book was at the Place of Temptation; a raised flat bed and part of the main Avenue of the Dead. The two men dedicated their flesh and bones to the Earth for its sustenance. They dug a small grave with a stone to bury themselves symbolically and surrender to death in preparation for re-birth. Birch left his grave open, leaving the stone inside.

One final visit of the day was to the Place of the Women, much of which was underground. Again Birch felt completely at home there. As he stood at the foot of a stairway he felt that he had walked up these stairs in the past.

The Place of the Women was where the priestesses lived and performed ceremony. They used their menses in these ceremonies. This was common practice in times past. Mystics and those that work with magical practices know that the female energy is enormously powerful psychically. When women live together it is common for their menstruation to become synchronised. At these times the priestesses of Teotihuacán would have used their powers.

It is claimed by some that the paternalistic religions know and fear this power. They feel it is greater than their own. Thus the power hungry and the control freaks of many religions have sought to suppress the psychic power of women. This is often done under a hidden agenda, for example, the witch hunts of the Middle Ages and the resistance to women becoming priests in the paternalistic religions.

At the end of the day it was back to the throng of twenty plus million Mexicans! The weather had been great. Birch was feeling tired but contented with their labours. On the bus back to Mexico City Birch reflected that he had seen three days of rain in five months, and yet there was no hose pipe ban. This jibe refers to England which, despite often continuous rain, a hosepipe ban is imposed most summers. Heavens above! It's a bloody island, isn't it?

(Unfortunately, at the time the manuscript for this book was being proofed, towns in Birch's own county of Gloucestershire had been hit by England's worst floods ever. A massive clean up operation was underway in the worst hit towns of Gloucester, Cheltenham and Tewkesbury. It was Tewkesbury where, tragically, three people lost their lives. Damage to property is estimated in the £100 millions.)

Birch shares a further reflection. He believes that when one has finished their individual work on themselves, then it's time to work for the benefit of the world. He thinks of two of his heroes, Yogananda and Gandhi. While still in Mexico City, he dreamed that he was back in England, relating to people and the environment. During the dream he realised that he was dreaming and that it was time to return to the 'waking' dream.

The next morning saw the intrepid two perform a meditation in their room as a review of their time so far in Teotihuacán. Birch had a vision of women and young girls sitting at the side of the road performing a function of purification at Tetitla. He felt that the negative vibrations dumped there were being drawn away through them into the cosmic. Birch couldn't ascertain if their role was conscious or not. He felt that these women had been priestesses at Tetitla in previous incarnations. They had reincarnated for this purpose; at least in his vision.

In addition tremendous vibrations came in through his base chakra. He asked that they continue throughout the day. It also came into consciousness that the two should re-visit the sites of their previous days' rituals.

The third day at Teotihuacán saw three ceremonies completed in separate plazas. The venues migrated up the Avenue of the Dead towards the Pyramids of the Sun and Moon; water, air, and fire being the themes. The whole day appeared to be monochrome, perhaps because the rituals were performed in very similar locations. The cumulative affect was powerful. The air around Birch was alive when he opened his eyes after the water meditation, very cleansing. The air ritual sought to give thanks for the breath of the person performing the ritual and to dedicate their last breath to God. Furthermore, the meditation sought to unite living in the 'now' with conscious breathing. Birch noticed that as he attempted to live in the 'now', his breathing deepened.

The last ceremony connected with fire was very powerful. The cumulative effect of the three ceremonies hit him so hard that he needed to rest under a shady tree for 90 minutes afterwards. In retrospect however, Birch wonders if this had been caused by his use of sacred geometry to connect with the fire energy, or perhaps it was the result of cumulative energy after the fire ceremony in Guatemala, Whatever the reason, during this rest Birch was facing one corner of the Temple of the Moon. It struck him as a fantastic sight, so massive yet so harmonious.

The chaps left the site at 4p.m. that day and returned to Mexico City. It was hot, missing the cool breezes of the two previous days. As they returned, Birch reflected on the relative gentleness of the hawkers in Teotihuacán. They seemed so much gentler than the female hawkers in Antigua. Perhaps achieving a sale in Teotihuacán was much easier rendering unnecessary the need for an aggressive hard sell?

These last three ceremonies were about being digested by the snake. The air completed the digestion and the fire allowed them to appreciate the facets of each person's soul unencumbered with the physical body. At the last, the vibrations in Birch's base chakra from the morning's meditation returned uniting him with the earth and his stability.

Sunday was a rest day. The two went to the Zocalo in the centre of the city. Birch and John performed a meditation in front of playing water jets. Come on chaps, give it a rest for at least one day.

A walk in the park was followed by a visit to a museum. Although much impressed by the exquisite art, pottery and paintings, they soon moved into the square to watch Aztec dancers performing their swirling entrancing moves made more hypnotic by their exotic plumes and costumes.

The two then walked to the Aztec ruins and yet another museum in one corner of the Zocalo. The ruins had, at the height of the Aztec civilisation, been the scene of the most appalling slaughter. The warped philosophy of the Aztec was that in order to maintain their power, it was necessary to kill as many people as they could lay their hands on; wholesale murder on an industrial scale. To top up the dwindling stock of victims, wars were fought with the object of capturing prisoners to sacrifice to their bloodthirsty gods. On one disgraceful occasion, 20,000 prisoners were murdered by having their hearts ripped out. The killing continued until the murdering priests dropped from exhaustion.

If there was anything good to come out of the Spanish invasion, and most of it wasn't, at least that disgrace to the human race stopped. Birch was glad to leave the ruins. The energy was decidedly creepy. He felt that a lot of cleansing was necessary to wipe out the energetic signature that had been left by these actions.

It is easy to feel envy at Birch's ability to sense these energies. What he feels may be linked to the phenomenon known as 'place memory'. Environments and inanimate objects may have the ability to absorb feelings, events and actions which can be felt centuries later. This may be in the form of a vague sensation to some while others of a sensitive nature can replay events as they happened. It has been likened to a tape recording. These places can be healed by sensitives invoking positive energies and drawing out the negative to be disposed of by cosmic forces.

As they ambled back to the Hotel Toledo they came across a martial arts demonstration. This caught John's attention while Birch strolled on. His reverie was broken when someone said, "Do you speak English?"

Startled he replied, "I am English."

Stood before him with a big smile on her face was a short Latin woman holding a cola bottle. Introductions done and Birch learned he was talking to Jaqueline, a 29 year old high school teacher. She was looking to improve her English by speaking with someone whose first language was English. Lucky choice or maybe it was a smart choice? Soon they were joined by John and Jaqueline's companion, José Luis. The two Mexicans offered to show the gringos some of the local sights on the following weekend. The visitors to this foreign land readily agreed, happy that they had made contact with locals who spoke English.

At a nearby bar, Birch explained the nature of the Englishmen's journey. They knew of the significance of the spring equinox and were interested in joining the pilgrimage to Teotihuacán on that auspicious day. The spring equinox is a time when great energy is made available to the material world. It is one of four quarter days, important in the spiritual calendar.

Birch places much emphasis on the spring equinox telling it has great significance. As the earth rotates, it does so at an angle. So, for half the year the northern hemisphere tilts towards the sun (approximately 20th March until 22nd September). For the other half of the year it is the southern hemisphere which enjoys the rays. When the sun is directly over the equator, those two occasions are the equinoxes (around 21st June and 21st December). At those times day and night are more or less the same duration. So the spring equinox in the northern hemisphere is in March and in September in the south.

This astronomical feature influences many cultures. For the Christian Church, it determines the date of Easter, (the first Sunday after the March equinox). Some calendars mark the beginning of their years from the March equinox, including the Iranian calendar. And many countries take a holiday on the day.

In some eastern European countries it is believed that only at the spring equinox can an egg be balanced on its pointed end. Sadly for this charming tale, given enough patience it can be successfully balanced on any day of the year.

For what it's worth, during equinoxes when the sun is almost directly behind geostationary satellites, the radiation can disrupt reception for several minutes or even an hour.

That night, Birch had a dream in which he was escaping in a boat with another person. The two fugitives found themselves on a rocky terrain in which the rocks were arranged in symmetrical rows; possibly to make walking through them easier. The next morning it occurred to Birch that the stones were a metaphor for his journey. All the hazards were laid out in such a way that they could be bypassed. I was reminded of les alignements at Carnac in Brittany. As I write this chapter, I wonder if it is a coincidence that Clive is visiting Carnac now? Who said there is no such thing as coincidence?

Monday to Friday of the following week was spent at Teo. Birch joked that it was as though the two men were working in the 'office' of Teotihuacán five days a week then had the weekend off to rest. Each day, the Toltec meditations were conducted in the temples and pyramids. It seemed so natural. It was only much later that it dawned on Birch how blessed they had been to perform their work in that fantastic place. All the rituals were completed and those that had been done before the weekend break were repeated.

It was on the following Sunday that Birch and John met Jaqueline once again. Gifts were exchanged which went down well. They spent a pleasant afternoon wandering around stalls and eating in the park. While the three were there they spoke with two women who were shepherding half a dozen children. One of them asked Birch to take her back to England. Jaqueline replied in Spanish. Needless to say the Englishmen couldn't understand. It was later when she translated to the laughing gringos, "He is my boyfriend!"

An enormous church dedicated to the Virgin of Guadeloupe was next on the itinerary. The Virgin of Guadeloupe, a Mexican Christian saint, had appeared on the site. The vibrations off the ground outside the church were powerful. As they stood there a Catholic service was taking place inside. Birch wondered which came first; the vibrations, the vision or the saint; the chicken or the egg? He soon settled on the vibrations.

As they left they were approached by a beggar, an old woman who claimed she had been robbed. She showed a split in her handbag as though to prove it. Jaqueline didn't believe her, and said so. The women stomped off, angry that Jaqueline had exposed her scam. Birch supposed that the woman loitered about the Cathedral waiting for tourists to approach with her hard luck story.

Birch and John had it in mind to contact Ian, a fellow Englishman, who was living with the family of his fiancée in the town of Atlixco, near the city of Puebla. Jaqueline succeeded in making contact with Ian despite the best efforts of the Mexican telephone system to frustrate her. It was agreed that they would travel up to Atlixco on the following Tuesday to meet Ian.

The next day, Monday, it was planned to go to Tula, 40 miles (65 kilometres) from Mexico City. The tourist guide book presented an impressive ancient site, well worth visiting. The night before, the men enjoyed TV programmes from England on the cable network. There was Five Nations Rugby followed by a quirky, typically English film with Stephen Fry and Hugh Laurie. English humour in Latin America? It seemed quite bizarre, incongruous, and the gringos laughed like drains. What the Mexicans made of it was anybody's guess.

The two arrived at Tula and walked the 1 or 2 miles (2 or 3 kilometres) to the ancient site. There they had a completely different experience from Teo. There were no high spiritual vibrations that they could sense. The most impressive element was the 5 metre (16.4 feet) high black stone figures set on a flat-topped, stepped pyramid. They were obviously of comparatively recent construction. As the two men moved around the bottom of the pyramid it felt totally dead vibrationally. Birch felt tired there as though he was being drained. From the vantage of the flat top, Birch and John took photographs.

I recall when, some years ago, I asked a professional photographer to "bang off some shots". Looking back, I could have been more respectful and chosen my words more carefully. But, oh dear, he pulled himself to his full 5 feet 6 inches (1.7 metres) and full of indignation said, "I do not bang off shots. I paint with light." So Birch and John did some painting with light then.

There was more energy at the top but it was of a low vibration. Neither man was happy with the vibrations. Birch belongs to the school which says that if something doesn't feel right, it almost certainly isn't right. The other side of that particular coin is worth remembering as we wade our way through the thick custard that is life. If something feels wrong, it almost certainly is wrong.

There was the ruin of another pyramid nearby which also felt dead. The two avoided it and left. As Birch left the site, he sensed that this had been a military and civil centre. This would account for the lack of a spiritual sense. The tall stone figures were certainly martial in character.

The next day the two travellers went to Atlixco to meet Ian. On the second leg of the journey in a local bus, Birch struck up a conversation with a man who spoke good English. He persuaded them to get off the bus at what they thought was the centre. It wasn't. They phoned Ian and fortunately got through, unlike several previous attempts. As they waited for Ian to arrive, two young Western men walked by, Jehovah's Witnesses, who offered to help.

Ian arrived and took them to a large house surrounded by a security fence. There they met his fiancée, Adriana, and her family. One of Birch's most vivid memories on this trip was the sheer joy of standing up in the back of a pickup in the cool of the evening, enjoying the speed and the cooling wind in the face. It was pleasant to be in different surroundings.

Ian took his guests near the lower slopes of Popocatépetl. This, an active volcano, is known locally as 'El Popo' or 'Don Goyo'. Meaning smoking mountain, Popocatépetl is Mexico's second highest peak, rising to 17,802 feet (5,426 metres) and lies just 43 miles (70 kilometres) south east of Mexico City. The top of the volcano is notorious for alleged sightings of UFOs. On 21st December, 2000 a local newspaper ran a front page story and a convincing photograph which, for all the world, suggested the presence of UFOs surrounding Popocatépetl volcano. On 7th July, 1991 Federal Agents of the State of Puebla were on duty when they saw and photographed a UFO. Throughout the July and August of 1991, many Mexicans and also foreign visitors reported strange aerial sightings to the authorities. Stories keep on coming to this day.

However, on this trip it was not UFOs that caught their attention. Rather disappointingly, it was the cops. They were followed by a police car to a vantage point in the foothills of Mount Popocatépetl. It hung around watching as the curious visitors scanned the skies for strange lights. They saw an aircraft then, funnily enough, they did spot something rather more interesting. A strange light moved very fast across the sky not far above the treetops in the distance. They left after little more than an hour since the lurking police car was, by now, slightly unnerving them. The police there have a reputation for corruption and 'discovering' that one has broken a law. Such criminal activity requires the immediate payment of an on-the-spot fine. Yeah, right!

On a later excursion Ian, John and Birch caught a 'combi', a microvan for passengers, to a local hill. From a distance the hill looked artificial with a church on the top. As the men climbed the hill it was clearly geological rather than artificial, although it may have been 'worked on' to change its shape. The sun beat down as the trio climbed the steep slope and steps. At the top, the vibrations were not so good. The church is only open one day a year for a single service. The walls were covered with graffiti, and rubbish was strewn around. An air of neglect pervaded the place. This was not a site of great spiritual power, precisely the reverse. The men prepared to leave after a very short time. Suddenly a wasp became entangled in John's hair. Struggling to release it, the wasp became angry. It flew onto Birch's right cheek and stung him. Unsurprisingly, and totally forgivably, Birch cried out.

Ian, acting with great presence of mind, quickly pulled out the sting from Birch's cheek and placed it on a nearby wall. He pointed out that the sting was still pulsating and pumping the poison. Ian said that human skin was the only animal substance that tears out the sting from the wasp's body. Bees and wasps can sting animals and not lose their sting. If the sting is ripped out, then the bee or wasp will die. Kindly, tolerant and understanding though Birch is, I find it difficult to believe he cared whether the creature lived or died at that moment.

It takes some seconds for all the poison to be pumped out, peristaltically extruded, so Ian's prompt action saved Birch from the maximum discomfort. The men immediately left the hill. They saw the attack as a sign that they were out of attunement with the low vibrations there. It wasn't long before Birch's face swelled. It felt as though he had been punched. John, with his medical knowledge, treated Birch with tea tree oil, cream, and anti-histamine tablets. After a rest, Birch started to feel better.

The travellers returned to Mexico City where Birch spent a couple of days with Jaqueline at her high school. He watched a very militaristic ceremony in which five children marched in a national flag ceremony. It was almost a goose step which would have other connotations in Europe. Here however, he was in a country which had remained practically untouched by the Second World War. This was seen as a

Mexican national ceremony only, and Birch was unable to find any reference to Hitler or the Third Reich.

Birch also spent a couple of fun sessions co-teaching some of Jaqueline's students; English classes with Jaqueline translating. He was impressed by the enthusiasm, intense interest and courtesy displayed by the young students. But then he thought, maybe he was probably the first Englishman they had ever seen.

The duo returned to Teotihuacán with just a few days remaining before the spring equinox. Birch and John meditated in the Temple of Butterflies, a place of high vibration for those prepared to stop and tune into them. Mostly, the two meditators were surrounded by sightseers, flowing in and flowing out, oblivious of the true energies. Some looked surprised or shocked and gave the duo a wide berth. John laid out crystals surrounding himself and Birch during the meditation. A guard approached and told John to put them away, not that he would have known their purpose of assisting in raising the vibrations.

The Temple of Butterflies, Quetzalpapalotl, is so named because of the carvings of butterflies and birds on the columns and patio. Their obsidian eyes are fascinating.

Later that same day the two climbed Moon Pyramid. They felt relaxed as they soaked up the atmosphere. Birch could feel the energies moving up through his spine and activating his throat chakra. This was the day when Birch bounced out of bed with unusual and unseemly energy for a gentleman of his years. He informed John that this was the day of attunement, when guides for the two men would be available to them. This leaping about was not a common event. By his own admission Birch claims that in the morning he is not the most positive or appealing sight. Fond though I am of Clive, all motivation for primary research eluded me. I found myself entirely happy to take him at his word.

Jaqueline had called to invite the two men to another party. Birch said he would not go. The following day was the spring equinox and he needed a good night's sleep in preparation. As he put the phone down John suggested that this was a test of his resolve. Was he committed to the task or, to put it another way, maybe it was an attempt by negative energies to distract Birch from his purpose?

Paradoxically, the two men felt a little sombre as the trip moved towards its end. Both knew that there were challenges waiting for them back home.

So the day of days arrived; spring equinox. All the planning, the travelling, the experiences, raced through Birch's mind as he started what for him, was a most auspicious day. The two men met Jaqueline at Terminal Norte. There they caught a packed bus to the site. Due to the packed roads it dropped them off some way away from the intended destination. It seemed as though half of Central America was going towards Teotihuacán for this important day.

Most people were dressed in the traditional white; tens of thousands of them. The three went immediately to the Sun Pyramid. There were so many people that it was necessary to queue. As the party looked up they could see far above them, people moving ant-like up the slopes of the incredible monument. There was no better place to be on this day.

At the top of the pyramid people were praying, meditating, performing salutation to the sun; the most extraordinary scenes. Birch could sense the thin barrier between the third dimension and spiritual reality. On this day at the culmination of his epic journey, he felt as though he was astride the two worlds with a foot in both realities. This was a gift from Teotihuacán. From then on throughout his future life, this gift would always be available to him. This was a true initiation.

A Rumanian named Chris joined the threesome as they descended the Sun Pyramid. At the bottom they rested for a short while, watching the twisting and twirling of Aztec dancers. Unbeknown to them then, this gave them just enough time and rest before the climb and meditation on the Moon Pyramid. The team was complete, the four in physical form at Teo, Audrey in England and two friends in Austin also tuning in.

The top of the Moon Pyramid was also crowded with white clad people, but the foursome found a place to sit. Birch went into a deep meditation. It was as though he was pulled into it without great concentration on his part. At the end of the meditation, he sensed a tearing; a separation of two worlds. Immediately, people around started clapping. It was precisely midday. Birch sensed intuitively that this was the precise moment of the splitting of two worlds of consciousness. This was the breaking apart of two realities of awareness.

Perhaps the spiritual forces had waited for this auspicious moment. It was only with the thoughts and aspirations of all those around, their combined energy, only then could this splitting apart happen. The work was done.

One final meditation, in the Palace of the Jaguar, was left for Birch and John. The energies generated found Birch twitching and shaking with the power of his being attempting to deal with those energies. One mystic had told him that if energies have an immediate effect on the body, then this is caused by physical blockages. There should be a perception of flow indicating no blockage.

The work was completely done. As the party returned to Mexico City, Birch had a sense of completion. John flew back to England and Birch back to the U.S.A. for a final week with Jeff in Austin before he too, took his return flight home to Blighty.

This momentous journey had one final gift for him. On a quiet street Birch walked back to the hostel in San Diego. This was the night before his flight home. He looked up to see a luminous disc crossing the sky in the opposite direction to the wind blown clouds. There was absolute silence at this archetypal sighting of a UFO.

There seems to be a postscript to this journey to the New World. Now back in Cheltenham, England, Birch rested at home. The weather was English dull, the people walked around the town wearing long faces and dull clothes. Despite Birch's need to return for family and other matters, he was regretting being back in this 'drizzly' environment.

In the U.S.A. he had enjoyed calling at cafés for an early morning breakfast, particularly in the small towns of the South West. Regularly the locals would greet each other with a cheery, "How ya doin'?" to be met with an equally cheery response, "I'm good, how are you?" These seemingly warm and genuine exchanges could so easily lift the spirits. Birch had the real feeling that over the Pond, pleasant conversations could break out spontaneously. Oh, how different from England with its reserved and standoffish culture which, at times, could appear cold and hostile.

For a couple of days after his return and before returning to his flat in Cheltenham, Birch stayed with his good friend, Audrey. One morning the door bell rang. Audrey opened the door giving the caller a cheery "Good morning" and asking how the caller was. A mournful male voice replied.

"Oh, I'm all right." The tone suggested that this person was carrying all the weight of the world on his shoulders.

"Oh, God," thought Birch. "I'm back in England."

He then took a short trip to the Isle of Man. This was part of his coming to terms with life back in England. While on the island Birch was given a reiki healing by a friend, Doreen; a very skilled healer. During the healing Doreen saw the still faithful Yogananda close by. With the spirit, there was also another being of light. Birch was still being looked after.

So there he was again; Yogananda. Just who was Birch's nocturnal visitor and protector, this man who seemed still to be around?

Paramahansa Yogananda was born Mukanda Lal Ghosh to a Bengali family in 1893. From his earliest years he was fascinated by the spiritual with particular interest in teachers, sages, scientists and saints.

In 1910 he met the man who was to become his guru, Swami Sri Yukteswar Giri. He later said that he sensed his guru knew God. Educated in Calcutta, Yogananda took his vows in 1915 and entered the Swami Order. Two years later he founded a boys' school in a remote village in Bengal. The curriculum was delivered using modern teaching methods and included yoga and spiritual training. Soon the school relocated to Ranchi and would later be integrated into Yogananda's American based global Fellowship.

1920 saw him in Boston, USA representing India at the International Congress of Religious Liberals. He soon founded his Self Realization Fellowship to develop and broadcast his teachings. By this time these included the study of ancient practices, philosophy, yoga and meditation. He became a popular speaker throughout the USA and made this country his home. He resided there for the rest of his life.

He attracted a following of many thousands throughout the world. He taught that belief alone was not a firm foundation for true religion. Instead it should be based on intuitive experience. Reminiscent of Hindu teachings he claimed that the universe is God's movie while people are merely the actors, changing roles through reincarnation.

'Autobiography of a Yogi' was published in 1946 and remains a best seller to this day. The book introduced meditation and yoga to the Western world.

Yogananda died in 1952, but the work he started lives on around the world. His Self Realization Fellowship maintains its headquarters in Los Angeles.

An interesting footnote is the claim that after death, his body didn't decompose. Even after twenty days there was no sign of mould, drying skin or odour. Indeed, it was claimed that his body was perfectly preserved.

For a couple of years after his return from the Americas, Birch sported a small beard and as if that wasn't bad enough, he also took to wearing an earring. As said before, whilst away on the trip he adopted some of the outer trappings of hippiedom. Maybe he saw himself as a free spirit, not without a certain amount of egotism? Perhaps these were badges to signify being a little different from the mainstream?

He had a few experiences which demonstrated the unnecessary nature of these outer signs. One morning he awoke, felt his ear and discovered the earring clip at the back of the earring was missing. Feeling around the bed he found and replaced it. He would have forgotten about this not very important event, except it crept into his mind as being slightly strange. It was a particularly strong clip. Some ten days later he awoke to find the whole earring missing. Feeling around, the earring was located under the pillow, firmly attached to the clip. Now, it is possible that in his sleep, Birch could have taken the earring out, re-attached it to the clip and then placed it under the pillow. It is conceivable, but unlikely. Maybe there is another explanation?

Whatever the truth of the matter, Birch saw it as a sign that it was time for the earrings to go. He disposed of them. Perhaps it was just a symbol of the past. In any case he was also feeling uncomfortable with metal next to his skin. There are those who say that metal is a subtle energy inhibitor. This idea would be in harmony with this experience.

The beard stayed until 2002. At this time Birch was working as a home delivery driver for a food retailer. One day as he stepped out of the van, he caught his appearance in the wing mirror. What he saw did not please him very much. There was this middle aged man wearing this comic opera facial hair on his chin. The most that could be said for it was that it wasn't just one boring colour. It comprised white, grey, and a small amount of brown. It was an untidy mess and the time for its removal.

Perhaps this was the true end of the journey; a psychological, subtle end.

Yucatan, Mexico 2000

Past life recalled and out of body experiences.

The Yucatan peninsula is the playground of gringos (male) and gringas (female), spectacular beaches and weather, ancient mysterious pyramid cities, good communications, miles of flat jungles, and all away from the madness and traffic of Mexico City. Cancun with its plush hotels is often the starting point for those seeking to experience the area's pleasures.

Yucatan means 'place of richness'. As far back as 3,000 years ago it was home to the Mayan civilisation as testified by its architecture. The cities collapsed at around the same time as Chichen Itza was born; around 900 AD. Over one hundred Mayan sites are still to be found on the peninsula. Cortez met with fierce Mayan resistance as they withstood the Spanish invaders from 1527 until 1546. While the Mayans adopted Christianity, rather than allowing it to replace their own beliefs, they incorporated it into their pre-Columbian religious culture.

Despite centuries of turbulence, parts of Yucatan flourished. The capital, Mérida, had electric street lights and trolley cars before Mexico City. By the latter half of the 19th century Mérida boasted more millionaires than any other city in the Americas. Today Yucatan enjoys trading relations with Cuba, USA, even Europe, and as a tourist destination it is thriving.

Now we've reached 2000 and Birch, now married, was on his first visit. Wife Jaqueline and he stayed in a downtown hotel used by Mexicans. It was a fraction of the cost of the tourist traps up the coast and of course, had a fraction of the facilities.

On their first day, a taxi took them on a 30 minute trip to the coast. They were looking forward to a boat tour. The boat took them out to some rocks a little way away from the beach, to snorkel. The multi-coloured fish were a revelation to Birch. They seemed so tame, they even sucked his fingers and legs. They were beautiful, all the colours of the rainbow. There was no pollution or effluent outlet. What a place to be after the dull, wet, cold British winter they had just left behind.

Next they sailed to a wooden staked enclosure built off a sandy beach. A captured shark, ('tiburun' in Spanish,) was imprisoned here. They were invited to swim and touch the fish. This was one invitation Jaqueline and Birch were happy to decline. "Not today, thank you." But some of their Argentinean shipmates accepted.

The beast was drugged, exhausted, frightened or perhaps, a particularly friendly variety for it tried to evade capture by squeezing itself into the corner of the deepest part of the stockade. The Argentineans wouldn't allow it to hide. They caught it and held it up to take photographs. Birch felt sorry for the beast as he assumed it was regularly manhandled in this way. Latin people generally don't seem to have the same sensitivity to animals that Westerners do. This performance certainly wouldn't be allowed in Western Europe.

The next day they took another boat trip from Cancun to an island called Isla De Mujeres; Island of Women. It was called this because when re-discovered, hundreds of terra cotta figures of women were found on its beaches. Very possibly a female cult was prevalent in ancient times. At the centre of the island was a statue of a goddess dedicated to female fertility. Birch joked with Jaqueline telling her not to stand too close.

As they returned to Cancun in the small boat the seas became uncomfortably rough. The boat was bobbing, cork-like, in the powerful waves that soaked every passenger. The waves became stronger and stronger. No-one spoke. Even the jollity of the crew on the outward journey had abated. It was with some relief that they eventually reached the harbour. During the journey Birch was comforting a terrified Jaqueline. She couldn't swim. Secretly, Birch needed someone to comfort him!

OK, that's enough of the water, time to head inland and onto serious and exciting stuff in the pyramid cities.

Tulum is a ruined Mayan city set on spectacular cliffs, overlooking the Caribbean. It may have been formerly known as Zama, or the City of the Dawn. Archaeologists say it was an important site for the worship of the Descending God. The site is relatively compact, certainly a lot smaller that the vast Teotihuacán complex of pyramids and temples. Tulum, formerly a major port for Cobá, was built between 1200 and 1450. Despite being abandoned in the late 16th century, Mayans returned to worship there right into the 20th century.

Now it was Birch's time to visit the site. As they entered the complex they saw a large lizard with a ruff around its neck, sunning itself on the entrance wall. Birch claims that it must have been four feet long. It no doubt provided an exotic introduction to this place. The reptile was relaxing with half closed eyes and enjoying the sun, not unlike Birch is apt to do.

Birch realised that each ancient site had its own vibratory note. He could sense the presence of a soft female energy. We revisit this topic later in the piece on Monte Alban.

The tour of the complex was followed by a bus trip to Tulum town. This was an unfortunate choice. They found Tulum to be a dusty, down at heel, expensive rip-off. They stayed in a barely acceptable room with barred windows, neither had the energy after their intense day to demand a change of room. Naturally, this presupposes there would have been an alternative.

The following morning they planned their escape with a bus trip to their next destination. As they waited for their bus they spoke to a couple of German tourists who had also stayed in the area. They had stayed in an equally over-priced hotel. Getting up in the middle of the night, one of them had gone to the kitchen, switched on the light only to find the floor alive with cockroaches. They immediately dispersed, scuttling to their hiding places. Gross! (The cockroaches that is, not the German tourists!)

One of the features of the town was the misery exhibited by the local people. Long faces and depression seemed to be the order there despite the fact, or perhaps because of it, they were ripping off the tourists. Perhaps abuse brings its own punishment.

The next planned stop was Chichen Itza. Built next to a natural well, Chichen Itza developed as a social centre when seafarers arrived in the 8th century. Not entirely surprisingly, Chichen Itza means 'mouth of the well of the Itza', the Itza being the merchant warriors. Today's phenomenal stepped pyramid had been erected around an earlier structure called the Temple of Kukulkan. On the spring and autumn equinoxes at the rising and setting of the sun, the corner of the structure casts a shadow in the shape of a plumed serpent – Kukulkan or Quetzalcoatl – along the side of the north staircase. On these two days the shadows from the corner tiers creep down the northern side of the pyramid with the sun's movements. There is a circular observatory which was used to record and monitor stellar and solar events. The Mayans were obsessive about the importance of these events in their religious affairs.

There is another fascinating anomaly about the ball court at Chichen Itza. Although over 500 feet (152 metres) long and 225 feet (69 metres) wide, words whispered at one end can be heard clearly at the other end. A clap in the centre produces nine distinct echoes. It has been said that the sound of the handclap echo is not unlike the call of the quetzal bird!

This is a truly enormous site, second only in importance to Teotihuacán, or so Birch believes.

While he rested under a tree towards the end of their visit, Jaqueline wandered off to view something else. Birch's consciousness was taken out of his body. He felt himself in another, more subtle, realm of existence. This wasn't planned or expected. He wasn't in a meditative state or even thinking about more rarefied matters. It happened spontaneously with no effort on his behalf. Almost as soon as it started, it stopped, and he was returned to an objective state of consciousness. Soon after this they left. But Birch felt he had received his gift from Chichen Itza.

They bussed it to the town of Vallodolid for a night's sleep before the next ruined pyramid city trip, this time to Uxmal. Vallodilid was an unremarkable town with a shortage of hotel accommodation due to a religious festival. The only item of note was the race in the hotel room. The competitors comprised Birch and a fat, large cockroach that ventured out from its lair. The cockroach was intent on reaching safety under the bed. Birch's rather unfriendly intention was to squash it to infinity. The cockroach won the race. It was quite amazing how fast it can move when it has a mind. It is said that cockroaches, those most ancient of creatures, can withstand and survive very high levels of radiation. As such, perhaps they would be one of the prime beneficiaries of a nuclear holocaust. Having considered this further, Birch felt they might be one surviving species among very few. They would almost certainly be no gringos around to hassle them.

As Jaqueline and Birch wandered around the city centre allowing their meal to digest, they came across a crowd gathered around a church. Many carried crosses and images of the Virgin of Guadeloupe, an important saint in Mexico. They mingled with the crowd. Suddenly a priest appeared, put his hand on Jaqueline's shoulder and said,

"Excuse me, daughter." The latter word is in common usage by priests to women in Mexico. They were standing on the kerb and the priest was eager to take his place on that very spot; no other spot would do. Within a minute they found out why. A very shiny, large, black limousine drew up, disgorging obviously luminaries of the church. The priest, like any subordinate in a business environment, was clearly anxious to give his superiors their due deference. No matter the organisation, the importance of the 'pecking order' is ubiquitous.

They found themselves swept along by the crowd which was no way to maintain their interest so soon they continued on our way. Birch annoyed Jaqueline over the next few days by referring to her as 'daughter'.

Birch much respects the beliefs of those who choose to be followers of a religion. On the other hand he struggles with the bureaucracies and power issues that have grown up around many organised religions as well as their dogmatic and theological constructs.

After the undistinguished stopover, they moved on to Uxmal. It was founded in 700AD, according to archaeologists. The layout of the buildings reveals knowledge of astronomy. The pyramid called 'Soothsayer' dominates the ceremonial centre where the buildings have motifs and sculptures depicting Chaac, the god of rain. Obviously the receipt of enough precipitation was a problem then, just as it is now.

The pyramid was fenced off. Unable to climb it, Birch spent time in a nearby plaza ruminating on what might have been when the civilisation was at its height. He imagined the priests and citizens busying themselves as they performed their duties. He imagined their clothes and their activities, ceremonial and mundane.

No-one knows why a city was built here. There are no rivers or local sources of water and no evidence that they ever existed. A feature of this city though, is the numerous cisterns which held water to sustain the population.

Leaving the complex Birch sat in the entrance while Jaqueline went to see about buses to Mérida. As he sat there quietly he was yet again taken out of his conscious self. Briefly he lost awareness of his surroundings and in a blissful state, but different again from his Chichen Itza experience. This out of body experience was softer than the previous occasion, but still strong. He came out of this altered state and back into normal consciousness, surprised and elated. Uxmal had also given him a gift.

Later, on his return to the UK, Birch discussed this with Audrey. She suggested that the two experiences had been of a short term nature because his body was not sufficiently attuned to hold the higher rates of vibration for any longer.

He received an interesting insight while relaxing in an outer part of the abandoned city. It was in another life that he had been a priest both in Uxmal and Chichen Itza. He had travelled between the two just as he was doing now, retracing steps through time.

Their next bus took them on the next leg of their journey, this time to Mérida. Not much joy on this ride; they had to stand all the way. Ah, wonderful Mérida with its plethora of good hotels, comfortable and, as far as they could see, cockroach free. And, joy of joys, this particular hostelry had a swimming pool; luxury. Jaqueline and Birch walked to the central plaza, the Zocalo. Mindful of practice in Mexico City, they kept looking behind to see if robbers were following them.

Evening time, and they were just in time to see the daily lowering of the huge Mexican flag. The ceremony was accompanied by the stiff-legged walk of the military detachment. Previous viewings of this spectacle were reminiscent of the Nazi goose step. This time Birch thought of Red Army soldiers marching across Red Square as Khrushchev on the balcony took their salute. The flag was then taken to its overnight resting place.

Perhaps the need for such overt displays of military protective nationalism was due to the relatively short period of Mexican independence. In historical terms, 200 years is not so long. Maybe also the close proximity of it's, some say, overbearing neighbour to the north, has an impact. Birch had not seen such a ceremony on a daily basis in a Western European city. This was followed by another ceremony in the Zocalo, and this time rather more charming. Children dressed all in white were acting out an indigenous wedding ceremony. In a sense it was as though the second, sweet and innocent ceremony energetically cancelled out the harsh and serious one earlier.

Two nights in Mérida and it was time for the final ruined pyramid city in their plan; Palenque. The ancient name for the ruined city was Lakam Ha, which translates as 'big water' or 'wide water'. Numerous springs found at the site suggest how this place acquired its name. Here reined arguably the best known Mayan lord; Pacal. He ruled from 615 AD to 683 AD, and is remembered most by one of the most magnificent tomb workings of ancient Central America; the Temple of Inscriptions. The temple sits atop a stepped pyramid, dedicated in 692.

The site is undeniably impressive; set in what was a very wet jungle on the day of their visit. There were no psychic impressions for Birch there, or even enhanced vibrations. He didn't feel connected to the site at all. It was more significant for Jaqueline. They toured the site doing the tourist bit and bought a magnificent 18 inches (46 centimetres) by 18 inches Aztec calendar. Sown onto real leather and painted by hand, it was undeniably beautiful. Bartering, they beat the seller down to 440 pesos, (£22). The seller had not sold anything that day according to him, so the negotiation was fairly brief.

Again their hotel was disappointing. The cynical reader might be asking a question or two by now. Why, for instance, does Birch have so many unhappy experiences with third rate hotels? Why, for instance, does he not check with the local tourist boards, websites, blogs, guide books? Is Birch just an unlucky chap? Well, actually, no, he is anything but unlucky. I have never ever met such a contented, amenable, cheerful man. I have never seen him wear any expression other than a smile. Some might suggest he is extraordinarily lucky.

The final leg of the trip was to Oaxaca City. Another story arose concerning the poverty and deprivation in this Third World country. One evening our travellers were walking around the city on the way to their evening meal. In the gathering dusk they passed a well lit cake shop. The window was crowded with mouth watering offerings. Standing outside and looking in was a thin, poorly dressed old man. He was gazing longingly at the wonders inside. All were so far out of reach for him. Jaqueline and Birch were hit by the emotion of it as they walked by. It was such a poignant moment, yet they walked on. Later, they felt that giving the man some money would have been a better option than just feeling sorry for him.

And then there was Acapulco. This former playground of the rich and famous is now bypassed. Today it is a slightly down at heel holiday resort with too much traffic pollution. Jaqueline and Birch, were having breakfast with Birch's mother-in-law and Jaqueline's sister, Coti. They were approached by a poorly dressed woman attempting to sell a Mayan style mask of polished stone. While very pretty, at that moment Birch was more interested in food rather than making a purchase. Twice she attempted a sale, twice they shooed her away. For a while she sat near the group, looking disconsolate. At last she made a third attempt saying she had not sold anything that day. This seemed a common comment when attempting to tug at the heart strings of comparatively affluent gringos. At that moment Birch's heart melted and a quick sale was made for 200 pesos, maybe £10, a fraction of what he would pay in his country for a similar piece. Sister-in-law said, "You could have beaten her down more."

Birch could not have done it, him with so much and her with so little. It isn't only the poor that poverty hurts.

Clive and wife Jaqueline at his
fathers grave in Villenave d'Ornon

De Havilland Mosquito as
piloted by Warrant Officer
Terry Birch and navigated by
Sergeant Ernest Stanley
Tickle during World War II

Lake crashsite of Terry
Birch's Mosquito in Certes

Jaqueline with Monsieur Normand in
Bordeaux - a 'delicious cliché'

A healthy and happy Clive on the Mexican subway

The Mayan ruins of Teotihuacan in Mexico

Chichen Itza in the Yucatan, Mexico

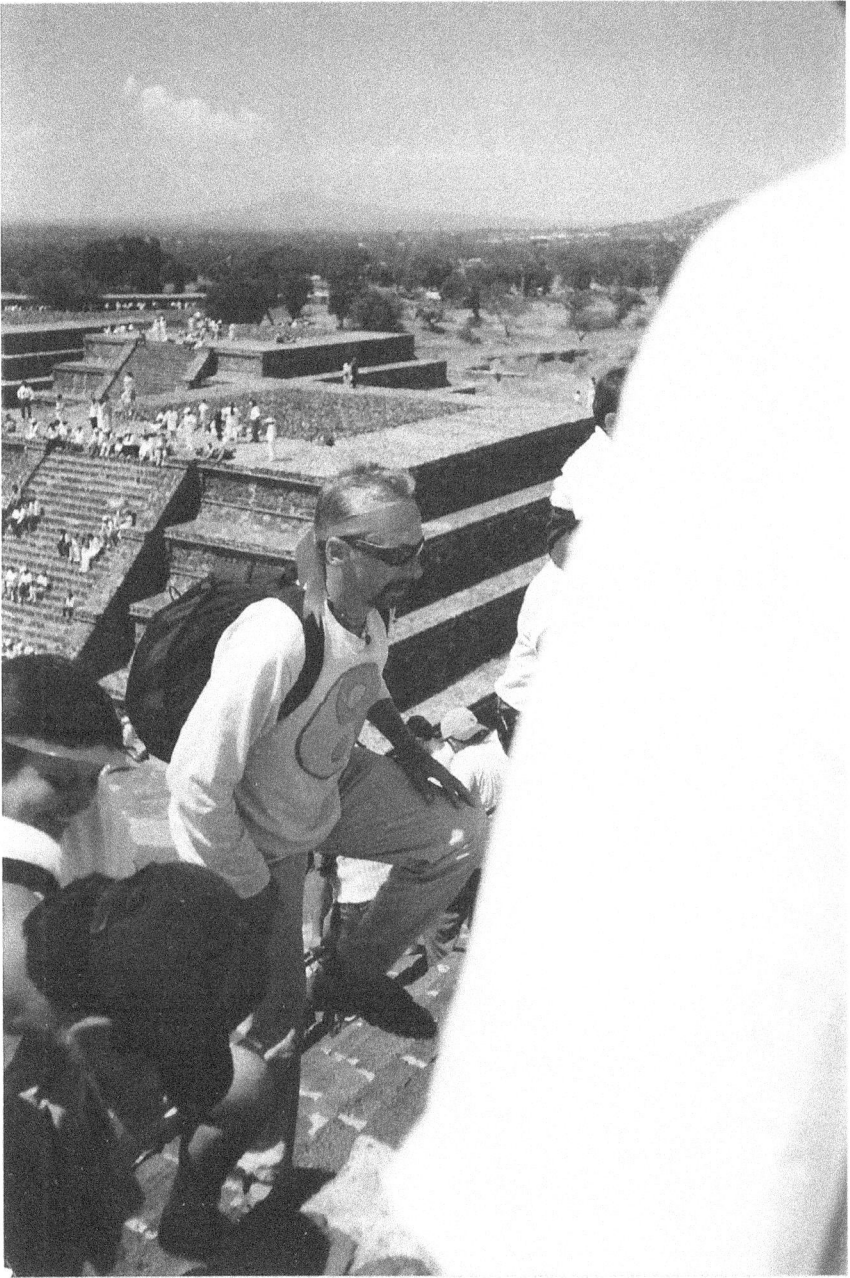

Clive ascending the Pyramid of the Sun in Teotihuacan

Clive and Jaqueline at Teotihuacan in
Mexico during the Spring Equinox

Clive at the Mayan site of Tikal in Guatemala

Chichen Itza - The Temple of One Thousand Pillars in the Yucatan, Mexico

A closer look at the Thousand Pillars

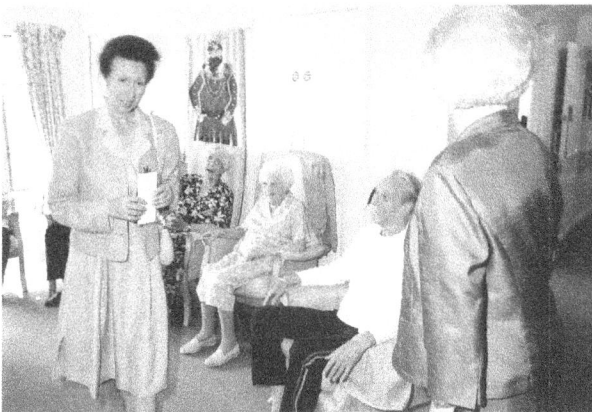

"No, I don't think I will join your class!" - A royal interruption during a *Chi Gong* session

"Don't stand too close!" - A statue of Ixchel,
the Goddess of fertilitity at Isla de Mujeres

The Wolf - Clive's power animal

The Travels Continue

Exotic resorts and intuitive generated journeys.

Inside Washington DC Airport, March 2002, and soldiers with big, scary guns. This was the first time Birch had seen this in the U.S.A. The aftermath of 9/11 was apparent.

Many people looked 'spaced out', almost completely unaware of their surroundings. Could this be caused by junk TV, junk food, junk societal values and relationships, or perhaps other things fed to them? This felt like the heart of Mammon to Birch. Other people appeared to lack in connectedness, a lack of dynamic with those with whom they were dealing. People moved around robot-like as though being moved by some external force beyond their personal control. Birch had the same scary feeling as the first time he saw an old friend who had been possessed by another entity.

Societies like this rot from the inside. For all its military, economic and technological might Birch wondered how long this material 'experiment' could last. Unlike his other visits to the U.S.A. this didn't feel good.

As Jaqueline and Birch went through the checking machines the tall elderly man in front walked away leaving his change in a bowl behind him. Birch shouted to him, he turned and collected it. There was no recognition, no acknowledgement, no vitality in his eyes, nada, nothing, no soul in residence. He simply picked up his change, ignored Birch and walked away. What was going on here?

The journey had not had a great start. Jaqueline's lack of a US visa had taken some time to get them through Heathrow check in and had cost $50. There was a blessing in Washington for they hadn't realised that their baggage needed to be re-checked until Jaqueline's 'minder' told them. They, in their blissful ignorance, would have carried on to Mexico, less baggage. The U.S. was still ramping up its security which was the reason for Jaqueline requiring a security minder wherever they were in the airport. This was due to Jaqueline being 'visaless'. This gave her the status not of a 'non-person', but of a 'half-person'. They went to have something to eat. The minder followed and sat with them. Jaqueline went to the toilet, mercifully the security women stood outside. It must have been her lucky day for, as Birch was such an English gentleman, his instinct told him to offer Ms Security something to eat with them. She accepted and ate with gusto.

Jaqueline had tried very hard to obtain a visa before this trip, but always the U.S. Embassy in London required more information. She couldn't avoid the conclusion that 'get lost' was their message. Birch wondered if it was something to do with Jaqueline's left-wing student activities in Mexico City. Thus her student marches may have marked her down as a 'potential threat'. He ruminated on what nature and level of risk to national security they thought Jaqueline was.

Jaqueline's brother collected them from Mexico City airport after an uneventful flight from Washington. Birch awoke at 7 a.m. after six hours sleep feeling OK. It seemed that jet lag was more severe on the eastbound journeys, something to do with flying with the spin of the earth, or not perhaps? Their 24 hour trek meant that their sleep was sound and deep.

Birch attempted to attune with Teotihuacán as he lay in bed in the morning. They were only a few miles away from the magnificent temple complex. The energy was so powerful that his head ached as the energy centres in the base of his coccyx and sacral area became stimulated. He worked with the energy to spread it evenly over and through his body. The energy emanating from Teotihuacán felt so close that it appeared the whole of the land was imbued with it.

He wondered if the city was stimulated by this energy, but now is hiding or suppressing it under the weight of concrete, and the materialistic and negative thought forms.

In Plato's 'Republic', the ideal society is portrayed by the author. He proposes a society that is rigidly defined, without flexibility for development of the individual or the group. This may have been a feature of the perspectives of civilisation at the time. As far as the original summary is concerned, the model does not account for outside influences; for example, the expansionist policies of other societies. The model proposed is linear and ignores the fluctuating, indeed cyclical, nature of civilisation or climate features. Civilisations in Birch's view, go through a cycle of rising, plateau, and decay. Given a rigid set of processes, no society can maintain its structure for long. One needs only to look at the Greek, Roman, and ancient Egyptian civilisations as examples to add credence to his theory. One could also look at the rise and fall of the British Empire.

Civilisations rot from the inside and are eventually invaded and conquered by stronger forces. Societies can also be destroyed by environmental forces such as climate change. The drowned cities off the coast of Malta, Japan and India probably destroyed by rising waters at the end of the ice age, exemplify this argument. The Mayan civilisation is claimed to have been destroyed by a reduction in rainfall causing drought and starvation.

There are those who claim that ancient Egypt, with a staggering civilisation lifespan of around 5,000 years, ensured its continuance by the priesthood performing powerful ritual to protect the borders. When the civilisation started to decline and the priesthood forgot or ignored the old rituals, then the border protection collapsed and so did the civilisation.

Co-operative measures with societies outside and planning for future difficulties such as strong reserves of food supply, are important features of current civilisations. The flexible use of individuals and the provision of opportunities are built-in features of current societies. This has provided the Western model of societies a considerable and relatively stable lifespan. This presupposes that corruption of the central structures in these 'civilisations' is controlled.

Perhaps more serious threats such as the result of environmental abuse are yet to come. This is the era of a one world society. No society can operate in isolation from any other.

These are the thoughts that rattle round Birch's head now that he is back in the megatropolis of Mexico City. Poor people migrate from the countryside in large numbers, all the time in search of a better life. Some make it to their dream, most live in some of the worst 'favellas' in the Americas. Who can blame them for trying?

And so to Zihuataneco. Jaqueline and Birch sat on the beach at 9am, already under shade to protect from the early heat. Sailing boats were anchored in the bay which had a narrow entrance to the sea. Birds skimmed the mist covered waters. Song birds sang out from the very coconut trees under which they were sitting waiting for their breakfast. This was great, this was the life. Back in wintry England just before they left on this trip, someone ironically said, "Ain't life a bitch for you, Birchy!"

He swam in the warm sea. His whole body relaxed as the travel weary and winter weary muscles and joints revelled in this health giving environment. Birch was distracted when a local man came down to the beach for a swim. There was nothing remarkable in that, except he was carrying a small crocodile-like animal with a head the shape of which was unfamiliar to Birch. Croc and man seemed in perfect harmony. It certainly created a sensation among the mostly Latinos on the beach. The man took his strange pet for a swim. Everyone gave it a wide berth as it lashed its tail contentedly in the blue Pacific Ocean.

As the man carried the five feet long creature back up the beach, a fascinated crowd gathered. Eager zoologists were charged 20 pesos for a photograph as they held the reptile. Birch soon grasped the reason for this mans presence on the shoreline. It was good business. He netted 250 pesos in a short period of time. Birch took his turn and was surprised at the weight of his new friend. Well, it seems Birch wasn't too sure if the creature viewed him as a friend. More like it was deciding if it was worth taking a good chunk out of his arm for a quick snack. As it was, cold to the touch, it nestled without complaint against his shoulder. It was obviously a salt water variety as it seemed totally at home in this environment.

For the next couple of days the morning ritual was to sit facing the sea, waiting for breakfast of fresh lobster and fresh fish. All this was served at a fraction of the price he would have to pay in Europe. This assumed he would be able to find a restaurant able to serve such luxurious fair for breakfast in Europe. Times were soon to change and this would be the last time that Jaqueline and Birch would be able to enjoy this place at these prices. On their next visit, Zihuataneco had been discovered by the American tourist trade and the prices had started to skyrocket.

They moved onto Guatemala after Birch had given his mother-in-law her first trip in an aeroplane. The flight had been initiated by a vision that he'd had concerning Lago de Atitlan which he had visited briefly with Don Alejandro and the Mayans four years before. In the vision he saw a vortex spiralling down into the lake from cosmic realms. The lake was beautiful, fresh water and set among the mountains of the Guatemalan highlands. One strange feature was that despite its very large size, there were no fish in it. The vision inspired him to visit the lake and the lakeside city of Panajachel. His plan was to visit for the spring equinox. This strategy had worked on previous journeys to places that he had been inspired to visit. What to do once there was a matter of inspiration and guidance.

Before Lago de Atitlan he wanted to experience other places of interest. First stop was Antigua. Jaqueline and Birch were taken there from Guatemala City airport by a charming young man who bombarded them with stories of his dangerous country. The driver described the trade in stolen passports which were worth hundreds of dollars each to the local gangsters. He was constantly asked by the local thieves to steal them from his fares. It seemed he would have been rewarded with a good price. He said that he always refused because of his Christian beliefs. Birch thought, "Welcome to Guatemala."

Birch was pleased to be travelling with Jaqueline. She was both a native speaker and very streetwise, after all. His tendency was to be trusting and not especially streetwise. They spent a day in Antigua. Somehow it had lost its charm from the previous, almost magical occasion. Jaqueline was bored by it. The following day they moved onto Santa Helena in preparation to visit another magnificent and famous centre of ancient Mayan culture; Tikal.

They had a bad experience with the bus driver on the economy bus line they selected. They were overcharged 20 quetzals each compared to the fare the locals were charged. They only discovered this towards the end of the journey. Two chaps from Germany had the same experience on the bus. They got their money back, or some of it, by asking for change. When our pair reached the terminus, Jaqueline made a fuss asking for the manager. The girl on the desk laughed in her face saying, "The manager isn't here." Jaqueline mentioned the magic words, 'tourist police' and suddenly a large man appeared. His function was to frighten and intimidate. He stood close to them, looming over them with his large bulk. He picked on the wrong one with Jaqueline. She is just five feet tall in her stockinged feet. What she lacks in altitude she more than compensates with attitude. Initially, the 'Hulk' was less than interested. Eventually, they did get their money back, although with inappropriate bad grace.

This was followed by an abusive experience with a taxi driver. Santa Helena was a sour experience.

Tikal, on the other hand, was an entirely magical experience on the next day. The jungle environment was filled with beautiful and exotic wildlife. Spider monkeys moved gymnastically among the upper reaches of the trees plucking the most succulent leaves to eat. In the distance howler monkeys made their deep throated calls. Brightly coloured and strange sounding birds flew through the greenery of the forest. A chocolate brown tapir-like animal with a long snout and a long ringed tail snuffled through the undergrowth seeking out its insect food. Birch was surprised to learn that these apparently docile animals are members of the horse family. These creatures were present in reasonably large numbers. They saw around 20 and one group of 13 was hunting together. Perhaps these animals were responsible for the small number of insects they saw? Small brown lizards scuttled in the forest and among the ruins. This was indeed a tropical paradise that was being protected from the rapacious advance of 'civilisation'.

The ruins were spectacular. Some had chambers in which Birch chanted sacred incantations. His diary tells how he felt the returning vibrations moving through his body and into the depth of his bones. There was a great sensation of peace and healing throughout the site. It was as though the healing could take place at a very deep level, perhaps even at a genetic level. He was reminded of the words of Christ and the Mayan people who said that it was possible to heal and impact in other ways, seven generations back and seven generations forward.

There were two enormous pyramids facing each other at the centre of the complex. They were very tall, graceful, much more spire-like than other pyramids he'd visited before. As they sat on the one scaleable pyramid Birch felt the flux of opposites between the two, yin and yang, the positive and negative, the male and female, the alpha and omega. This magical site was the antithesis of the very negative atmosphere in Santa Helena. It reminded him of other experiences at ancient sites close to towns with essentially negative vibrations; Tulum and Palenque.

From Tikal they moved on to Panajachel. It was there while lying in bed listening to a dog howling that Jaqueline started off on a story of dogs in Mexico. She claimed they cry in a certain way when the death of a human in the area is imminent. Just before her father died a nearby dog yowled for two days and just before the actual death, other dogs joined in.

Visiting exotic and colourful places such as Guatemala, Mexico or Honduras tourists see idyllic and glamorous locations. Sometimes it takes contact with people living there to bring reality crashing into the visitors' dreamlike perceptions.

One day before the spring equinox, Jaqueline and Birch decided to take a walk to an animal sanctuary. An hour of tramping through the hot countryside and close to their intended destination, they came upon a local man. He wore local dress and carried a wicker basket on his head. After a few pleasantries with Spanish-speaking Jaqueline, he opened his basket to display a very frightened and shocked looking hawk which had a damaged claw. He offered to sell it to them as the animal shelter did not have the funds to buy it. After the obligatory Central American haggling, a price of 200 quetzals was agreed; perhaps £10. Their Western conditioned charitable consciences were stimulated. His need was to generate income; theirs, to release the avian. Triumphantly they set off for the animal sanctuary, holding said bird. The seller faded into the surrounding greenery.

At the sanctuary the bird was placed on a pedestal from which it immediately fell due to its damaged claw. It remained on the floor. As the two walked back to Panajachel, they were met once again by the bird seller who had re-emerged from the jungle greenery. To their open-mouthed shock he now attempted to sell them a young child. He claimed there would be no problem obtaining the necessary paperwork.

"What about the mother?"

"No problem," he said, "too many mouths to feed for the poor people."

They were absolutely astounded by this and unsurprisingly refused with some haste. One of the outstanding elements of all this was the casually relaxed manner in which it took place. It was as though this type of transaction was a regular occurrence. After further discussion they learned that he was a poor dirt farmer, subsistence level most likely, struggling to support a large family. He had seven children. Later it crossed Birch's mind that there was no certainty that the transaction would have been above board. Children 'disappear' from their homes and loved ones on a daily basis. The struggles of the poor are mostly hidden from the relaxing, vacuum-packed, hermetically sealed tourist.

In a similar incident the following year the travellers were visiting Jaqueline's uncle, a farmer in Oaxaca State, Mexico. He told them of an offer by a fellow villager, to give him a baby. The mother could not afford to feed it, he said. The sadness and desperation of the poor is alien, unknown to the rich Westerner.

We in the Western world may be tempted to think that we are not wealthy compared to some of our compatriots. In fact, we are infinitely blessed. Healthcare, education, plentiful food, social support systems are all available to us. The poor of Central America and those in other regions of the world would think that they were in heaven if transferred to our home environment.

Jaqueline's uncle, Fortino, refused the offer. He had an extended family of his own. Now in his 70s, he still needs to work. Yet, he is considered to be relatively comfortably off in his community. He has land to grow crops for consumption and sale, and animals for slaughter and food.

Jaqueline tells the story of visiting him when she was a teenager. She became involved with the capture of Fortino's bull which had become dangerous. A number of the men of the village assisted in the capture. The bull's head was tied, a spike inserted into the top of the head and his throat slit on the spot. No slaughter houses there. The bull collapsed in a death paroxysm. As soon as the blood started to spurt from the throat of the unfortunate beast a steel tray was thrust under the fountain of liquid. The thick coagulating liquid was then passed round for all to take a restorative drink after the exertions of the afternoon. Jaqueline was invited to join the party. She fled, revolted by what she had seen and was then invited to share.

Fortino features in another interesting story, this time more psychically based. He was walking in the mountains looking for lost animals. This was in a region remote from cities and towns, or most other forms of human habitation for that matter. Dirt roads connected what hamlets there were. As he walked up a hillside path he was suddenly surrounded by 'little people', laughing and dancing around him. He must have blacked out. The next thing he remembered was waking up to find himself on his hands and knees on the path. The 'little people' had disappeared. This was not a man given to flights of fancy. He was a well grounded, practical individual.

Now back to Panajachel and Lago de Atitlan. Jaqueline and Birch stayed in the town for ten days. This seemed a little long for both of them. However they had done a lot of travelling leading up to being there. Maybe it was best for mind and body. They particularly enjoyed their breakfasts in one or other of the open air restaurants. These eateries were used by Americans mostly, and the fare suited Jaqueline and Birch well.

Most mornings an old woman would go by selling trinkets. They didn't really want any, but regularly they bought from her. Barefoot and appearing very poor, they found the purchases irresistible.

Jaqueline felt that the old woman lived on the street and fondly called her 'grandmother'.

So, we move to the main event of this trip. The spring equinox arrived and the weather was wonderful as usual. They took a ferry which visited most of the other villages on the lake. Birch's intention was to meditate as they travelled on the ferry as this, he thought, would be most appropriate given the nature of the vision that had seemingly summoned him there.

One village they visited presented the opportunity to purchase a beautiful rug. To this day it is spread on their bed during the coldest, deepest times of winters in the U.K. In a rough poor church they found a memorial to all the people who had died in the civil war that had raged there for many years. As said before, the U.K. was largely unencumbered and undisturbed by information concerning this horrendous conflict. The two travellers stood in front of the memorial in deep quiet prayer and meditation for the souls of the departed.

The last village they visited was set against a very steep hillside. The stepped terraces for growing of crops swept up the precarious slope as far as physically possible. This terracing can be found in many areas of the world where land is short and the need to grow crops vital.

One women in a craft shop asked them to change a Mexican 200 peso note. This would have been a relatively large sum for her but was useless in Guatemala. They told her to go to a bank to change it. Perhaps she though the local bank would not pay her a proper rate. They left to return to the ferry and back to Panajachel.

The next morning when Birch awoke he felt disappointed. He had received no feedback from his meditation labours. This was unusual. Normally there would be a flow of energy, a message, something. Within a couple of days they were out of there, back to Guatemala City, then through the U.S.A. and back home.

He forgot all about the non-feedback journey as he returned to the maelstrom of life in the U.K. Well, he did until he was reminded, two and a half years later. One winter evening he was watching the TV news, almost idly. An item came with pictures of a village in Guatemala. It had been devastated by a landslide. As he watched the pictures he realised, with dawning shock and horror, that this was the last village that he'd visited on that ferry trip across the Lago de Atitlan. The image of the ascending, very steep terraces, returned to his consciousness. He was distraught.

He could not understand the enormity of the catastrophe in which hundreds of people had died. "Why had I been drawn to that place?" he asked, again and again. He was so shaken by the news he couldn't do any spiritual work for several weeks after.

Even today emotions well up inside him. Did the people he saw there survive the disaster? Did the woman in the shop with the 200 peso note survive? These were questions to which he could find no answer. The only comfort was the thought that maybe, in some small way, his presence there might have made a difference. As a man once said, "It is better to light a candle than curse the darkness."

In 2003 Birch, along with Jaqueline, returned to Oaxaca, Mexico. While looking in the guide book he saw Mitla on the map. Thus Mitla entered his consciousness for the first time. It was not part of the itinerary when he left England. He read that Mitla had a blood soaked past. It was, or so he read, the last place in Central America where human sacrifices were conducted. Subsequently the Spanish behaved very badly there as they had elsewhere on the Continent.

Mitla was occupied as long ago as 500 BC. The arrival of the conquistadores in the 1520s halted its architectural and cultural development. Some of Mitla's buildings including the palace are decorated with geometric mosaics comprising millions of stone tesserae.

So it was that the guide book had grabbed his interest. On the corridor wall in his hotel in Oaxaca City was a big poster advertising Mitla. As on previous trips it seemed as if he was being pointed in a direction that had not featured in his planning. So be it.

The very next day they changed hotel. In the reception they were told that there were tours of Monte Alban and Mitla. O.K, Birch had got the message. Perhaps there was some healing work to be done there? Jaqueline and he went on the tour; first stop, Mitla. This was an impressive place and not because of pyramids or energies. There was a very large Aztec style ball court and well spread out, ancient buildings. He seated himself in a corner of the ball court. He wanted to work on healing in this place. The very second he sat, the driver of their coach came into the ball court. He asked them to return to the coach and take their seats. They left. No healing meditation to be performed in Mitla, then.

The next ride took them to Monte Alban just outside Oaxaca City. This ancient site of pyramids, plazas and temples had been built after the top of a mountain had been scraped away. Another information filled tour finished with them frozen with cold on top of a plaza 7,000 feet (2134 metres) above sea level. There was no energy or time for meditating at this sacred place of the past.

The impacts of these two visits made their appearance that night. At 2 am Birch awoke with a start. He was very hot and vibrating with energy. Information came in through his intuition. He was told that every sacred site vibrated with its own sound. The pyramids were a means of focussing this energy which was a reflection of the Earth sound and energy. This energy was also a source of learning for the humans attuned to it. So, it seemed that he needed to be in those two places to receive information and not to conduct a healing.

Some of the places Birch has visited in Central America, along with his experiences there, seemed to suggest to him that he had visited, lived and worked in those locations in other lifetimes. To we Westerners this is a concept with which we struggle. Yet, there are many other cultures which readily embrace reincarnation. Reincarnation is a vast and contentious subject, and one we will visit in a later chapter. Another explanation for the purpose of these ancient sites is that they are places of healing. Birch claims to have a very limited understanding of what is going on if that is the case. He says that sometimes it is important just to be in the places of power and experience without rationalising.

A second visit a couple of years later was a strange and inexplicable experience. When they arrived in Oaxaca City next to the site, Birch became quite ill. For two nights he had a high fever. Because he was so sick Jaqueline was planning for them to leave by plane rather than retrace the long coach journey that had brought them there in the first place. However he was determined to visit the Monte Albán site, sick or not.

A few days later Birch struggled onto a microbus. He felt sick and nauseous. At the time he assumed he'd eaten something that disagreed with him. As they approached the site he felt worse; terrible. Jaqueline was so concerned she wanted them to return to the hotel. Birch was adamant; they would continue. Something was urging him on; he must continue to the site. But once there he received no insights or strong vibrations. He felt so sick he was past caring about such matters. He did however conduct a tiling ritual in order to build up energy at the site. (The spiritual process of circling a space changes the energies inside the circle.)

They left the site to return to the city. Almost immediately he began to feel better. As the minutes past he felt better and better. By the evening he was completely healed apart from a weakness that was cured by a good meal and a good night's sleep. Had he drawn to the surface an ancient buried illness which was healed in Monte Albán? Was it psychosomatic? In the latter case, he wondered why was he sick before the visit, and unaware that he might be healed merely by visiting the pyramid city.

Initiation or the raising of consciousness occurs in small steps. So says Harvey Spencer Lewis, the man who started Rosicrucian Order, AMORC. Sometimes it can occur in a controlled ritualistic manner or be invoked by an advanced being of consciousness such as Sri Yukteswar. It was he who did this with his student, Paramahansa Yogananda. Sometimes it can occur in the most suddenly. For the spring equinox of 2004 Birch was internally inspired to visit and do some spiritual work in Mesa Verde, Colorado. This is an ancient abandoned Native American village built into the clefts of rock set in a narrow valley.

Birch planned the trip making his first visit to the site a few days before the energy influx which he knew would be brought by the spring equinox. On 21st March, he drove back to Mesa Verde. As he drove up the winding road playing atmospheric music on the car radio, he became aware of psychic changes in his being. It was as though he was being dragged through a psychic doorway. That was his internal perception while his physical body and mental attention was still driving the car.

Thus, he felt a change in consciousness, not in his planned location, but on the road to it. Thankfully Birch hesitates to compare this experience with another that occurred on the road to Damascus? Nevertheless, it is difficult to avoid such a thought.

After Mesa Verde he decided to drive up to Colorado to relax in some hot springs. He stopped in a motel on the way. During the course of the evening he turned on the TV. What he saw on the news was the bombing of the compound in Baghdad by US and British warplanes. As the explosions ripped through the night sky, a reporter in a nearby hotel described the scenes and filmed the explosions. Reporters back in their US studios spoke with an almost reverend air, describing 'shock and awe.' Birch wondered what if there were innocent people being blown up and maimed in the carnage and mayhem? The triumphalist attitude may have been different if the reporters, or their loved ones, were in the middle of all that. Birch turned the TV off after a few minutes. This was not right. He thought of the military, and those making the bullets behind them. And then he wondered, why start this slaughter on the highly energetic day of the spring equinox? It was the evening of 21st after all. Were they consciously aware of the importance of starting an event now, whether it is perceived as positive or negative? Birch thinks that they probably were. It was interesting that the President of the United States stood on the deck of the aircraft carrier weeks later to announce the end of the war. This announcement was made on Beltane, another important day of energy in the Earth spirit calendar. Were these start and end dates 'accidents' Birch wonders?

His very last thought before closing his eyes on this momentous day, was that of comparing his simple and quiet work at Mesa Verde with the attack on Baghdad. Could his work to some extent offset the carnage and mayhem? He would never know.

To Bordeaux

*Birch revisits his father's grave, lays
ghosts to rest and heals the past.*

Birch had long wondered if it would be possible to discover more about his father's death. Warrant Officer Terry Birch's Mosquito had been shot down on 10th June 1994 close to Bordeaux. He had died in hospital the following day. There seemed to be so much to be explained. But would it be possible to discover anything more. It had been 61 years. He knew that the Resistance had been able to advise the Air Ministry that the crew had been captured and taken to a local hospital. Perhaps there might be someone still living in the area? Maybe there would be records in the mairie? (Every French town and village has a mairie, or town hall.)

Birch, Jaqueline and son, Matthew, flew to Bordeaux on Monday 23rd March 2004. Birch's heart sank as the taxi dropped them off at their hotel. Had he been right in trusting in a fly/accommodation booking by a Cheltenham travel agent? At the time it had seemed like a good idea. Now it seemed like maybe it hadn't been such a good idea. The hotel was on the outskirts of Bordeaux, in a 'zone industriale'. It seemed isolated, miles from anywhere. Not too auspicious, he thought.

It didn't immediately get much better. As is the custom in many French hotels, especially those which are not situated centrally, it is merely a roof under which to spend a night. Facilities are scant and a restaurant is more often than not, non existent. This seems most confusing. Since there are few restaurants on the outskirts of towns, especially in industrial areas, and since hotels in those areas have no restaurants, it can all be most trying. And if one is fortunate enough to find a restaurant in the evening, it will almost certainly be shut. Catastrophe! However, fortune smiled on them and the three found an eatery. It provided a simple but welcome meal. The walk back to the hotel seemed long and cold. They felt fortunate that a receptionist was still on duty. Birch decided to grasp the opportunity to sort out some geography. Perhaps she could tell them the way to Villenave d'Ornon, where Terry Birch was buried. Now the next problem presented itself.

It is an odd thing about the French who are passionate about their language; and quite right, too. They do whatever they can to preserve their native tongue, even to the extent of passing legislation to prevent advertisers using English to promote products. So it is that if an Englishman tries to speak to a French host in English, he will not understand a single word. The moment he tries to muddle through in French, even by uttering a sentence or two, he will discover his host speaks English well, and will then insist on speaking English throughout the conversation. Protest if you will, but you'll be told they want to practice their English. This experience has been shared by Birch and many more Anglophones when they visit this delightful country. Yet how was it that he had now happened upon the only receptionist in the whole country who didn't speak English?

Birch opened the conversation in his halting French, expecting her to immediately interrupt and insist on speaking English. To his surprise and disappointment, she didn't. It was a long job to make himself understood. As he recollects this delightful scene Birch smiles, reminded of that wonderful moment in Fawlty Towers when Basil, pleading with Manuel, says "Please try to understand before one of us dies."

Then suddenly, as if by magic, all became clear. "Villenave d'Ornon!" she cried. "You are in it."

To say the pilgrims were surprised would be understating the case. It was at that point that Birch realised that help from other realms was assisting the party in that hotel. The graveyard was only one kilometre away. It was with a mix of joy and anxiety that Birch went to bed that night. Tomorrow would be difficult, an emotional roller coaster, he believed.

The following morning started with croissants and coffee, one of the great delights of being in France. All three walked the short way to the graveyard. Birch found it a profound experience. His pace slowed noticeably as they approached the cemetery. Worry intensified. Would they be able to find the grave? What if the information was wrong and the grave wasn't there? Jaqueline grabbed Birch's arm and gently shoved him through the gates.

After a short search they found the military part of the cemetery set in the middle. Terry's grave was at the front of six British and Canadian dead. Behind were the graves of some forty Polish war dead. Birch, Jaqueline and Matthew spent about an hour in this special place. Mainly they didn't speak, each preferring to remain alone with their thoughts. After taking a few photographs they said a short prayer for healing. They talked about how they felt about the experience. The rain came and they departed the cemetery to return to the hotel. Walking in silence through the pitter patter of the raindrops, Birch felt serious but not sad; no, not sad, but something else.

Back at the hotel they found chaos. People where running to and fro with towels. It was pandemonium.

"Desolée," said the receptionist. "Nous avons des problemes avec l'eau." At this point, Birch's French let him down as the receptionist chattered on. Fortunately linguistic help soon arrived in the form of the owner. It seemed there had been a burst pipe and much of the hotel was flooded.

"We will have to transfer you to our sister hotel dans la centre ville."

This news was not welcomed by Birch. He'd found, quite by chance, a hotel which was ideally located. Now he was going to have to reorientate himself. Right, first things first. Let's get to the new hotel and then find the railway station. He knew that the crash site of his father's aircraft was out of town and fairly close to the SNCF railway station. This was their next point of pilgrimage. What a nuisance and inconvenience it all was. Off they went to the town centre.

As they left there was some consolation in the fact that the rain had stopped. They found their new hotel quickly and were surprised to see that it was no more than 200 yards (183 metres) from the railway station. More help from those beyond third dimensional reality!

A short train ride took them to a small town close to the crash site. There they found a little mairie. Neither Jaqueline nor Matthew spoke any French. Spoken communication continued to be the responsibility of Birch. Mounting one flight of stairs, offices were found on the first floor. Sweating in his effort to communicate his needs, Birch found a sympathetic official who immediately lifted the telephone receiver. Dialling several times, he spoke to a number of people. Eventually he handed the telephone to Birch.

"Pour vous," he said. Birch caught his drift.

Both Birch and the person on the other end of the phone struggled to understand each other. Eventually, through the fog of misunderstanding, M. Normand made himself understood.

"Je peux vous aidez," he said. "If you meet me outside the mairie tomorrow you will find out more."

Intrigued, the threesome returned to their hotel where they spent a restful night. The next morning Matthew was sick so Birch and Jaqueline struck out on their own back to the mairie. The trip was uneventful apart from the intrepid duo sitting in the first class compartment of the train with second class tickets; unknowingly of course. The ticket collector was graciousness itself waving away their offer to go to second class. Who said the French don't like the English?

Throughout the journey Birch had time to review the events and synchronicities that had brought the three of them to this place.

"What did your husband's father do in the war?"

The question jolted Jaqueline out of her concentration as she sat in front of her computer at her office. She looked up to see one of her colleagues, Stephen, with a questioning look on his face.

"Terry Birch was shot down somewhere in France towards the end of World War II. He was a pilot," she said.

Jaqueline was happy to answer his question. She knew that Stephen had been in the military and retained an interest in military matters. She thought no more about the apparently innocent question during that day. As a supervisor in a busy office this was just one of a hundred questions she would have answered.

The next day, to her jaw dropping surprise, Stephen triumphantly presented her with official details of Terry Birch's demise, the location of the grave, as well as War Grave Commission details. In addition he'd located the family of a colleague of Terry Birch's. This colleague had not only been in the same squadron but he had also shared the same billet.

"I found all this on the internet," Stephen announced triumphantly.

Jaqueline was so amazed, she wasn't sure how husband Clive would take this information. When she arrived home that evening, it was with some trepidation she spoke.

"I think that you had better sit down. I have something to show you."

As Birch absorbed the information he was shocked and pleased at the same time. The realisation started to dawn that now was the time to consider visiting the grave and crash site.

There was also another element of this story, dawning in his consciousness that was synchronous with this story so far. For the last 11 years he had been a member of the Temple Study Group. He had joined this Group since his withdrawal from the Rosicrucian Order, AMORC. The Group joined together some 50 souls to work on their own spiritual development and where possible to give service to others.

Over the years the psychic connections, trust, and caring friendships had grown apace. Most members of the group had been working on their own spiritual development for decades. Over time the psychic connections between the members became stronger and stronger. If some members of the group were working on a particular area of spiritual development, then those members not present at the time benefited psychically. They might not have known intellectually what the working group was doing.

Prior to Stephen's inspired and considerate battle with his search engine, a party of Temple Study Group members had travelled to Chartres Cathedral, an initiatory temple for mystics of many persuasions. Birch knew that they had gone to Chartres. What he didn't know was that they had worked on healing of the ancestors. He didn't discover this until after he'd planned his trip to Bordeaux to visit his father's resting place. So what amazing energies work with us all, physically, mentally and spiritually to help us gently towards our destinies?

Had the Temple Study Group work subtly inspired Birch to at last make the trip? Had the spiritual forces used the energy generated in Chartres to inspire Birch? Was Terry Birch's influence now able to call on his son from the realm in which he now dwelt?

It is unlikely that time will reveal the full extent of spiritual or material involvement in this fascinating adventure. Enough to say that all the elements came together in harmony and the trip was made.

The little group was being guided and helped along the way. It was at this point that Birch remembered the urgency with which Jaqueline had encouraged him to make this family pilgrimage. Until this time he had resisted. Previously there had been family pressure to make the trip. Birch comments that, "Perversely perhaps, family pressure had turned me off making the trip by the mere fact that pressure had been applied at all." Perverse maybe, but so very human.

We now return to our story and the meeting with M. Normand. As they turned up at the mairie Birch and Jaqueline were surprised how beautiful it was. While spring was some way off back in Cheltenham, the hanging baskets and pots were bursting into life there in France. The mairie showed every sign of love and pride. Everywhere was spotless just as if the surroundings where swept every day.

Standing ramrod straight in the designated meeting place was a man with the most impressive waxed moustache. Birch found the sight extremely humorous. Struggling to straighten his face he shook Monsieur Normand by the hand. For Birch, here was a delicious cliché. M. Normand looked, for all the world, just as a foreigner would imagine he might look. He was the archetypal French onion seller; the wide horizontal striped jersey and the beret tipped at a rakish angle. Perfect! Birch couldn't resist the thought that here was someone having a joke at his expense, or at the expense of the English. It really was just too stereotypical to be true.

Thankfully his doubts were soon dispelled. The handshake was warm and genuine. Without too much ado M. Normand pulled a folder from under his arm. Normand retrieved a photograph of Terry Birch, handing it to Birch. To say that Birch was staggered hardly did justice to his level of amazement. This was followed by a bundle of correspondence between Normand and a distant relative of Birch's. It seemed that this relative had contacted Normand concerning Terry Birch's crash. Birch had no idea this had been going on. The angels were still working overtime to help. Birch was struck by the harmonious nature of it all. He couldn't believe that all these coincidences were chance. Then again, Birch didn't believe in chance. No, there were higher forces at work.

Conversing in Birch's broken French and Jaqueline's native tongue, Spanish, (fortunately Normand had some Spanish,) communication presented no great problem; by way of a change. He invited the couple to go with him. Normand drove them to a nearby nature reserve. They stopped at the gates which were heavily padlocked. This did not deter their host. He chatted into his mobile phone. Within 20 minutes someone with a key turned up. Moments later the key bearer was joined by a second man, this time a reporter. Clearly M. Normand was someone with clout in the community.

M. le journaliste made copious notes. This scoop had excited his Gallic temperament. The keyholder unlocked the gates and gestured enthusiastically for them to follow him. They did as they were told and walked in. Birch felt sorry that Matthew wasn't with them. They walked through the tranquil countryside for 30 minutes before they came upon a lake.

"This is where your father's aircraft crashed," explained Normand.

Jaqueline and Birch separated themselves from the other two. They wanted to spend some time with their own thoughts; to experience the profundity of the place. Everyone was silent. Even the birds seemed to mute their songs. Maybe they felt something of the serenity and depth of emotion below? The lake was the last resting place of the Mosquito. Birch and Jaqueline prayed for the departed souls and the fallen from WWII, but especially Birch's father and navigator Sergeant Tickle.

As they walked slowly from the lake, Birch's emotions were in turmoil. The four converged at the gate. Once again there was a moment of awkward silence. M. Normand came to the rescue. He invited Jaqueline and Birch to his home to meet Madame Normand and share an aperitif.

At his home M. Normand showed Birch a bullet case from W/O Birch's aircraft. He had rescued it from the mud. Birch held the bullet in his hand. He wondered if across the decades, his father had also once held this in his hand. This was a poignant and special moment. Once again, time seemed to stand still. Time had no meaning for these precious few seconds; a bridge across the decades and generations. He wondered if Normand was going to offer it to him. He didn't. The time came to make their goodbyes and there was genuine warmth as they shook hands and kissed.

The trip wasn't yet complete. Birch had one last task on his pilgrimage. His father and Sergeant Tickle, seriously injured but still alive, had been dragged from the aircraft. (This much was known from intelligence received from the Resistance.) German soldiers had quickly arrived at the crash site and arrested the two airmen. They transported them to the German military hospital in Bordeaux. There they succumbed to their wounds. The hospital was now a French military hospital. Birch hoped that there might be records still remaining from 1944. Staff members were helpful and sympathetic, but Birch was disappointed to learn that no such records remained. With hindsight, he realised that Germans have a reputation for documentation and bureaucracy. During WWII they also had a reputation for destroying all documents as they retreated before the Allies in 1944 and 1945.

Pilgrimage complete, Birch knew he could now lay that ghost to rest. He paid his respects to Bordeaux, sent healing to the past and to those still grieving. He wondered if in some way they had helped close a chapter for the family and loved ones. He knew they had played their parts as best they could.

There was one last duty to perform. Terry's widow, Birch's mother, had never visited the grave, although it had always retained a place of important memory in her heart. Birch had recorded incidents and events of the trip on a personal recorder, and he'd taken photographs throughout. Lastly, he brought a handful of gravel from the grave.

All these he presented to his ageing and, by this time, ailing 85 year old mother. She was delighted with the report and the mementos.

Within less than 2 years, Joyce Birch had passed to the greater beyond to be with her still beloved Terry.

The article that appeared in the local French newspaper makes interesting reading. It appears here translated from the French.

AUDENGE *Clive Birch, son of the English pilot who's fighter was brought down in the swamp of Certes on June 10th 1944, ... of the drama.*

A fighter crashed in the swamp of Certes

Sixty years later, Clive Birch, accompanied by his wife, Jaqueline, came from Cheltenham, 150 kilometres north of Cheltenham to collect themselves in the place where his father was killed 60 years earlier, during the crash of his plane.

June 10th 1944 airman W/O Terence Birch, 23 year old pilot, and his navigator, Sergeant Ernest Stanley Tickle (29 years old) from 151 Squadron RAF, crash landed. Their plane, Mosquito Mk XIII, having been shot in the right wing during an air battle above the (Arcachon Basin). Aiming at the domain of Certes, their plane crashed in the swamp.

The two English airmen, seriously injured, taken out of the device by German soldiers, were transported at the military hospital Robert Picqué in Bordeaux.

During the crash of the plane, Clive Birch, the son of the pilot, was only 11 months old. He thus came on the 'Bassin d'Arcachon' to collect himself on the grave of his dad interred in the cemetery of Villenave d'Ornon. Then he took himself on the site where the plane crashed and where it is always. In a big moving silence, he threw a handle of gravels brought from the grave of his father.

(I make no apology for the inaccuracy of the geography. Cheltenham lies 80 miles [129 kilometres] west of London.)

Hawaii as 2005 closes

Work with a sacred crystal. Three come together for another lifetime's activity.

Marco Polo had nothing on Birch when it came to globe trotting. While talking to his friend, Hazel Barnes one day, casually she mentioned that she had visited Hawaii the previous year. Although she saw the place almost as paradise, her trip had functioned solely in material existence with no spiritual perspective. But now for her next visit she lacked companions who would share in a deeper adventure. Birch's curiosity and interest were roused. In no time at all they were planning the trip together, sensing other companions they felt would be attracted to it. One of the major interests was the presence of a so-called 'Earth Keeper' crystal, held in a Hindu Temple. The story was that twelve of these crystals would be located around the world. Their purpose was to 'hold the energy' of the emerging higher consciousness of the Earth. Birch was interested enough to follow this story and perhaps participate in an adventure or two on this 'project'.

The next element of this story was when he arrived for a meditation at the organiser's house. These meditation sessions were held once every six weeks. As Paul the organiser opened the door to Birch, he stared at him in mild surprise.

"The meetings are held on Sundays." Birch knew this full well. He'd been attending for a couple of years. "This is bank holiday Monday," Paul continued with a smile. "Come in anyway and we'll have a chat and a cup of tea."

They sat and chatted. After a few minutes the discussion turned to Hawaii.

"I know about the Earth Keeper crystals," said Paul. "In fact I have some photographs upstairs of the alleged Earth Keeper crystal held in a country house in the Midlands. I'll collect them from another room and, by the way, why don't you hold this ET (Extra Terrestrial) crystal while I search them out."

He handed Birch a rocket shaped crystal with a pointed nose and fin-like protuberances before disappearing from the room. He turned back with the words, "I don't normally allow other people to hold that, but I feel drawn to put it in your hands."

While Paul was out of the room Birch gazed at the ET crystal in his hand. Immediately he felt energy pulsing through his lower spine. Throbbing, it was as if some previously closed, energetic pathway was being opened. It wasn't consciously directed by Birch. It just seemed to happen and he was the passive observer. It wasn't long before Paul re-appeared with the photographs.

"I don't know if this Earth Keeper crystal has been activated yet, but I've visited the country house, looked and meditated on the crystal for some time. I didn't receive any impressions from it," said Paul.

By this time, given the apparent accidental timing of Birch's visit and the information and energy that had manifested, he was fully engaged with the idea of the Earth Keeper crystal. He thought of the possible adventures ahead in Hawaii. He left Paul's house fired up at the prospect of the potential trip.

The one other element to the pre-Hawaiian puzzle was the lack of response from others. Here was a great opportunity, yet it was only Marissa who signed up to join Hazel and Birch on this adventure. He was initially disappointed at the response; or lack of it. Both he and Hazel knew many adventurous souls. However, as it turned out those that needed to be there were there.

So, on with the adventure.... next stop Kauai Island, Hawaii.

It is a long journey from the UK to the west coast of the US; further still to the Islands of Hawaii in middle of the Pacific. 'Door to door' it took 30 hours. They arrived on Kauai to find that Birch had not brought his driving licence. Hazel and Marissa were going to be responsible for all the driving. He claims he felt a little guilty about this but as it turned out, particularly on their last adventure, it was the 'right thing' to happen.

It was late by the time they had chosen a rental car. The first two they rejected; too complicated the first one, not comfortable the second. It was too late to find their pre-booked rental house in the dark. Exhaustion was setting in after 30 hours travelling so they booked into a good hotel and 'collapsed into the arms of Morpheus'.

The next morning Birch awoke refreshed enough to do some *chi gong* on his hotel room's balcony. This he followed with a slap-up breakfast with the restaurant doors open. The warm sea air blew through contributing to the invigoration of travel weary bodies.

Suitably strengthened they drove from the hot and wet side of the island to the dry. Most oddly the microclimates changed within yards of each other. This island is blessed with numerous rainbows caused by alternating sun and rain. As they neared their rental house they were greeted with the most fantastic sight. Driving over a rise, a rainbow was laid out on the road and fields before them just like a carpet. It was the most amazing welcome to this wondrous island. The first few days were spent relaxing, shopping, a little swimming, and enjoying the sun.

One sight that puzzled Birch initially, but was to become part of potent symbolism later, was the flag that flew throughout the island. It contained the 'Union Flag' in one corner. A digression here to clear up some confusion might be in order. The Union Flag represents the union of England, Scotland and Wales. While commonly referred to as the 'Union Jack', this is, officially at least, a recent development. The name 'Jack' was only sanctioned by the Admiralty and Parliament in the early 20th century. Historian, David Starkey suggests that 'Jack' refers to James I. It was he who introduced the flag after his accession to the throne. Others suggest it was so named after the 'jack staff' on naval vessels from which the Union Flag originally flew.

But what was the British flag doing, of all places, on an island that was part of the United States, in the middle of the Pacific, and halfway around the world? It seemed very strange. After a few days it dawned on Birch that this was the state flag of Hawaii. Still, the connection with the British Isles remained a mystery until later.

One day while shopping in the down-at-heel town next to their rental house they came across a statue of Captain Cook, He looked regal, or perhaps imperious, in the centre of a grass square. The English explorer had 'discovered' the islands in the 18th century. Hawaii was of course inhabited by indigenous people. Captain Cook, lionised in England, 'discovered' them so that the native peoples could be exploited by the English. James Cook landed in 1776 and was surprised at the rapturous greeting. The islanders believed him to be a Polynesian god. It was eventually on Hawaii that Cook met his end, being stabbed. By this time adulation had been replaced by another emotion due not least to exploitation by the Captain and his crew. In fact, Cook had taken a chieftain hostage at one point.

Thus the statue, the man, the Union Flag on the state flag, all made a powerful and psychological connection between the two sacred isles, as Birch came to see them. He began to meditate on the connection. It came to him in a flash. He felt that all three, Hazel, Marissa, and him, were connected with the Western 'discovery' of the island. More of reincarnation later, but his insight told him that he was involved with the planning of the Captain Cook journey to these paradisiacal islands, Marissa had been one of the crew, and Hazel was one of the native population.

So there they were re-tracing the journey made in another lifetime, reinforcing the energies, perhaps closing a chapter somewhere in all the myriad lives of their beings. So just maybe the trip wasn't just about the crystal. Maybe it was a way of attracting the three of them in order to explore other areas.

Certainly this appeared to be the case as the adventurous journey unfolded. Two health issues emerged which surprised Hazel. The first was the upsurge in Birch's asthma. She wondered if it was caused while Birch was in the sea. The vision of the enormity of the endless blue yonder took him out of his comfortable city 'box'. The second was energetic difficulties that he experienced on the sacred mountain of Helakalala on the island of Maui. The pilgrimage to this sacred place was part of Hazel's spiritual journey, but not part of Birch's. The energies, physical and psychic, of that place were not invigorating for him. He was at 10,000 feet (3,048 metres) plus, and the thin oxygen content at the summit was not great for his struggling lungs.

Now back to Kauai. The down-at-heel feeling in the back streets of the area in which they stayed reflected the poor economic conditions on that part of the island. It was largely a sugar cane growing area owned by one man. The fields looked uncared for. The area did not strike Birch as being vibrant and alive.

He realised that poverty happens all over the world, but he was shocked by seeing people living on the beach in this otherwise affluent society. This was a sobering sight for the relatively well heeled visitors. They were told that many of the 'beach people' were indigenous, those of the racial stock that had been there when Captain Cook landed. Most of the inhabitants of these islands were now of different racial stock. Besides the whites there were people there from the Orient and from the Indian sub-continent.

On his return to the UK someone referred to Hawaii as paradise. To some extent Birch agreed as exemplified by the hilarious warning nailed to a coconut tree on the beach.

DANGER FALLING COCONUTS

To him it seemed so incongruous when he considered other problems there, not the least of which was whole families living on the beach.

Towards the end of their eight days on Kuaui they took a trip on a large sailing boat. They sailed around the picturesque and relatively uninhabited end of the island. Interestingly the sugar cane grower also owned this out-of-the-way corner. The extreme tip of the island was completely uninhabited. There were no buildings or people there, but visitors were allowed to hike into it. One of the reasons the area managed to retain its pristine natural environment was the presence of large stinging insects. This made life extremely uncomfortable for human visitors.

As they sailed around the area Birch felt that this part of the island was protected by Quan Yin, the female spiritual being. This was an area of the Earth, he also felt, where such spirituality was mercifully free, not only of developers, but nearly all infringement from human mental consciousness. Hazel felt that the consciousness embedded in the rocks was also an unconscious protector.

From their boat they saw flying fish and dolphins disport themselves perilously under the bow. While the dolphins showed off the flying fish were merely doing what came naturally. Birch refrains from calling the dolphins 'creatures'. He says that they are mammals and by that criteria a higher order of creation and consciousness. Many people have commented on the psychic and mental connections that they have made with dolphins. Birch sensed that they were showing off, giving a display of their athletic talents in their natural element of water.

A couple of days after the boat trip Birch visited the 'Earth Keeper' crystal. He meditated in front of it while Hazel and Marissa did a tour of the Hindu Temple complex that was home to the crystal. He had no psychic insights concerning the crystal or its message. Hazel felt that that the consciousness of the crystal was not yet fully present. Nevertheless, perhaps he was able to add a little energy to it as a result of his meditation. One reason for the lack of 'presence' may be due to the Hindu 'protectors'. It was they who built a temple around the crystal and Birch felt they saw themselves as its owners. Birch sees the ownership quite differently believing it to be owned by the consciousness of the Earth. There were Hindu beads and paraphernalia around it. This would tend to limit the externalisation of a non-religious, pure vibration. Birch implies no criticism for the temple does protect the 'Earth Keeper' which is a sacred duty and responsibility. This visit also precipitated the vision that he was given from inner contacts and which are highlighted at the end of this chapter.

Although they couldn't visit it, they did hear of an off-shore island where the old indigenous ways were being resurrected and protected. Indigenous people lived there. No vehicles were allowed on the island, again owned by the sugar planter, and visitors were only allowed by special permission. Birch felt that the sugar cane owner was being used, consciously or unconsciously, by those forces working to maintain the natural purity of the environment.

It was time for the trusty trio to move on, this time to Maui, a further eight days for the adventurers.

On their arrival on Maui, one small but bizarre incident occurred as the travellers left the aeroplane. As Birch stood to leave the plane, the man behind him commented on the words on the back of Birch's tee shirt which said, 'Bring back the wolf'. The man asked what was on the front. Birch turned to show him. 'Red Riding Hood was wrong!'

The man was tickled pink and kept commenting on it as they all shuffled off the aircraft. Birch noticed that he was a grown man carrying a Star Wars light sabre. As Birch left the aircraft Birch wondered which person was crazy him, Mr Light Sabre or both.

After picking up a second rental car they moved to a rental house close to the beach. Protecting the beach was a ring of rocks which inhibited the power of the rollers. They were very strong thereabouts in that popular surfing centre. They were told that recently a surfer had underestimated his ability to control the 'ride'. He was smashed on the rocks and killed. The protective rocks in the bay created an idyllic pool in which a certain asthmatic person could splash around to his heart's content, free of potential dangers. At the beach and pool Birch worked on his tan. This was in preparation for the return to wintry Britain. It also stimulated and allowed the inner processes to work, or so he chose to assume.

Hazel and Birch, looking for an outer mechanism for their inner work, found a Zen Buddhist temple nearby. They discovered it wasn't the vehicle for them. They found the meditation process quite rigid, stilted and uninspiring. Disappointed, they rejected it. Fortunately in the nearby town there was a Tibetan Buddhist temple. That was much more relaxed in its approach. They were welcome to enter and to meditate when it suited. They felt most relaxed there. It was there they started their days with meditation for an hour. On each occasion they were accompanied by the temple cat keeping a wary eye on them. Birch wondered if this feline was a spiritual guardian and more than a pleasant appendage to the atmosphere.

One morning as they left the Temple Hazel walked straight through the outer mosquito door, demolishing it. She immediately burst into tears and asked for a hug. Nonplussed and taken aback, Birch duly obliged. This was quite something for the slightly repressed and shy Englishman hailing from a WASP (White Anglo-Saxon Protestant) background. When she had gathered herself she told him of an insight that she had just been given. It concerned Birch being her father in another lifetime, and he had also been Marissa's father at least one time. When he had absorbed this information he recommended that when she had further insights it would be sensible to refrain from demolishing the buildings within her reach. Such behaviour might 'disturb the natives'. In any case, the owners might have a use for them.

Birch's son, Matthew, arrived for this part of the trip. Immediately he and Marissa started a relationship which lasted all of the seven days of their time in Maui. So, there they were. Clive, Hazel, Marissa, father and daughters in other lives plus Clive and Matthew father and son in this life, interesting. (Not to mention confusing.) Birch had previously received an insight that he had been Marissa's father in another lifetime.

Some in the spiritual fraternity make an extraordinary claim. In the 25 year period leading up to this universe lining up with the galactic centre at winter equinox 2012, much is being resolved in human consciousness. Birch smiles and says, "Again cycles within cycles within cycles." Unknowingly the four of them may have been acting out and resolving relationship patterns that had been initiated at a different time in a different place.

There was one final part of this adventure to be played out. On the last day the group visited a part of the island as yet unexplored by them. Hazel and Marissa were in the front of the car, driver and passenger. Birch was in the back, quiet and meditative. Matthew had already returned to the UK. As they drove, Birch sank into a deep meditative state, again without any effort or deliberate intent. At the same time he was aware of the goings on around him; the scenery and the two in the front of the car chatting away. It was akin to being in two worlds at the same time. He felt no stress or disharmony in this dual conscious state. In his inner state, he sensed two beings. He sensed that twins had entered his consciousness. They spoke to his inner consciousness.

"We are the guardians of this sacred place."

OK, he thought, another normal day in the life of Clive's consciousness. They stayed with him throughout the drive without further communication. He said nothing to the two friends in the front until they reached their destination, the sacred place that the 'twins' were guarding. They parked the car and walked to the seafront. Unfortunately they were unable to reach the sacred place, honoured by local people. It was blocked off for protection and to maintain its purity.

They sat by the sea absorbing the environment and talking, reviewing their trip. After a while they walked back to the car. There in the car park were two 'low energy' men sitting in a van. They made Birch's skin crawl as he passed them. It occurred to him they might be drug dealers. They tried to involve the group in conversation, but were ignored. Birch felt protective toward his two female companions. As with many other visits to sacred places, so often the dark energies are attracted to energies of the light.

So what was this trip all about? After their return Birch received inner messages. We may accept some, part, or none of the following. He passes on what was given to him. The vision commenced with the connection of the two sets of 'sacred isles', Hawaii and Albion (the ancient name for the British Isles). They were connected by a psychic rainbow of energy. Having this insight gave him the hope that the three of them had somehow been able to reinforce this subtle connection.

Another insight was connected to the crystal. This told him that there are, or will be, thirteen crystals. (Some commentators say there are twelve.) In his vision the twelve outer crystals in various locations were connected to a 'master crystal' at or near the centre of the Earth, thus making the thirteen. Each crystal is waking up and when all are fully awake in the near future, they will create a matrix of energy which will hold the new consciousness of the Earth in place. The Earth, which is going through its own initiation, (as all living beings have the opportunity to do,) will vibrate at a higher rate from winter equinox 2012.

This crystal grid will have a profound effect on the human body. During its development period, as all the crystals switch on and start their interaction phase, mankind will have the opportunity to develop further its crystalline structure. Each human has crystal in substantial quantities in their body, particularly in the bones and in liquid form in the blood. In this way man can move towards 'homo superioris'. This can work in conjunction with the awakening of the DNA structure and its movement towards multi-stranding. The latter has been identified by other commentators. Teachers will appear who will pass on methods of development of DNA and crystalline structure and their co-ordination.

Finally, fully developed 'homo superioris' will have the potential of living to 1,000 years or longer, depending on individual development and the final conditions on the planet. The grid structure at one of its levels will function geometrically as a rainbow does in a perfect semi-circle. Birch's insight told him that this is an important structure which, "You Clive, were shown when you came to Hawaii."

When the UK crystal is activated, Hawaii and the UK will form a binary system with connection being made through the co-ordinating crystal in the centre of the Earth. In addition there will be the overarching rainbow style mentioned above. The energy of the binary system will be tremendous. Time is short. The structure needs to be in place very soon to give time for the other crystals in the system to be activated.

Once in place, the binary system, because of its tremendous power and transformative energy potential, will cause the collapse of many of the systems that are not synchronous with it. We are talking here of the Hawaii-US-UK social and geographic system. There are third-dimensional energies working with cosmic powers to minimise negative Earth changes during this cycle of activity. Birch was informed that he will be contacted with information on work that can be done to help this 'project' forward.

Damage to the eco-system, land masses, vegetable and animal kingdoms will depend on the positive levels that can be achieved by workers of the light and others. Mankind will be pushed in many ways. "Listen intently to your intuition," he was told. "Act on the impulses. Avoid distractions. Many of them will disappear in the changed consciousness.

"Karma will be playing itself out in this scenario. The whole is greater than you, Birch, can imagine. The project is managed by the

'Lords of Time'. The US is most at risk of serious problems because of its accumulated karma and its continuing failure to move into the new consciousness. Hawaii and the UK are the most favourable locations. They are the pivots of this particular phase of the plan. However, much needs to be done. You heard today how few of the Kahuna people (indigenous Hawaiian magicians and healers) are incarnate at this time. Those incarnate are aware and are working with their part of the plan. It is they who have been waking up the Hawaiian crystal. The Hindus are indeed the 'guardians'. The most 'awake' of the Hindus are aware of the work of the crystal. This is beyond religion.

"The Northern Siberian/Arctic crystal will form the next part of the sub system. We call it this because the poles are likely to shift as a result of these changes. There is limited time for the whole system to be in place. 2012 is the cut off point because after that your universe will begin to move away from the galactic centre and thus the energies of change rapidly reduce. Whatever is in place, or in course of preparation at this time, will be the final. Therefore the 'Lords of Time' are planning a change in the 'wake up' plan for the other crystals. They will be woken up simultaneously, or nearly so, and then the connecting grid put in place. This supersedes the plan of 'waking up' one at a time.

"Your energies and physical conditions will continue to fluctuate as your whole being seeks to co-ordinate the accelerating changes. Drink plenty of water, rest more, worry less. Every person has their own path. Whatever happens to others is right for them. Stand back and be compassionate. Live and love life to the full. You have chosen to be here, make the most of it. You will have the option to stay, or leave this reality after winter equinox 2012. Listen to your inner promptings. They will guide you through.

That is the finish of the guidance."

Perhaps the three had a small part to play in these connective energy processes. It was worth going to Hawaii for that thought alone.

Scott and Lexi

*A troublesome ghost and
attempts to dislodge it.*

This story started with a text message from Scott, the elder stepson of a dear friend, Pete. Now Scott, all 300 pounds (136 kilograms) of him, marshal artist, weightlifter, night club bouncer, is not by nature a shrinking violet. Neither is he easily spooked. Even as a young child, Scott's mum and stepfather, Pete, realised he was remarkably sensitive. To this day, he can see the ghost of a young female who is invariably standing at the top of the stairs at Pete's house. She stands there just watching the comings and goings of the family. Whatever can be of such interest in the house to a ghost is a mystery to Pete.

Scott and his partner, Alexis, had recently moved into their new home in Stourport, Worcestershire. A Victorian terraced house, roomy and peaceful, they were faced with much to do both inside and in their back garden. Just hours into the New Year, 2007, Pete received this text.

"Pete. Odd question for you but when you stayed at ours (house) did you see a male shadow in the garden when you were out with the dog at night? Get a really menacing feeling out there at the mo (moment) and wondered if you had noticed him as well?"

Well, no, not really, but Pete hadn't been entirely unaffected by spirit energy in that large, dark garden. There had been two occasions when he had been out there smoking a cigarette. On each of these occasions he became aware of energy which was strong enough to make him wander round the garden to see (or sense) more. He couldn't, and that was that, or so he thought. The first text was followed by another.

"The bugger moved from the bottom of the garden and stood by next door's shed last night. Had to carry the bloody dog to the garden. Staffies are supposed to be fearless, aren't they?"

For those ignorant of canine types, a Staffie is a Staffordshire bull terrier. Jack was just a puppy but looks every bit the doggy equivalent of his master. Big, heavy standing four-square; don't mess with me, sort of thing. As the days passed the spirit energy seemed to move closer to the back of the house. There was only one thing for it. Pete phoned Birch seeking his help. Having briefed him, the two found themselves driving northwards to Stourport.

It was a cold, dark, winter's evening. Birch confessed to mild anxiety as they drove up the M5. The night and the weather were perfect if being scared was the objective.

The long narrow garden with a shed at the bottom at first seemed to Birch to be clear of nefarious vibrations. He walked down to the shed. When he reached it he felt an oppressive energy. He started to work there, invoking a protection rune, chanting its name and drawing it in the air. This was an attempt to create an environment that would deter the troublesome spirit. Walking back up the garden, he joined Scott and Pete who were standing outside the house, leaning on the garden fence. Pete said that he had a pain down one side of his body. In discussion later they considered the possibility that this was the result of an injury in the ghost's physical life. Scott felt a light headedness at the same time as Pete's side pain. The three stood silently for a few minutes. Birch jumped as Scott and Pete wheeled round together.

"There he is! The Ghost!" yelled Scott.

Together, Scott and Pete each saw the ghost in his customary position in front of the shed. Then Harry, Scott's younger brother, saw it fleetingly in the adjacent narrow garden. That was it, end of the sightings.

They returned to the house where Birch drew out on paper the rune for Scott, and wrote its name down for him to use. His previous experience of invoking this rune had demonstrated that the protective energy can deteriorate over time. Thus the energy needs to be reinforced regularly.

Birch had suggested to Scott that he speak to the ghost and ask it to leave. Scott said that he had already done this. The ghost's reaction was to come closer to the house. Birch then suggested that, if the ghost returned, that Scott gives it a 'get out'. Scott might wish to say that if he, for it is the shadow of a large male, follows the source of a light that would present itself, then there would be beings there to help him. In any case, this garden now belonged to him (Scott).

As they drove home Birch said that he felt that the ghost was attracted to Scott personally. No-one else had a strong impression of the ghost. Pete, who regularly sees ghosts, confirmed that discarnate spirits seem to be attracted to particular individuals as well as to familiar places that they have experienced in lifetime.

The following morning after sleeping on the issue, Birch felt that he needed to discuss what had happened with a friend, more experienced than he in these matters. This friend, Hazel, was of the view that Scott should communicate further with the ghost should it re-appear. She advised Scott to first go outside, close his eyes and put out loving thoughts towards the ghost. Scott should explain that he was not fearful or stressed. Next, communicate the date, either by holding up a board with the current date on, or put a newspaper at the end of the garden highlighting the date.

Hazel confirmed the view that the ghost probably saw Scott as a fellow work-mate from his lifetime.

Some weeks later, Scott told Pete that the ghost had migrated into the house. Clearly, Birch says, more work needed to be done. Pete has failed to connect with this entity inside the house.

Clearing energies from buildings whether connected to entities, ghosts or negative energies, has never been work to which Birch has been drawn. It has not, until recently, been within his field of interest.

The work done at Scott and Lexi's house was in fact the first of three clearing requests to which he has responded. The second clearing came out of some chance remarks with Sue and Roger, two of Birch's *chi gong* students, whom he taught in their home. Because of our mutual interest in energies, (Sue is an acupuncturist,) they spoke one day of energetic problems they were having in Roger's office over the garage and in their garden.

For this clearing Birch prepared a physical rune protective symbol, making it from wood. This, he left in the disturbed office. He also created further sticks which he placed in the river at the bottom of his own garden. A third was given to Sue to bury in their garden. Yet another, a fourth, Birch burned in the office. Naturally he observed health and safety requirements, so essential in Health & Safety Executive racked Britain. No-one wants to get on the wrong side of these safety czars. In this way, he invoked the four elements to assist with the clearing.

He sensed that there was an outside influence that was corrupting the energies. Previously, the atmosphere had been harmonious then for no identifiable reason there was deterioration. In his office Roger was having headaches and a considerable lowering of his physical and mental energy.

Birch asked the couple if there had been issues with two former business colleagues. He felt they may have been sending negative thoughts. Sue confirmed that there were two ex-colleagues and their relationship with Roger might easily have been less than amicable.

Birch worked with the protective rune, another sacred geometric symbol, incense and his trusty Tibetan bowl. When he felt the work was complete he asked Sue and Roger to keep him informed of any changes, and left.

Nearly a week had passed before Sue updated Birch by email. Roger felt a definite difference in his office space. 'Lighter' was the word he used and Sue felt similarly. Sue also said that the atmosphere was clearer, less stagnant and felt safe. The garden felt much safer too. Strangely enough the garden hadn't been perceived as having a problem until the difference was noted after the clearing. Sue was now prepared to walk round it after dark. She hadn't been prepared to do so before. It was now how it used to feel, yet Sue hadn't realised it had changed.

Birch had an insight into the reason for the increased 'lightness' of energy in the garden. He believed that the change was picked up and continued by the deva kingdom. Deva beings are not in this reality. They are responsible for the health and growth of nature. Stories of fairies originate from this source of beings.

Human structures pretty much exclude belief and working with such entities. This closed mind attitude adds to the already great difficulty in connecting with their energies. Churches, temples, meditation rooms, healing rooms, as well as harmonious places in nature, all encourage spiritual-being involvement. That is one reason why they feel so different.

Barbara Piranty, she of the *chi gong* inspiration that will come later, was the third request to which Birch responded. Barbara was unhappy with the atmosphere in her office. She said that it was an extremely depressing experience to walk into it. Birch had been so busy with *chi gong* classes that he'd let the first request slide, forgetting about it until Barbara reminded him. She conveyed that this was important to her and so finally, Birch was prompted into action.

As Birch entered her office the depressive energy was striking. It was certainly not helped by the dull and old paintwork on the walls. It was as though the depressing energies were, at least in part, held in the very fabric of the walls. The clearing work commenced with creating vibratory tones with the Tibetan bowl. This raised the energy of the space and the air in the room. As the sound of the Tibetan bowl died away Birch used a previously lit incense stick to draw a protective symbol against each wall in the room. He had previously asked Barbara to stay believing her positive energy would contribute to the process. They progressed to a quiet meditative period to allow the energies to settle. Next Birch placed a previously cleansed crystal on the window sill. It was dark in colour with a touch of protective 'tiger's eye' in it. He had asked the consciousness of the crystal to transfer any inharmonious vibrations to other realms of existence where they could be purified. He also suggested to Barbara that she open the very difficult sash window. This should be done regularly to help the seeping negative vibrations of the whole building to escape.

That was it, job done. He asked Barbara to keep him updated with any changes in the room. She did just that and Birch was pleased to hear that the energy in the room became lighter and more relaxing.

The crystal itself presented an interesting event. He had previously intended to use it in the clearing of Sue and Roger's house and office. As he was preparing to leave home to go to their house, the crystal went AWOL. He couldn't find it anywhere. Upon his return home, there it was sitting in the middle of the coffee table. Clearly it wasn't meant to be used in that clearing. This had happened to Birch before when using crystals. It was as though they make themselves available and then withdraw, sometimes re-appearing, sometimes not.

So, those are the three clearings so far. Whether they are the fore-runners of other, similar requests, Birch waits to discover.

Working with Audrey and Faye

Meeting 'SuperAud' and the 'Head Witch'.

Anyone meeting Audrey Sinclair in a social setting couldn't fail to be charmed by her. Audrey is everybody's image of their favourite 'granny'. Audrey is a white haired, slightly stooping figure with a welcoming smile and gentle manner. She is almost a perfect grandmother stereotype, except for the twinkle in her eye and the tinkle of her laughter. It is that laughter which is perhaps the first indication that there is a lot more to this lady than first meets the eye.

Indeed there is so much more. As a young woman Audrey lived and worked in Africa, spending time in Aden with her surveyor husband. It was there she raised her daughter. The time that she spent in Aden was during the latter days of the British Empire. There is a book to be written about Audrey's adventures in these 'foreign parts', of her careering around the desert in pursuit of local bandits in the company of the local police! Birch's pet name for her is 'SuperAud'.

Audrey has a very special talent. She has access to the Akashic record at will. This record is the repository of all the events that have happened to humanity in this third dimension. One of Audrey's particular skills is to 'read' a person's past lives, then giving the enquirer a synopsis of key events in those particular past lives.

Birch first met Audrey in 1992 when they both joined the Temple Study Group at the invitation of Jacques Rangasamy. They quickly became firm friends, enjoying each other's company, personalities, and sharing much personal interest in psychic and spiritual matters. Audrey was to play an important role in his preparation for the six months' adventure in the Americas in 1998/9. As we have seen already there was much 'psychic clearing and preparation' before he was completely ready for the trip. Audrey conducted a series of readings in the summer of 1998 investigating some key 'other' lives of Birch's, all to assist him on his way.

On these occasions Audrey holds an object belonging to the enquirer. She goes into a light meditation and 'sees' a relevant lifetime that is appropriate to the now. This 'seeing' is similar to a film passing through her consciousness. As she 'sees' she recounts the highlights. Birch smiles here. "I know what you're thinking," he said. "You're thinking, OK, this is all very interesting, but what's the point of this given that you believe it in the first place? Well, I'll tell you. For me, it helped me to understand elements of my personality in a stronger, deeper way."

It transpired that two of Birch's previous two lives were in the military. In his last life, he was born in Bayreuth, Germany, the son of a respectable 'burgher' family. In the life before that he was born into a white family in Georgia, USA and fought in the American Civil War. Both these lives are described more fully in the section on reincarnation. After Audrey recounted these 'lives' it brought to the centre of his attention a number of elements in his consciousness and personality. One is his hatred of violence and antipathy to uniforms in this life. Also at times there is an aggressive streak that arises in his being, or so he claims. Knowing Birch makes this difficult to believe. He is affability incarnate. He seems totally unwavering in his good nature and tolerance. Nevertheless, he says this temper comes from nowhere that he can identify. Occasionally, he even feels engulfed by it.

Being given the information about the military lives, and his awareness of his tendency to anger, Birch inferred that he really needed to deal with it this time around. He felt it a waste of energy to pollute further existence with this negative emotion. In addition he has often become extremely upset at scenes from the American Civil War. The cause of this intense emotion had been confusing and a mystery to him.

Paradoxically, his interest in World War I had always been immense. He has studied the subject in some depth and his knowledge is legendary among his circle of friends. Once having had these things explained to him by Audrey, he was able to put them into context, to work with them, and gradually put the negative elements of them aside, leaving them behind. There were more lives revealed to him that did not have the same powerful impact at the time.

Discovering these other lives was a healing experience. Others who have sought Audrey's help because of trauma or illness in their lives, have found help, solace and success. They have been able to link present problems to far distant causes in many instances. The process of self healing could then begin.

Audrey has another talent. She is able to read people's thoughts; not all the time, but enough to give her considerable insights into the people she meets. If someone is saying something to her while thinking something different, then Audrey is frequently aware of this. More often than not though, she will keep it to herself having had the benefit of a genteel English lady upbringing.

So the next time you pass a 'granny' in the street, or have a simple conversation with one in a shop, it might just be that there is more to her than first meets the eye!

Birch recalls a conversation early in their relationship. They had been watching a deep film about the sphinx, the pharaoh, and the phoenix. Audrey gave Birch an eruditely mystical perspective of this trinity. She said that she saw the sphinx as a symbol of the beginning of the search for enlightenment and, in an objective way, it represented the physical body with the face of a human. The pharaoh in the next stage became the priest of the people, manifesting the spiritual life for the masses. She felt at that time (1994) the Temple Study Group was doing the second stage work. She went on to say that they were aiming to become the phoenix; to work with the Holy Spirit in a mystical, rather than a religious sense. They sought to become as childlike as possible to enable them to be taken into the realm of the highest forces that humanity could possibly work with. This work needed to be done through the feminine and the Christ consciousness (again from a mystical perspective) so that the work could be balanced in duality. However, the feminine is the source of this development work.

Audrey claimed that when we embark on the spiritual path we are living in darkness. At this point, if we are being kind, it is an unconscious path. When we start asking questions about why we are here, we are shining a light into the darkness and this is the beginning of creation within ourselves.

Birch felt that he was listening to a master class as Audrey explained these principles. They were expounded with gentleness, no hint of ego or self righteousness. Birch was impressed. The things Audrey explained resonated in his being. It was a deeply mystical perspective that he struggled to grasp and understand, yet he knew it was an important series of truths. He thought at the time, that this was a woman of profound understanding. He would like to get to know her better.

One September years later, Audrey and Birch travelled to Glen Lyon, Scotland; the longest glen in the country. There is a story that Jesus and Joseph of Arimethea landed on the west coast of Scotland. Disembarking from their ship they walked along the glen to the site of a mystery school that existed at that time. It was situated at the inland end of the glen at a place called Dull.

This would have been easy to arrange as it is claimed that Joseph, Jesus' uncle, was a ship owning merchant. He regularly traded with Cornwall for tin. He would have had a good relationship with the Roman rulers of Britain, not least because of his metal trading links. It may well have been easy for him and his companions to move around freely. Having read the story Birch felt enthused to walk in their footsteps. They flew to Scotland and collected a rental car at the airport. First stop was the amazing chapel of Rosslyn made famous in Dan Brown's book and subsequent film, 'The Da Vinci Code.'

Rosslyn Chapel hadn't registered on most people's radar until the publication and subsequent court case of this global best seller. It was founded in 1446 by Sir William St Clair. His last resting place is in the Chapel which was unfinished at the time of his death. It is believed the original plan was for a much larger construction. During the English Civil War, in 1650 Cromwell's troops stabled their horses in the Chapel. HRH Prince Charles visited Rosslyn in 1998, the last in a long line of Royals to do so.

From Rosslyn they drove northward. Reaching Glen Lyon they travelled along its length tuning in to the energies as they went. During this journey Birch received the impression that they were somehow, in a way that he finds difficult for him to explain, reinforcing the energy simply by travelling along the glen's length. He felt strongly that others had made this same journey, performing the same task. At one point they stopped on the side of the road. Audrey tuned in and received the psychic impression that Jesus and Joseph had indeed travelled the route. Birch felt that Glen Lyon was the male energy. They later came across the female energy at Mount Schiehallion which provided the female counterpart. This mountain had tremendous power. It is commonly known in the area as a magic mountain, associated with fairies and devas.

At the end of the Schiehallion visit they drove back towards London to return the rental car there. As they drove towards the border with

England, Audrey asked Birch if he would like to visit Hadrian's Wall. He responded with a spontaneous burst of apathy, however they were led by circumstance, to stay in a bed and breakfast in Northumberland. Lo and behold, when they spoke with the owner it turned out that the B&B, a farmhouse, was built directly on the Wall. That night the two meditated, tuning into the Roman soldiers that had been garrisoned there. They sensed that these souls from two millennia ago were cold, bored, miserable and far from home. There were skirmishes but no major battles for them. The power of the Roman army was a major disincentive for the local tribesmen to 'have a go'. Birch gave Audrey a reiki healing session. During this a young, round-faced Japanese man came into her consciousness. He had a black fringe of hair and wore a red silk coat, embroidered and long. He had his hands tucked into the long sleeves. Both of them were then visited, in consciousness, by a Chinese master, scholarly looking, who also 'kept his eye on them'. Birch had seen the latter gentlemen on a number of occasions, particularly when practicing or teaching *chi gong*. This technique will be explained later. Subsequently the Chinese master said to Audrey, "I am the quiet master".

Audrey and Birch had a great mutual friend, Faye; another fascinating woman. Birch was certain that there was psychic and spiritual work for the three of them working as a team. At the time of writing they haven't got round to it yet. In the 1960s, Faye was working in Delhi in the Diplomatic Service. As with many people she loved to visit the small shops and haggle with the merchants to get the best deals. Some of her colleagues found this haggling very difficult; a bit un-English. They would enlist Faye's help on their forays to the shops and markets. One day Faye was in a shop haggling away as normal. The shopkeeper stopped in mid-haggle, opened his eyes wide and pointed his finger at Faye.

"It's you," he said. "You are the person attracting all these people into my shop."

Faye looked around and indeed the shop was full to overflowing with potential customers. The shopkeeper was convinced that it was Faye's presence that was attracting all these people.

"If you come into my shop regularly, I will pay you."

Faye politely declined, but from then on she noticed that her entrance into previously empty shops caused an influx of potential customers, no matter which country she is in. One day, in more recent times, Faye and Audrey were in a restaurant in Leominster, well away from a centre of population. When they arrived they were the only two people in the place, apart from a couple of bored waitresses. Within a very short time, the place filled with people, much to the chagrin of the waitresses who took to tearing their hair out at the unexpected influx.

This shopper magnet talent is not her only gift. Birch and Audrey call her 'Head Witch'. In one of her employments she worked as a PA to a manager. Part of her role was to organise a conference for her company. When it came to the invitation list, it appeared that Faye was not on it despite all her hard work in setting it up. In a fit of semi-humorous pique, she said to her boss, "May your back be covered in boils." Within days, the boss's back was covered in boils.

Now we in our Western European Judeao-Christian psychological box, are aware of the power of suggestion. Maybe that same power was enough for the boss to persuade himself, through guilt, to cover his own back with boils. One could argue however, that some are better at suggestion than others. Faye lives in Harefield. The hare is the symbol of the Mother Goddess.

OK, one last Faye story for no better reason than Birch likes it. Faye tells this story concerning her window cleaner. One day she met him on the doorstep, opening her door to him.

"How are you Faye?"

"Not too good," she replied.

"Would you like some healing?"

"Yes please, she replies," thinking that he would send her some absent healing from his church as Leslie, let us call him, is a born again Christian member of a 'happy clappy' sect.

To Faye's affirmative reply and to her consternation, Leslie immediately seizes her hands on the doorstep and starts calling on his Lord in a loud voice.

"Oh Lord, heal this poor person, give her your grace lord. We ask this in the name of the holy spirit, blah, blah, blah." This went on, without any interruption for half an hour, all the while Faye wishing that she could drop through the floor. The postman walks by.

"Aye, aye, what are you two up to?" He says as he whistles along his way.

The neighbour walks by. "Hello Faye and Leslie. Are you having a nice time?" Isn't this the way of the British treat everything as though it was normal? Never on any account make a fuss. Undeterred Leslie continued, oblivious to the comments and stares of other passers by.

"Oh Lord grant thy servant eternal peace and make her walk in the steps of the Lord, etc, etc, etc."

Eventually Faye was able to escape. Now when Leslie arrives to clean the windows, Faye hides if she is at home. So, dear reader, be careful about passing on your state of your health to those that you don't know.

It was Faye who, when in a meditation with Audrey and Birch, saw a Mayan shaman standing on a rock outcrop overlooking a valley. Next to the shaman was a wolf. Faye received the message that the work was done. Birch's power animal, as we've said elsewhere, is a wolf. They both took this vision as a sign that the work that he had done in Central America was now complete.

Suggestion as a control tool may be a new concept to some. Two stories highlight the deliberate use of suggestion. When Francoise Mitterrand was electioneering in one of his campaigns to become President of France, a political advertisement was broadcast on French TV. Unbeknown to the viewing public, a subliminal insert was placed in the ad. This can be done by flashing, very briefly, an image which is so quick it is not picked up by our everyday objective consciousness. However, because of their very nature such images do stimulate the unconscious, are retained, and can become part of our 'knowledge' without being explored by our critical faculties.

What went wrong with this subliminal insert was the flash was allowed to go on too long. Thus it was picked up by viewers' normal outer, objective consciousness. This caused many complaints as the viewers realised that that they had been 'had'. It is no surprise that this practice, once called subliminal advertising, is outlawed in Britain.

Birch was told another story by a friend. This friend was part French, and he had a friend in the French TV service. Some years ago there was a war in the North African country of Chad. Chad had once been part of the French Empire and was thus of newsworthy interest in France. The French TV journalist was sent to Chad to do a piece for the French news that evening. He stood in the desert in that very dry country, with the blue sky as backdrop, and did his piece to camera. It was sent back to France for transmission. Something changed from the point when the piece was recorded to the point when it was broadcast. What changed was the presence of two military jet aircraft flying overhead in the broadcast piece. They had been added later. What was the point of this addition? The point was that the presence of the military was highlighted to settle nerves in metropolitan France, to show that 'something was being done'. They were not in Chad, at least not when the item was recorded.

Reincarnation

*Birch introduces a modern perspective
and extracts from his past lives.*

There are many ways of looking at reincarnation. It would be surprising, even disappointing, if Birch didn't have some perspectives on this emotive subject.

Throughout the East the concept of each human being living lifetime after lifetime, is part of everyday belief. It pervades philosophy, religions, and social contexts. In the West it is for the most part disregarded, derided, spun as a belief of 'backward people'. Myths are spread concerning the beliefs and practices of those using reincarnation ideas in their lives. For instance, one lie commonly aired is the idea that humans can reincarnate as animals and, as such, is backward and abhorrent. This myth is most certainly not one shared by the believers. Birch questions why these lies and deliberate misunderstandings have been propagated?

For an answer let's go back to the Council of Nicea in 325 AD. This Council was an early meeting of the Christian Church to propound its dogma and theology. Before that date, reincarnation was an accepted element of Christian teaching. During the Council it was written out of Christian belief. Why might this have been so?

For any possible illumination on this we must examine a central tenet of the workings of reincarnation theory. A central plank of any such belief is that in each lifetime we have the opportunity to right the wrongs in our characters and personalities. Each birth is an opportunity to progress further along the path towards spiritual development and complete self-realisation. We come into each lifetime with a 'shopping list of experiences' that we wish to go through. We choose our parents and place of birth that will best facilitate these experiences. As we move from the spirit world to this physical existence we forget the decisions previously made and have free will to follow the path previously set out; or not, as the case may be. Nevertheless we have set the vibratory pattern of our life to come, and the experiences will present themselves to us whether we have awareness and realisation or not.

Now, this causes a problem for Western religions. In this scenario we are totally responsible for ourselves. This is our spiritual journey mapped out by us, for us. Good experiences, or bad, develop our soul personalities and characters. Thus there are no divine interventions, no retribution from a stern discarnate being pointing the finger at our weaknesses and failures, and no moral code laid out by a God for all others to follow. We are living out our own moral code, minute by minute, and certainly no need for a human intermediary between us and the divine source. We are our own priests.

What are we to believe the church fathers thought of that? What, no specialist priest, no archdeacons, no archbishops, bishops, cardinals, or popes? It would rather stifle career development. No control over the masses. What about the church building programmes, church investments, power over kings, princes, and we commoners? No hell, or threats and punishments to be perpetrated upon ordinary folk by self appointed clerics. All these constructs would disappear into thin air, at a stroke.

Thus throughout the last 1800 years reincarnation has been suppressed as a belief system in those countries heavily influenced by Western religions, Christianity and Judaism. The exquisite simplicity and harmonious nature of the ideas of reincarnation are seeping into Western thought, more and more. People become more open and questioning about the nature of reality. As people become free from the dogma imposed by those seeking to continue to dine at the table of imposed power over others, belief in this system gathers momentum.

Some may find the prospect of reincarnation perplexing, others reassuring. Good or bad, this is Birch's perspective. How have these ideas shaped his life? What affect does he perceive that these other lifetimes are having on him now? How have they contributed to his development? Birch tries to shed some light on some of these questions. By the very nature of being human and living in this three dimensional reality, we attract those experiences that will contribute to our development. If we fail to learn the first time round, then these events and people will be re-presented to us time after time until we take the lesson on-board in our march towards spiritual perfection. This re-presentation time after time can be extremely frustrating for many people; those who don't have the insight that it is they who are attracting conditions to themselves. They may blame fate or a vengeful God.

However, in Birch's way of looking at reality there is no fate, no luck and no accidents. All the while we are attracting the conditions to ourselves that we face in this life. It is our responsibility to solve them and move on; this is the opportunity we have been given. It may be that we will live hundreds of lifetimes. There is much to learn. There is no end time by which we are required to attain perfection. All is in our hands.

This can be very scary for many people. Birch has a very dear friend whom he describes as being intelligent, articulate and mature. She simply cannot accept Birch's viewpoint. Her rejection is nothing to do with logical argument. She has told him that she has an emotional need for someone else to tell her what to do; for instance, the local priest. She needs another to comfort her and reassure her that she has value as a person.

Birch finds this really sad. In his friend's case, her feelings of self worth are so fragile she cannot think for herself or make up her own mind. Birch does not suggest that she should take his perspectives lock, stock, and barrel. It would be beneficial for her, he believes, if she could formulate her own perspectives. After all, we all have a slightly different view of reality. This unique view, person by person, is part of the genius of the human race.

Before the Chinese invaded Tibet, over the lintel at the entrances to the monasteries was the admonition, 'A thousand monks, a thousand religions.'

The major Western religions don't like reincarnation because this belief helps create a self assured, self responsible person. A thinking adherent is no adherent at all when all the rules and regulations are laid out for them to swallow wholesale, or be banished to hell as a heretic by structured religions. It is Birch's view that a major failing of the Western religions is the attempt to shoehorn us all into a more or less one world view of spirituality. This is doomed to failure given that we have all had the opportunities of many experiences and are at different places in our spiritual development.

Birch likes to compare the soul personality (the sum total of talents, characteristics, preferences, and abhorrence's,) to a diamond. Each lifetime we present another facet to be polished on the wheel of experience until all are shining and the wheel of re-birth is no longer necessary. That could be some way off. One would need to be a Gandhi figure to have resolved most of life's vicissitudes. In adversity and danger we can reach back into ourselves, discovering talents that we had no idea we possessed. In this way we re-explore other facets of the diamond.

Many lives are simple and mundane much of the time, but all the while learning opportunities are presented, no matter the nature of our existence. Sometimes lives of simple service are as valuable as ones of excitement filled with happenings.

Those who see themselves as Cleopatra or Bonaparte in previous lives are, for the most part, kidding themselves. The current ego is most likely over inflated in these cases.

So these are the personal perspectives of Clive Birch. He seeks to convert no-one to a belief in reincarnation. There have been enough 'conversions' on this planet to last until eternity. He presents his thoughts as a model with which he is comfortable. He hopes that those who are unfamiliar with the concepts, and those who have an open mind, enjoy these ideas. Birch has described some stories extracted from some of his previous lives. Most have come from insights to these lives, extracted by his dear friend and spiritual sister, Audrey. It is she with the 'direct line' to the Akashic.

Some years ago he had a visionary experience from ancient times. In this vision he was a central character moving from scene to scene, much as actors do in a film or TV drama. He felt so emotionally drawn into the experience, during and after the vision, that he believed it to be a past life experience. This belief was reinforced later. He was a spear carrying soldier, marching in a cohort with other spear carriers. They were lightly clothed and lightly armed. The landscape was dusty desert terrain. Marching next to him was his great friend at that time.

On one occasion, as a group, they slept in a room with very bright white-washed walls. Some illness or accident befell the friend for in the next marching scene his face was covered in a mask of cloth with eye holes covering the disfigurement. This mask flapped as they walked. In the final scene the friend and Birch had been captured, or were being disciplined within their own army. He saw and felt that they were surrounded by threatening men, at least three. There, before his eyes, the friend was killed. Birch went into great shock and grief inside the vision and, significantly for him, still felt the shock and the grief as he emerged from the altered state. For him, this was a real life experience, just as valid as any that he experiences in his day-to-day life now, in the 21st century. For the time being this was where the vision rested. The year of the vision was 1997.

In 2007 Birch contracted an attack of shingles. The painful spots appeared on his right chest, just below and to the right of the nipple. The discomfort extended around his body and terminated in the right shoulder. He believes that shingles follow nerve ganglia wherever they are on the body.

Prior to this he had been very healthy. He was taken aback by the sudden arrival of the malady. He went into meditation to try to ascertain the cause or background information concerning the attack. In the meditation he saw a spear of light entering his back where the discomfort ended. It emerged from his chest where the shingle spots were located. His intuition made an instant connection with the lifetime experience mentioned above. This was somewhat of a surprise to him. There had been such a time lag since the first connection with the spear carrier life.

One of the nurses who looked at the rash on his chest said, "This is the strangest shingles I've ever seen. It looks more like a wound." Birch's version of the stigmata perhaps?

The story appeared to become stranger and stranger. As he didn't receive any further vision he determined to ask Audrey to look into the Akashic to attempt to find out more. Audrey saw him in the spear carrier life, as part of an army besieging a castle or ancient city with high protective walls. Rough ladders were thrown against the walls by the besiegers in an attempt to scale them. The defenders threw missiles down in attempts to dislodge the attackers. He climbed a ladder, reached the top, and scrambled over the parapet. At that precise moment, before he could gather himself, one of the defenders speared him from the side. The spear entered and exited his body precisely where he saw the spear of light in his meditation and where the shingles had manifested.

In Birch's way of looking at reality, somehow the suppressed memories had been released from the unconscious into memory and into the cells of the body, as far as the shingles were concerned. This was in order to be cleared out with healing methods. So in this case he was clearing, or having cleared, the trauma from a past life.

In Niamh Clunes book 'The Coming of the Female Christ', she speaks of the spear representing 'intuition' in the archetype of ideas. She also says that in the grail myth, the spear that wounds is the spear that heals.

Birch suggests that a message here is to give intuition even more credence over intellect in negotiating one's life path, day-by-day. To some extent he does this. He claims he needs to do it more. In addition, the healing of the wound, for him, is most profound.

Working roughly chronologically, he had a life as a Chinese mandarin at the court of the emperor. With many others, he was an advisor at court. This life was relatively uneventful except that, as one of his tasks, he undertook the teaching of *tai chi* and *chi gong* movements to others. In his current life the teaching of such systems has been his livelihood for 3 years. He has been fascinated with these movements for many years. However it was only recently, long after he had started teaching, that this Chinese life was revealed to him.

In this Chinese life, he died peacefully in the bosom of his family. Seemingly then ancient interests and talents bled through into this life.

In another ancient life he was advisor to an emir or sheikh of an Arab city state. The ruler was extremely cruel, tormenting criminals, enemies, and those he didn't like with dreadful tortures which invariably led to their deaths. He was revolted by these practices and sought to ameliorate these punishments whenever he could. Birch or whatever his name was in that life needed to be careful not to alert the emir to his moderating practices for fear of similar reprisals on himself. He would escape to the desert when he could and live among the Bedouin tribes-people to relax and free himself from the pressures of the court.

The 'bleed through' into this life is his predilection for fair and honourable treatment of others. One of the sources of anger within him is the perceiving of injustices perpetrated on others. Curiously, injustices practiced on him don't generate the same amount of righteous indignation.

In another life he was the dancing master, or master of ceremonies, in a big house of rich and powerful people, somewhere in Central Europe in the 16th and 17th centuries. It was common in those times for the elite to host big parties for their fellows. His role was to host these parties, organising the entertainment and ensuring the event was a big success. He would dress in frock coat and purple high heeled shoes, and carry a silver-topped cane. He lived in a room at the top of the house, more or less in the roof space. As he aged he trained a younger man to take over his duties. He eventually died peacefully in his bed.

Even today he likes brightly coloured clothes and shoes. At the time of writing he is 64 years old; his wife, Jaqueline is 38. She tells him that he dresses younger than her. This is not a conscious decision on his part. He dresses as he likes. He doesn't care if it is younger or older than anyone else.

There were at least two lives in the Christian religion. Birch does not doubt that these lives have had a significant impact on his current beliefs concerning this religion. In one he was an official in the Vatican. He was born into a wealthy Italian family. Being the third son he was not entitled to inherit the family estates. This would pass to the eldest son under the law of primogeniture. The second son would go into the military as was the tradition. The third son, Birch, was packed off to the church, again according to tradition. He was sent as a young boy.

Eventually he attained the rank of cardinal. The role was primarily political. He was obliged to take part in a certain amount of religious ceremony. However, he would not equate this situation with a spiritual one. It was very worldly and emotionally empty. One very bright spark entered this life in the form of a young priest. He became Birch's 'good friend'. This relationship did not last as the young priest died at an early age. Birch was devastated. The only thing that he had ever loved was taken from him.

He carried out his duties with a broken heart and, to ease the emotional pain, he started to drink alcohol heavily. In the end the booze killed him releasing him from a miserable life. The last scene was of the funeral in the Vatican, carried out with all the pomp of that religion.

In another existence as a Catholic priest, much lower in the pecking order this time, he was serving in Central America. He has had a vision of him in a black monk-like vestment with a hood and a rope around the waist. He was standing next to a pyramid in the jungle. This was a very emotive scene, given the story of the Mayan life following. He was given the task of marching deep into the jungle in order 'to convert the savages to the true religion!' This is what he did, except things did not turn out as planned. In the jungle, he met his nemesis in the form of a shaman. This shaman had far more knowledge of spiritual and psychic matters than anyone he had met in the church. He had more compassionate human understanding as well. Birch was totally fascinated and instead of converting the shaman to 'the true religion', Birch became a student convert of this 'ignorant savage'. He forgot himself so much that the church sent out a rescue party to bring him back to civilisation.

He returned from whence he'd come hoping to return with some of the knowledge gained in the jungle. It was hope doomed for disappointment. He was given lowly duties and watched by his colleagues. He was now a suspect who had 'gone native'. He needed to be careful just to survive, for the Inquisition was still very much a force to dread and fear. This life introduced him to a more mystical and spiritual version of reality away from dead dogma and theology. Thus he has carried this mystical awareness and approach into this life. This past life was a springboard for his current mystical and spiritual approach.

As Lisa Simpson said, "Everyone needs a nemesis".

Sometimes personalities recur time and time again in different lifetimes. There is an example of that in the American Civil War lifetime following. In the next two examples Birch tells of other lifetimes with his wife, Jaqueline.

They were in Atlantis together as partners. She was pregnant at the time of the final deluge and sinking of that continent. Although they were not part of the priesthood, they had been warned by them that the end was near. They knew that the final destruction was close. Because of the pregnancy they left it late to attempt to make their escape. After the baby was born they did make their way to one of the last ships leaving. Too late; the final deluge came. Birch's wife, standing near the edge of the boat, experienced the horror of the baby being washed out of her arms and over the side. Sadly they were not destined to escape either. The force of the terrible inundation caused the boat to sink. All were drowned.

Is there significance that Atlantis was raised again? Atlantis has captured the imagination of many for centuries, yet we are captivated on scant evidence, mostly folklore. Some suggest there is a link between Mayan culture and Atlantis. Sadly for our purposes, even the most assiduous research fails to provide any compulsive association. Indeed, most historians refer us back to Plato. Are we really to believe that an ancient, advanced civilisation disappeared under the waves leaving no trace? Plato tells of a great naval power which conquered much of Western Europe and Africa. All this happened around 9400 BC, before Atlantis sank beneath the waves "in a single day and night of misfortune."

Historians, archaeologists and adventure seekers have suggested a number of possibilities for its location. But do they hold up to scrutiny? Over the years, hundreds of locations have been suggested but most do not stand even superficial scrutiny. For now, it appears we are left with four main contenders.

Malta seems to offer some hope. Some 24 temple sites can be found on Malta and Gozo and new sites are discovered from time to time on the sea bed. In the last 5,000 years the level of the Mediterranean has risen some 15 metres (49 feet). Plato talks of elephants on Atlantis and, unlikely as it sounds, 500,000 year old remains of pygmy elephants have indeed been discovered on Malta. Perhaps they were marooned on the island when Malta broke away from the African continent? Unfortunately that seems to be it; no cast iron evidence

We now move to the coast off the Americas, a location favoured by Edgar Cayce. Back in the early 20th century he suggested Bimini Island. There, in 1968 an aviator spotted buildings under the sea. Now called Bimini Road, there are square outlines and symmetrical blocks suggesting they are man-made. Similar submerged shapes were discovered off Andros in the Bahamas in 2003. It seems possible that the Mayans could have settled on the Bahamas. But the earliest signs of habitation are dated only as far back as 1000 AD. Was there an earlier culture there? If so, maybe it could have been swept away by a tsunami. Again we seem to be destined for disappointment. Geologists tell us that the blocks are natural and there is no record of any tsunami.

Let's try Cuba. There are huge structures there, submerged 600 metres (1969 feet) beneath the waves. Their presence was detected by sonar and they are definitely symmetrical. Their layout is similar to Mayan cities with their temples. The site covers some twenty square kilometres. Strikingly, some of the structures are 45 metres (148 feet) tall. But 600 metres deep is considered by many to be far too deep. It would have required massive tectonic activity to depress the land to that depth.

Yucatan folklore tells of an advanced culture lying to the east. Maybe this was it? Scientists believe more investigation is necessary before the site can be dismissed entirely.

Finally we return to Europe, to Greece. In 1967 an ancient Minoan city was discovered buried on Santorini Island. This city disappeared some 3,400 years ago. Its advanced architecture included internal plumbing and aqueducts. For good measure, just like the Mayans, the Minoans worshipped bulls. Santorini was all but destroyed by a massive volcanic eruption 90 times bigger that that of Mount St Helens. The pyroclastic flow wiped out the city and the island collapsed, water rushed in and this ended the world of the Minoans in 1630 BC.

In another lifetime together, this time in the magnificent pyramid city of Teotihuacán, Mexico, Birch was a priest and she a priestess. This was the time of a takeover of dark forces of that magnificent temple complex. They were part of the existing spiritual network seeking the light. As the enemy succeeded in overthrowing the forces of light, Birch was incarcerated. Again the wife was pregnant. She managed to see him in prison and he persuaded her to flee into the countryside to save herself and the baby. He was not so fortunate. He suffered a horrible death, being buried up to his neck until dead. Birds pecked out my eyes. Not the nicest way to leave this life.

We have already seen that Birch is fascinated by the mystery of Teotihuacán. But he says he has visited and worked meditatively there long before this current lifetime. The connection has remained strong across the eons of time.

He detests wearing uniforms, particularly military ones. Perhaps the next two life experiences explain why? At the time of the American Civil War, he was the son of a mill owner in Georgia. The mill was situated near a river. Although of ordinary artisan background, his family owned a black slave. He and the slave were great friends and companions. In larger social environments this would have been frowned upon and disallowed. The social division between black and white was total in the South. Because of the social environment, he needed to be very careful concerning his friendship with the black friend, especially so when visiting the local town. Birch has the strong intuitive impression that this friend is one of his sons in this life.

Sadly the Civil War erupted. Birch joined the forces of the Confederacy. He was, after all, loyal to his state of Georgia and to the South. This decision to fight was not out of commitment to the slave industry which he was against. He took part in skirmishes, seeing horrible sights of mangled and dead bodies. His greatest comrade choked out his life next to him in the fields. He wasn't injured physically, but greatly traumatised by his experiences. This psychological damage was almost too much to bear. The war was lost and the army disbanded. He was simply demobbed and told to go home. He walked many miles back to his home in Georgia. There was no food. He scavenged what he could, coming across others doing the same.

He found his way back, subsequently managing to eke out a living as a clerk. He married a woman who would have been above his station before the war. Her family had lost everything. Beggars can't be choosers, particularly after being on the losing side of the war. She and her mother looked down on him. He was little more than a necessary evil. He could never hope to fulfil their expectations and was soon past caring to try. He had a dog that was his loving companion. They would escape to the wild together to try to soothe the pain in his mind and heart. Then one day, his beloved dog was killed violently by a pack of wild dogs. This was the final straw. His heart was broken by his experiences. It was at this point that he vowed never to open his heart again.

It is only now, in this life in the 21st century, that Birch is working to reverse that commitment. He had lived a simple, carefree life, and was thrown headlong into the hell of slaughter. He died pretty soon after. Interestingly, he believes his wife's mother in that life was his mother in this one.

Throughout this life, and long before he was shown this life experiences by Audrey, he would become extremely upset by TV and film presentations of the War from the Confederacy side. So much so, he couldn't watch for long, the emotional discomfort being too great. Another 'bleed through' to this life?

Bill Bryson in the 'The Lost Continent' talks of his surprise at visiting the University of Mississippi and finding that the black and white students were living and working happily together. Twenty-five 25 years before there had been a riot at the enrolment of the first black student. This resulted in the death of two journalists and the wounding of 30 Marshals.

A possible reason for the illogical hatred of black people by certain sections of the white community in the south of the US occurred to Birch in an intuitive flash. Could it be that they blamed the black people for their part in the Confederacy losing of the Civil War. This is a totally spurious reason of course. Nevertheless their unconscious reaction would be passed on through the genetic sequencing down the generations.

It is fascinating and extremely sad that each generation is incapable of dealing with its own negative issues. Awareness of them, and the realisation that they do not serve positively, would help with resolving them individually and at the social group level.

In fact the Confederacy never had a prayer of winning the Civil War. The North was overwhelmingly powerful in manpower and resources. By the standards of the day, its manufacturing capability was astounding. There is something about the tide of history here that the eighteenth century society in the Deep South, with its slave culture and rural attitude was missing. This approach to society was finished. It was just that the South did not realise it. The industrial nineteenth century, right or wrong, was the way forward for the Western societies, despite its manifold weaknesses. The Confederacy was really the last bunker of the old. Its time was gone. It is such a waste that so much pain and suffering was a by-product of this tide of history.

Birch feels able to express the above because of his life in Georgia and his time in the Confederate Army. It is part of his being, part of his history. He believes that he has the right.

The last life, chronologically speaking, saw him being born into a 'respectable' burgher family in Bayreuth, Germany. His father was a banker. His upbringing throughout childhood and young adulthood was extremely strict. At a very young age he was sent off to military academy where martial discipline was rigidly applied. Although respectable on the outside, there were pressures on the inside. One time he caught his father in the bedroom of a young woman who lived in the house. He was not sure if it was his sister, a servant, or a relative.

This was not the behaviour of a respectable, middle class pillar of society. He and his father fought on the staircase as he sought to defend the honour of this young woman. His relationship with his father was fractured by this event. He never spoke to his father again, such was the rage of the youth. Even when the father lay on his deathbed, the son refused to go and see him. He supposes that this incident would have been covered up in 'respectable' society.

Time marched on. As he entered young manhood, he joined the army and, because of family connections, he became an officer appointed to the general staff. It seems that one of his uncles was a general in the Prussian elite of the army. He tried to find happiness with a partner and once there was a young woman around. Perhaps because of his stiffness and buttoned-up personality, happiness never quite happened.

On one occasion as the staff stood around a map table during military manoeuvres, the Kaiser joined them. The First World War came. He commanded men on the Western Front. He witnessed more terrible slaughter, this time on an industrial scale. At one point he prayed on his knees in church, seeking a meaning to all this horror. The almost inevitable happened. He was shot in the back, and died.

He is certain that he has had enough of martial lives. The unnecessary and futile nature of it appals him now. Perhaps that's the point. In the development opportunities presented to him, he has seen violence in its true light. Someone once said, "Violence is the last refuge of the incompetent". As Churchill said, "Better jaw jaw than war war".

An interesting story concerns an insight Birch had of someone else's past lives. It came out of the blue and surprised him because he didn't feel connected to this work with other people normally. It is not his field.

The story starts on New Years Eve 2003. Wife Jaqueline was away visiting relatives in Mexico. He was invited to stay with friends in Milton Keynes over the New Year period. On the night of the New Year, his friends and he attended a party. There he met a larger-than-life character, who we will call Dan. He was a big man, muscular with shoulders that would not disgrace the front row of the England rugby squad. He had hands the size of plates and fingers that looked like pork sausages. Yet his size was in no way menacing, not least because of his sunny, extrovert personality. He boogied the night away, moving with great smoothness and balance that belied his size. He was great fun.

At the end of the party Birch and his friends staggered back home to recover from the night's activities. As he lay in bed awaiting the arms of Morpheus, he suddenly had a vision of Dan in what he sensed was a past life. In this life he was a priest in ancient Egypt, very stern and forbidding in persona, unlike his present life. He had responsibility for conducting ceremonies that were to aid the fertility of the Earth and the bounty of good crops. Most certainly this would have been a very important function in an ancient society. Because of the perceived importance of this role, he had access to, and influence with, the highest of the aristocracy. He was very aware of the important role that he held, and he let every one know this by his words and actions. Not a man to be liked or crossed. Most people would avoid him unless forced to consult him concerning his priestly duties.

As he walked across the plazas to perform and supervise the rituals for which he was responsible, he spoke to no-one as he passed. He would wear his high crowned hat of office. Such was the expanded nature of his ego and sense of self importance. The children would make faces behind his back. One of his nicknames was 'Mr Stiff Neck', a name that would only be voiced out of his earshot. Time marched on. In his dotage he lay dying on the floor with a single attendant to care for his final needs. No other person bothered to pay him any attention.

Through his friend in Milton Keynes, Birch contacted Dan. He told him of his vision. He was very open to the idea and asked Birch for more information. Birch suggested that Dan send him a crystal or some other object that was his. It would have absorbed and be carrying his vibration. The crystal duly arrived and Birch went into meditation while holding it. What came to him were the fragments of two other lives.

In the first Dan was the chief of a small tribe of Africans. This tribe, and their lands, were threatened by a much larger tribe that surrounded them. Birch saw Dan sitting outside his hut, worried and troubled by the threat to him and his people. The inevitable happened. He saw spears and then darkness. This was the end of his insight into this life.

In the next life he saw Dan again as an African. He was captured by slave traders and shipped to Cuba as a slave. He was intelligent, young, and perceptive. His life however, was one of unremitting toil, as it was for most slaves. Nevertheless, in his unpleasant life the light of spiritual interest was lit in his breast.

In April 2004 Birch wrote to Dan, gave him all the insights that he'd received, and forgot about it quickly in the maelstrom of life. Dan never wrote back. At the end of the year, Birch returned to Milton Keynes for the New Year celebrations once again. As he sat with his friends, bringing each other up to date, he asked casually how Dan was. He was intrigued. His friend dropped a bombshell.

"He is dead. He died of cancer very suddenly, within weeks of diagnosis."

Birch's jaw dropped. He was staggered. The whole series of events between the two of them flooded back into memory. Over the next few hours and days, Birch struggled to make sense of this news in respect of the past life histories. Yet he felt he had been privileged to share in the dramatic insights, maybe particularly so at that time at the end of Dan's life.

The conclusion Birch reached was that Dan needed to know this information before he passed over into the spirit world. The reason that it was Birch that was the messenger was perhaps to do with the need, from his perspective, to be impressed from outside his circle of family and friends. "A prophet is without honour in his own country" seems an appropriate adage. Birch had already discovered this to his cost, in the past. Or maybe it had something to do with Birch being the most sensitive to Dan's psychic needs at the time. Whatever the reason, the whole situation had a very profound effect on him. He explains that if we make ourselves available for good works, or ill, then the cosmic and spiritual forces will use our talents and communication skills. However the impetus must come from us. We live in a free will universe.

Above we see a perspective from Birch's point of view. To him it makes sense, in a crazy, material world, filled with heroism, strength, genius, intelligence, illness, suffering, and death. The above for him is the building block, GCSE, grade C, Reincarnation 101, the basis.

For those interested in exploring this fascinating field a little further, Birch offers more.

In this three dimensional material world, we see time as an ever flowing stream. One event follows another. The whole process is linear. One lifetime follows another. This linear process does not work in the spiritual realms, for time is a material construct. We use it to make sense of the reality in which we currently find ourselves. It gives us a frame of reference.

In the spiritual worlds, as time does not exist and events do not follow a linear path, our lifetimes exist and are all happening at the same time. Thus Birch's life as spear carrier, as master of ceremonies in 17th century Central Europe, as a Chinese mandarin at the court the emperor, are all being played out now; yes, right now. But what does that mean for the relationship of this current life with those that we perceive as being in the past. It means that each lifetime is equally as valid as all the others. In this equality of lifetimes, it gives us enormous power not only over our present life, but over all the other lifetimes, now, in this moment.

Being aware of other lifetimes is merely the first step to having an expanded view of our individual humanity. We are thus far larger in consciousness than our previous perceptions of ourselves. Of course we need to be prepared to move outside the 'mental box' to appreciate this expanded perception of self. In this mode of consciousness we are able to turn to other of our lifetimes, heal ourselves, heal the traumas that we experienced, heal the injustices, heal the pain that we are inflicting, and thereby move towards experiencing ourselves as balanced human beings; physically, emotionally, mentally, and spiritually. Not only are we greater than we imagine, we are greater than we can imagine.

We are indeed spiritual beings having human experiences. Birch is not keen on the model that places the soul somewhere in the region of the heart, and is only accessed from time to time. This creates the physical as superior, of greater importance than the spiritual, when the reverse is the case. His belief is of a physical body travelling in a spiritual one.

We are bound to question his perspective along these lines. "This is all very fine and dandy, Birch. This may make perfect sense to you, but how can one work with these ideas if we have no perspective of these other lifetimes going on, and no access to a sensitive who can tell us."

We can all work with the notion of *timelines*. The stream of consciousness that you are currently in is a *timeline*, your current life if you like. Your other lives are *timelines*. Every time you face a decision or make a choice, you are creating the next moment of the *timeline* that you are in. The other choices that you rejected are entry points for other *timelines*. If we don't put our decision into any other particular choice, then that is an entry into a potential *timeline* that will disintegrate back into the cosmic melting pot. We have thus not put our consciousness into that potential *timeline*. It is moribund and will break down.

So if we accept this premise of *timelines*, then it is a model for changing our reality. We can, in meditation or quiet thinking time, create an alternative reality. Thoughts are things, so by creating such a thought pattern we create an alternative set of experiences for our lives, in fact or in potential. This works. Birch's own experience includes an alternative *timeline* that came to his consciousness. This one was presented to him by his inner, spiritual self, rather than an objective externalisation of desire by him.

Without warning he was placed in a vision where he felt himself coming down the birth canal and out into the very cold, very bright world. He saw himself as a young boy in school uniform with a striped school tie. Education finished, he moved to a hot climate with palm trees, discovered the spiritual life, and then this alternative *timeline* merged into the present moment. He was then free to work with this *timeline*, filling in the gaps, and helping to create a new future with the revised *timeline*, free of certain personality 'baggage' accumulated in the present life *timeline*. He works with this to this day viewing it as a 'project' for his own development, (albeit a never-ending project.)

Are there any other reasons for believing in, and creating, *timelines*? Birch helps us with this when he addresses the battle between dark and light forces elsewhere in this book.

So does all this have truth, or is it all contained in what psychologists call *racial memory*? Or is the information of our forebears held in our DNA? Perhaps all are true.

Certainly DNA codes are being constantly unlocked. We are understanding more and more about this source. Birch has experimented in this area of 'unlocking' information from DNA, psychically. Within the possibility of all three aspects above being true, Birch believes that Audrey's skill is manifestly what it appears to be.

He now believes he can access his own DNA information through meditative techniques. He reckons to have proved this, at least to himself. It is much more difficult, or impossible, for Audrey to access his DNA. It is much more likely that Audrey, as has been argued above, has access to this 'field of human experience' known as the Akashic record.

Before we leave the subject of DNA, here's a discomforting thought. We assume that DNA is something that enables us to exist as we do, to have developed as we have and to enable our children to become very much like us. We view DNA almost as a servant for us. But what if... what if we are servants of DNA, as are all other living organisms on earth? What if the prime organism is DNA, and it is our function to provide a body, a vehicle, if you will, to enable DNA to exist and perpetuate itself? That would make us hosts, wouldn't it?

Birch presents one alternative view. This is from 'Healing Celebrations Lecture' by Leonard G. Horowitz. He suggests that one does not need to believe in reincarnation to explain why many people feel they have ancient memories - lucid flashbacks to age-old emotion-packed events - or even divine callings. These experiences may be associated with ancestral memories transmitted through hydro-electrified DNA. This theory is adequately supported by recent advances in electrogenetics, protein crystal science, and structured water biochemistry. Simply consider the subtle yet powerful frequency transmission capabilities and energy capacitance facilitated by DNA-clustered-water-nucleosome resonances. Some of these may be encoded with a spiritual flow containing ancient data.

Birch will finish this section by paraphrasing Spike Milligan's comment that he wished to place on his gravestone which was. 'I told you I was sick'. Birch's version of it for concluding this section is, 'I told you I would stretch your minds'.

DNA as a Start Point for our Development

*Some perspectives on the role of DNA
in our development. Psychic exercises
and meditations for the student.*

This section started as an exploration of the use of DNA in Birch's work. It rapidly developed into an exploration of how he had been able to move his consciousness forward and be happier in the process. Sharing it now might be useful.

What does the study of DNA, a scientific postulation after all, have in connection with spirituality and the energy bodies? It is hoped to answer this with the perspectives in this chapter. Let's start with a simple scientific guide? Deoxyribonucleic Acid or DNA is a nucleic acid molecule that contains the genetic instructions used in the development and functioning of all known living organisms. The main role, as far as the three dimensional world is concerned, is the long term storage of information and is often compared to a set of blueprints. DNA contains the instructions needed to build the components of cells such as proteins. The DNA segments that carry the genetic information are called genes.

Chemically DNA is a long polymer of simple units with a backbone of composed of sugars and phosphate atoms joined by bonds; the oft referred to double helix. Attached to each sugar is one of four types of molecules called bases. It is the sequence of these bases along the backbone that encodes information. This information is read using the genetic code.

In 1953 James Watson and Frances Crick published the first accurate model of DNA structures in the journal *Nature*.

The following perspectives are partly visionary and partly mental projections from those visions. As we visualise the interior of a cell nucleus we see the binary strand of DNA twisting upward, each bead of DNA threaded to its neighbour and the two strands connected across the divide with filaments of light energy. These filaments are so strong that they have the constituency of a fish bone skeleton.

There are those that say we utilise only 60% of our DNA but much work can be done to awaken the remainder of the 'sleeping' DNA. This can be done in psychic terms by meditation techniques, breathing, movement, and toning techniques. *Chi gong* can do this for us. Regular practice will prevent the shutting down of elements of DNA which is a major factor in the ageing process and will assist in the waking up process of dormant DNA. There is information on the slowing of the ageing process in the section on *chi gong*.

In visualisation we can fill the beads with light 'stroke' or 'pulse' them with movements of energy so that they can be fully activated. Some of the beads may be only partially active due to lack of use, misuse, pollution and negative thinking. Therefore it is appropriate to stroke and visualise the whole of the DNA spirals. Birch recommends sitting or lying comfortably in a quiet environment when we practice visualisation. As far as possible ensure that you will not be disturbed during the practice. Relax and set aside issues and problems of everyday life. Concentrate on that which you wish to achieve for a few minutes at first. As you become accustomed to the practice it is possible to extend the time. It may be difficult to hold concentration at the beginning. We in the West do not train our minds in this way. Regular practice and concentration are the keys.

From Birch's perspective DNA is the generator, the repository or library reference of our consciousness. The more that we awaken our DNA, the more we increase the strength and subtlety of our consciousness. We become more sensitive, more aware, better able to cope with the events of our lives, 'the slings and arrows of outrageous fortune'.

Viewed from a spiritual perspective, working with a visualisation process enhances our facility for integrating more of our higher self, the soul, into our beings. The more that the higher self is integrated into the being the easier it is to graduate onto higher consciousness states for those that wish to take that road.

Raising our vibratory rate through DNA visualisations, as well as other spiritual development activities, will bring out our demons, shadow side, negative traits of character into our objective consciousness. This may seem a negative aspect at first but is inevitable as night follows day and must be dealt with if we are to succeed. These negative traits knock on our door of consciousness. They challenge us with "Hello Mr Seeker. Here we are, we are you. What are you going to do about it?"

And do about it we must, for here they are in our faces instead of locked away in some dark corner of our psyche. We may wish that they return from where they came. Too late, the genie is out of the bottle. As we continue to awaken more of our binary DNA, there will be times when we become de-energised or sick. This is an entirely natural process.

During these periods much rest, relaxation and quiet reflection should be the order of the day. You may be given insights during these periods to aid these transitional states. No, you are not 'losing it' or deteriorating into madness. These events are necessary preludes to your next level of awareness and should be welcomed as such. It is part of the process. This will help relaxation concerning such phenomena.

Harvey Spencer Lewis, the 20th century mystic said that initiatory experiences occur in small steps. This is indeed what you are experiencing in these periods. Sometimes these changes of consciousness will occur 'out of time', when you are least expecting them. The other realms and our psyche do not work in linear time. The more work that you do in this way will encourage developments in your being which will occur with increasing frequency. Of course consequent negative perspectives will arise along with them. These remain to be cleared.

This is the way it works. Birch thinks that the term 'no pain, no gain' is appropriate here. It is worth it however to be clear of one's so-called 'baggage' coupled with a greater awareness. One word of warning, watch that ego, it will rise up and bite you when empowerment arrives. Every guru on the planet will have gone through such issues. Whether they arrive at a place of realisation or manipulation is up to them.

One other thing that will happen during these times is that your lifestyle will change. Radical alterations in your relationships can take place. People who are no longer contributing to your higher good will disappear from your life. Inappropriate employment and living spaces will fall away. Redundant habit patterns must be left behind. You will know in your heart which attitude or response will best serve you.

This whole approach takes considerable courage to just 'hang in there'. Do just that. This phase is in the hands of the cosmic forces and your higher self. You are being and will be fully supported. Be confident that the universe is unfolding as it should. Seek the company of like minded people. Open your consciousness to these influences. They will come to you.

Increased psychological and physical health is a major bonus in the work as well as a contribution to vigorous old age. The Temple Study Group of which Birch is a member and which works with this and other techniques meets, in the physical, once a year, every year. Members meet for a weekend and have done for the last 13 years. It still consists of members that joined at or near the start of its activities. As Birch sits with his brothers and sisters, who call themselves' the family of love', Birch detects very little ageing in them. He does sense vigour, energy, mental and spiritual acuity. Only one of the group has died in the 15 years, a friend who was severely disabled for decades. Birch is 64 years old and one of the younger members of the group.

So dear readers, adopt the techniques with enthusiasm and energy and you may be able to dispense with the pharmaceuticals. That has to be a great bonus.

Years ago Birch saw an interview with the father of Britain's number one sprinter who had been accused of drug taking in order to enhance performances. The father, an immensely dignified and proud man, said to the camera, "My son. He don tek drogs."

Well, "Clive he don tek drogs," apart from an inhaler for mild asthma, and he is working on that.

Sometimes a sense of the psychic can lift your spirits as well as give you a good laugh. That is very healthy. The friend that Birch spoke of above was severely disabled. Eventually she gave up her spirit and the struggle with her disintegrating body. She is remembered every year at the Temple Study Group's annual meeting. The year after her death, as the group meditated sending her love and making their final goodbyes, Birch saw her clearly flying through the cosmos free of her unworkable body. As she flew she was shouting in exultation. "Wheeee." Her cry of joy at her new found freedom reverberated around the cosmos. It was one of the highlights of the weekend for him.

OK, let's do a little more work with the DNA. "DNA is a specific vibration of light that comes from the sun and becomes matter," according to the Toltec visionary Miguel Ruiz. He goes on to assert that every kind of life on Earth from stones to humans has a specific vibration of light that comes from the sun. Each plant, animal, virus and bacterium has a specific ray of light. It is condensed by Mother Earth and the information carried in the light becomes matter. This reproduction is the method whereby the silent knowledge is passed from generation to generation. DNA is specific to every form of life. Science has not yet differentiated the subtle distinctions in forms of DNA.

The spirit is a little piece of sun trapped in matter. Our DNA is in direct connection with the spirit. What we are, is spirit.

There are those who say that humanity, in its highest states, could and would incorporate twelve strands of DNA. Birch has no insight whether this is true or not. The following inspirations have been released to Birch and he shares them with us.

Another level of DNA activation is, or can be, the creation and activation of a third strand of DNA. Some psychics say that children are being born with the third strand of DNA or more. Medical authorities are keeping this secret as they suspect that it is an aberration and a function of pollution or stress. More likely it is a result of the higher rates of vibration entering this quadrant of the universe at this time, and the increasing consciousness of humanity at the mass consciousness level. So for those of us not born with the advantage of this third strand, how does it manifest and how can we develop it? DNA powers our physical, mental, emotional, psychic and spiritual natures. It is the repository of our memory personal, genetic and racial. Some of the memories that we have concerning previous incarnations can be memories of events stored by our forefathers and mothers connected with their lives and retained within the DNA.

Other experiences may be conscious connections with other elements of one's being. More research and inspiration would help. These experiences can be extremely valuable to us for if we absorb the lessons and experiences available to us, then it is not necessary for us to live through them in our own conscious human lives. This reminds Birch of an apt historical quotation. 'Those who ignore history are doomed to repeat it,' according to George Santayana.

Now here is a good trick. The Earth and the creations for which it is responsible (mineral, vegetable) will move into a new consciousness. In fact, it is already moving into its new consciousness or higher dimensional frequency. Many say that this will happen by the time our universe lines up with the galactic centre at winter equinox 2012. In Birch's view this is an inevitable consequence beyond our conscious control.

The trick for humanity is to align itself with these changes, create the necessary raising of consciousness and activation of increased sophistication of DNA, and move smoothly and elegantly into the phase shift in alignment with the remainder of reality. Some challenge, huh?

Throughout, Birch has attempted to demonstrate ways of raising individual human consciousness. Obviously we are free to accept or reject any or all of them. This is by no means a prescriptive list. It is Birch's list. A genius of humanity is that it will find a multitude of ways to get where it wants to go. Let's all enjoy the ride.

This is what Pat Cori in 'No More Secrets, No More Lies' has to say about DNA.

The receptive quality of a water molecule is identified in the molecule's capacity to reverberate at those specific resonant frequencies that create the ideal vibrational field into which the third strand of DNA, the first etheric strand to be re-integrated into the double helix, can be eventually crystallised and ultimately anchored as a material reality first at the molecular level of awareness, then at the cellular level and so on. The integration of the third strand is the most important progression of all that will follow, for it weaves in to your essence the consciousness of all the celestial bodies of your solar system, the intent of the extra dimensional beings who served you at the seeding and the higher consciousness of your souls creating triangulation within every cell of your being. Correctly executed the process of the stranding instantaneously activates the Thymus – the master gland and central control tower of your light bodies – like the flick of a switch floods a dark room with light.

The above complements the elements that have been raised in this text and also raises more interesting points. For those that wish to explore Pat Cori's ideas further, her book is heartily recommended.

And now for two exercises that you may wish to try for yourself. First, have a go at this 'cell exercise'.

Every cell in your body, and there are trillions of them, has an important vital part to play in your life. Each cell is a small world performing its vital function and communicating with its companions. Birch's guidance tells him that the shape of a cell can be compared to two convex lenses or plates stuck together a little like the shape of a UFO. Now, the cell, again from guidance, gathers energy around its rim. This energy proceeds in a circular motion and each cell then externalises its output after transmuting energy into usable elements for the body. In the same way waste products are rejected.

Normally all our cells perform their functions without our conscious interference. The unconscious effectively manages this element of our physical organisation and we, most of the time, are unaware of the tremendous activity continuously being performed 24/7. Only when the system breaks down in some regard, and we feel sick or in pain, or when we attempt to perform an extra energetic task are we aware of the individual and group tasks constantly being undertaken.

Now the energy of the cells, both physical and non-physical can be affected by our conscious will. Indeed our physical health and psychic abilities can be changed by our normal thinking for better or worse. Thus we can improve the quality of cell activity, physical and psychic, by our meditations. This we will start to do in the following meditation exercise.

When you have time and no distractions sit comfortably and quietly Close your eyes and relax. Breathe deeply. If any thoughts come, let them come and let them go. With your mind's eye visualise the cells of your toes, the cells of flesh, bones, blood. Now with the conscious will fill each cell with love and light. See the cells become brighter, more energised, increasing in light intensity and love. Feel the physical effects of the change. Take your time.

Move your consciousness to your feet and repeat the exercise. Continue the exercise moving your consciousness to each part of your body. Try following this list... ankles, fingers, throat and neck, lower legs, hands, lower jaw, knees, wrists, teeth, upper legs, lower arms, upper jaw, abdomen and hips, elbows, cheekbones, rib cage, upper arms, nose, eyes, liver and kidneys, shoulders, forehead, lungs and heart, back, scalp, thymus gland, spine, brain and finally, the interlocking bones of the skull.

Now take a mental step back. See the whole of your body vibrating to this new energy. Feel a surge of energy, lightness, running through your being. Feel your blocks and stuck energy being moved out and away. Relax and stay with the feeling. Gradually return to normal consciousness. This completes the meditation.

This takes a lot of concentration and effort. However, performed regularly and with commitment it will have a profound and positive effect on your health. Birch has used it to great effect over many years.

Here's a second cell exercise. Prepare yourself as advised in the above meditation.

Imagine your physical body shrinking in size, becoming small enough to enter one of your cells. Approach a cell seeing it large, round and shining with health. Now float in through the cell membrane. As you move through the cell you see the cell nucleus. Move through the nucleus wall and you will be confronted by the binary strands of DNA twisting upwards. Each bead of DNA is threaded to its neighbour. The two strands connected across the divide with filaments of light energy. You see that some of the beads of DNA are switched on and working, some are not.

You can now awaken those beads that are ready for activation by stroking or pulsing them with movements of energy. Do this throughout the whole of the DNA spiral, filling each inactive bead with activation and strengthening those which are active. Take as long as you need. When you feel you have done as much as you can, gradually move back from the cell nucleus, the outer part of the cell and return to your normal body consciousness. That completes your meditation. How did it go?

DNA is the generator, the repository or library reference of our consciousness. The more that we awaken our DNA, the more we increase the vibration and strength of our consciousness. Thus we have greater facility for integrating more of the higher self into our being and consciousness.

The Struggle between Light and Dark Forces

*Why we need both in our reality and
how we can work to balance ourselves
when confronted by both.*

A friend said to Birch that, as a spiritually inspired person, the route that we take is a little like walking the plank. We are on this narrow path with the possibility of falling off, one side or the other. Another friend once told him of a vision he had in which his higher self offered him the option of moving with the light side, or with the dark. This sounds a little like the first of the *Star Wars* trilogy.

Some time ago, as a Rosicrucian, Birch would go for walks with a friend who was also in the Order. When they reached junctions in the route, Birch would joke with her that maybe it was time to take the left-hand path. (Left being the notional sinister or dark side – sinister being the Latin, left.) There is a serious side to this debate. We all have choices in the way we respond to life, and in which direction we wish to go. As is commonly agreed, and has been mentioned before, we all live in a universe of free will. This allows humanity and other non-physical entities, free rein in their thinking and behaviour. Birch makes one proviso.

In the path which careers toward self destruction, Birch believes there are forces (forces of light) in the universe which will inhibit one particular madness. A nuclear war on Planet Earth would cause much instability elsewhere in the universe. Thus he believes that stupidity would be stopped. However, and for the most part, mankind and other entities in this particular quadrant of the universe can progress or deteriorate as they may. The latter is possible. Birch's great friend, Jacques Rangasamy is of the view that there was a reality before this one. This reality before the 'Big Bang' deteriorated to such a state that it collapsed in on itself, and that this reality we inhabit now is a second opportunity for mankind and other beings, to develop towards greater understanding.

So, given the opportunities for free will, all beings, physical and non-physical, have the opportunity to move towards a positive frame of reference or to a negative. In this scenario if there are forces that could be deemed to be of the light, then it is self evident that there would be forces that would move towards the dark. We are in polarity consciousness.

It amuses Birch to consider this idea when he watches the cowboy films and TV programmes of his boyhood in the 1950s. In these simple stories the hero and all-round good guy would invariably dress in light clothes, ride a white horse, tote silver pistols, and be accompanied by a sidekick who was very much number 2 in the pecking order. One of the most potent symbols of being the good guy was the white stetson that he invariably wore. The bad guys on the other hand wore dark clothes, were invariably unshaven, spoke in a harsher manner, rode dark coloured horses and of course wore dark hats. The Lone Ranger was his hero in those simple times.

The reality of the light and dark conflict is of course much more subtle in this timeline that we have constructed for ourselves. Because of this conflict we are constantly working with the opposing forces in our daily lives. In this way we have the opportunity to develop further along our chosen path. Without the dichotomy of these apparently opposing forces, the result would be stagnation and the slide backwards would continue unabated. The likely outcome would be ultimate extinction. It is perhaps difficult to accept, but the dark influences are a blessing as much as the light. In this interplay between the two we have the opportunity to move forward or not. It is our series of choices.

This brings us to the subject of the ultimate deity, the being of which we are all part. This is a potentially delicate area. Everyone has a view and all are equally valid. God is what we perceive her to be. She is also both the light and dark sides. Ancient Egyptians understood this and exemplified this combination in the form of Sekhmet, the creator/destroyer Goddess. The Indians also exemplified the principal in the form of Kali. Deepak Chopra asked the question, "Does God know that we exist and if so, does she care?" Birch claims to have no appetite for deep philosophical debate on this question. Nor does he possess the intellectual equipment to follow this path, or so he claims. His awareness and perception has changed, and will continue to change, as his awareness of reality changes. Those that believe in an unchanging nature of their belief in God are doomed to disappointment. As reality changes around us, these beliefs will be consigned to the bunker of history.

To return to Deepak Chopra's point, Birch believes that she does care, for God is you and me, the hero on the TV, the boss at work that we loathe, the dog that passes us by. God is in all of us. We are God. God is not a venerable old bloke sat in some distant venue dispensing justice and telling us what to do. We are perfectly capable of doing the latter for ourselves.

So this brings us back to human nature and its proclivity to respond to different influences, light and dark, in our lives. Nearly everybody on this planet would consider themselves to be 'good people'. Hitler, Idi Amin, Stalin, all probably considered themselves 'good people'. We are probably less contentious figures to add to the list of 'good people'. However we, or certainly most of us, admire those who are less than reputable characters.

Clint Eastwood's out of control policeman in the film *Dirty Harry* stood over a very nearly helpless adversary. He pointed his Magnum - "the world's most powerful handgun" - at the near helpless man on the floor. Through gritted teeth Clint grunts, "You gotta ask yourself one question. Do I feel lucky? Well, do ya punk?" Well, it was something like that as he implied he was bustin' to blow the squirrel's head off. At that moment how many of us revelled in righteous indignation, even willing Clint to pull the trigger. It's an idea which might make one or two of us squirm on our seats.

This revelling in righteous indignation was clearly brought home to Birch, at the time this section of the book was being planned. Surprise, surprise, his higher self confronted him with his own demon. An item on the TV news spoke of a pensioner who had fought in World War II being denied a drug treatment that would save his eyesight. This decision was made on grounds of it being too expensive. To make this more tragic, he was the sole carer for his wife. Birch felt anger, indignation and a sense of injustice when he compared the lifetime contribution of this man to the life of another. That other was the Prime Minister who was about to leave Number 10. The latter would depart with a fat pension, and take up a new role in the Middle East, and all this from the man who was complicit - allegedly - in the starting of two wars, resulting in the death of hundreds of thousands, and untold misery for countless people. For this pensioner, the lecture circuit beckoned and that alone would ensure his pension would receive a generous boost.

Righteous indignation is an interesting emotion that has been utilised by religions, the military, politicians and rulers, throughout time. Another country, religious minority, philosophy, alternative social belief, is somehow of a lower standard than our own. We must 'convert' the others to a 'proper' understanding.

Some years ago, when manager of government training initiatives, Birch came across an intelligent woman who was making good use of the training that was being offered. She spoke with enthusiastic zeal, of the number of people who had been 'converted' at a recent religious gathering she had attended. Birch chose not to enter into debate. There was no point. There is plenty of evidence that those that come forward for 'conversion' at these events, mostly renege afterwards. The emotion has died down, and they have had the opportunity to review the decision in the cold light of day.

Those that would rule us use this emotion of righteous indignation to move the goalposts of morality to suit their own preconceptions. This dictator must be eliminated. He is a nasty man and anyway our guns are bigger than his. We can kill more of the 'enemy' than they can kill of our precious sons. Their sons are not here, so they must be less precious. So, in this scenario, who are the good guys and who the bad? Who are wearing the white hats and who, the black?

So the concept of forces of light and forces of dark can be a matter of opinion, religious and spiritual development, social convenience and personal prejudice. That said, there is also another perspective to this debate. In Birch's experience, there are forces or beings, primarily or completely, of one polarity. But it is rare for humans to be of one polarity because of the very nature of being human. Openness to both is the norm. Those who practice black magic may be of one polarity; that is the dark side. Many of them have been subverted and are possessed by negative personalities or energies. Birch is convinced of this due to his experience of people he knows, who show all the signs of possession.

Years ago as a single man, Birch had a girlfriend of jolly personality and 'comfortable' body shape. She was fun to go out with. Eventually, they split. Years later, on returning from a long journey, he saw her. She was maybe a hundred yards away from him as he strolled through his home town. He had a big shock which also scared him. As they looked at each other and recognition grew, he saw staring back at him another personality. The face was that of his old girlfriend, but there was another being sharing her body. Of that he was convinced. The body shape had changed completely. Where there had been a jolly shape before, now there was a very slim figure.

A mutual friend confirmed Birch's perception because, quite independently, she'd also shunned Birch's old girlfriend. The change was also very shocking for the friend.

One day Birch was having a meal with a group of people one of whom was known to be schizophrenic. At times the schizophrenic woman had an extremely violent temper going into rages that could end violently. Birch wasn't thinking of anything much during this meal, except enjoying the food and chatting. He suddenly noticed this schizophrenic person go very quiet, exhibit mannerisms not associated with her, and externalise a distinctly masculine presence. With shock, Birch realised that she was possessed. Her body language, demeanour and attitude all changed together. He had known this person for years, but had never before linked her psychological condition to possession.

Another mutual friend has a partner who is regularly possessed. Because she has deep spiritual knowledge, she has the experience to 'clear' invading entities from his being. This work never stops.

Many people are ill because they are possessed, Birch believes. Lower your vibrations and you will attract entities that have the same agenda. These lower vibrations can be attracted through alcohol, drugs, certain sexual practices, or black magic. Morals are very important. They transmit a message saying for what we are available. Overweight people could be doing the eating because of possession, while sexual orientation can change because the possessor is of opposite sexuality. In his book 'Demons of the Inner World', Alfred Ribi claims that the demons and spirits that plagued the lives of ancient and mediaeval peoples have re-appeared today as our psychological complexes. As a result, our anxieties and compulsions - related to achievement, power, money, sex, ideologies and other obsessions - threaten to overwhelm us and sabotage our conscious efforts and intentions.

At one time in the 1980s Birch was friendly with a shaman and they did some spiritual work together. However, the contact faded; deliberately on Birch's part. He felt the shaman had a guru complex. He saw himself as the teacher/ leader and Birch as the acolyte. This did not suit Birch one bit.

On one occasion, Birch visited the shaman at his Snowdonia home. The shaman was quite keen on creating manipulative situations around him. He persuaded Birch to sleep overnight in a tent. There he was alone in the mountains, on a particular shoulder or spur. Before dark descended he walked up to the appointed place, set up the tent and enjoyed the magnificent scenery; peace beyond words, and great fresh air. But his joy was short-lived. As soon as he climbed into the tent he was disturbed by noises and movement. It was as if someone was walking around the tent. This went on all night. Birch was petrified and frozen into immobility. There was no disturbance of the tent itself, just this constant shuffling. He slept not one wink. As soon as dawn broke he leapt out of the tent, disassembled it and retreated down the mountain. He reached the shaman's house and recounted the story.

"Yes, I do believe it's haunted," said the shaman with a twinkle in his eye.

One of Birch's teenage sons, full of testosterone fuelled bravery, marched off to repeat the lone night on the mountain. He was going to show the old, cowardly 'wrinkly' how it should be done. He was soon back in the house, pale and shaking. He didn't get as far as pitching his tent.

There was one other event of note on this visit to Wales; Birch's only sight of a ghost. There was one part of the building that was particularly cold and forbidding. The shaman told him that this part was haunted. Birch immediately went into a visionary experience. The current three dimensional realm of existence disappeared and he stood in front of a young, brown haired woman. She casually leaned against a wall. He didn't recognise her. The one outstanding feature of her appearance was that she was wearing cherry red shoes. Birch immediately dropped back into three dimensional reality. The shaman confirmed that his vision had been correct.

To this day Birch hasn't decided if his experience presented a conflict between light and dark. Perhaps many of the situations that arise in our lives are such battles? Either way, it was a fascinating experience.

One simple way of staying on the path that he's chosen for himself is to visualise a stream of light connecting him to the forces of light. It is very easy to become disheartened by the anger, negativity, obsession with intellect and the chaos around us. Those forces that would control us would be very happy to perceive us constantly linked to these negativities. For when we think about them we are giving them succour and our own personal energy. His method is simple; some may even see it as naïve. It works for Birch however, and that must be good enough. In any case, sometimes the simplest things are the best.

According to a fragment of Vedic lore, the light of a single candle is stronger than all the darkness of the universe. As someone else said, "It is better to light a candle than curse the darkness."

Gradually over time Birch has realised that those possessing abilities in the psychic and spiritual realms, does not necessarily mean that they are not balanced in other fields of their being. By that he means physical, mental or psychological balance. In short, some members of society consider those with claimed psychic abilities are crazy. They go further, suggesting that those with such abilities have no place in the conventional Western world. Birch finds this unacceptable. Take the following example.

Some years ago he was conducting an exit interview with an employee who was about to leave the company. Suddenly in the middle of the interview, she interrupted him. "Are you psychic?" she asked. He was shocked. He believed he had been successful keeping his business life separate from spiritual and psychic interests.

Slightly befuddled he asked why she might say this. "Because during our working relationship you spoke knowledgeably of events for which I had been responsible. You could not possibly have known about them from our normal contact point of view." He was flabbergasted. There he was, believing he'd maintained this very mundane, professional front, yet all the while talking and being knowledgeable of events that were physically unknown to him. It demonstrated that trying to hide his light under a bush might not always be entirely successful.

There must be ways of being more open about these matters 'without frightening the natives'. The Chinese have an interesting way of demonstrating the balance of light and dark forces. The symbol of the yin and yang consists of a circle with a division inside it. On one side is a white space, on the other a dark area. Within each division there is an element of the other. So the 'dark' contains the 'light' and the 'light' contains the 'dark.' This is a wonderful metaphor for the human condition. Always we, as humans, have access to the other polarity, whichever one is the predominant in our lives at any given time.

Yin and Yang

But now Birch provides a warning concerning using magical and spiritual techniques. In 1992 Birch went to the Isle of Man and did some magical work with a friend who lived there. Every day they had a session of chanting, meditation, and visualisation. It was intense work, probably made more so by the bedrock of the island being largely composed of crystal. Towards the end of his time there he started to feel quite unbalanced and physically unwell. His friend felt similarly. Later they both needed to call on other friends to give them healing to help them balance and regain physical health. The symptoms included coldness, shaking, general malaise and feeling 'spaced out'. Perhaps this is better described as feeling not completely in their bodies. The healing from their friends helped them to return to normal.

Birch tells this story to point out the potential dangers of meddling with energies with which we are ill prepared to deal. It is important that we make haste slowly when working with magical, visualisation and spiritual techniques. In order to help us do this it is important that we find, and work with individuals and groups that have experience in these matters. Seek out those groups and individuals you believe are balanced and as ego free as possible. "Look around," Birch says. "They are out there. Work with a number of individuals and groups until you find those with which you are comfortable. Be careful that they have no agendas that are contrary to your best interests. Read widely. Think long and deeply about the principles that you come into contact with. If in doubt, don't. Move on."

During the Christmas period before making his first trip to the USA, he was encouraged by a friend to make a psychic experiment. The friend was at his home accompanied by his father-in-law and stepson. He couched his encouragement in the form of a challenge. "Go on," he said during a telephone conversation with Birch. "Make something happen." Birch rose to the bait. He sat in a chair, meditated and projected part of his consciousness into the room in which the friend was sitting. Within an hour the friend rang him back. Excited, he said that as they all sat, relaxed and chatting, suddenly there was a loud crack, crack, crack, crack, one after the other, in each corner of the room. The noise was above and beyond any normal sounds, by far.

Birch put the phone down feeling strangely unsettled by the whole affair. As he reviewed it he realised that he'd acted in response to an impulse of the ego. There was absolutely no need to create this manifestation other than to satisfy the friend's passing interest and to demonstrate some potential through this ego impulse. How easy it is to be sucked into the ego consciousness and, through this, subvert the work of the light.

He vowed from that moment on, never to work psychically again in order to satisfy idle curiosity. He felt, and feels to this day, that this is a downward slippery slope toward negative manipulation. It was most definitely a perversion of the use of the cosmic forces available to humanity. From that point on he vowed, so far as was humanly possible, to utilise those cosmic energies for positive benefit to humanity and all the Earth.

The greatest challenge in the battle between light and dark is the battle with ourselves.

Timeslip

*A quick look at the baffling phenomenon
of timeslip. It's nothing new.*

While researching this book, two odd events took place for which *timeslip* might provide an answer. They each happened to me and after discussing them with Clive he suggested *timeslip*. Maybe he's right. Our home in Gloucestershire had been devastated by the summer floods of 2007. The ground floor was a mess and it was a stressful and unpleasant time.

I'd spent the morning upstairs in my study working on the manuscript. It was time for a break and as I was about to wrap up a chapter when I heard the front door open. Then there was the sound of a footfall on the tiles of the hall followed by the door closing. Clearly my wife was home for lunch. It was usual for her to shout a greeting to me, but on this occasion there was nothing but silence. Odd, thought I. I shouted, "Hello darling." Still no response. Odder still. I went downstairs to investigate but there was no sign of my wife. I opened the front door and looked around outside. No, she definitely wasn't home.

For a moment I forgot about this while I made a cup of tea and went into the back garden for a smoke. Then my wife appeared with a bemused look on her face. She had just arrived home that very second. "That was funny," she said. "When I came in I heard you shout 'hello darling'. But you're out here." By 'out here' she meant that it would have been impossible to hear me shout anything from the back garden. I am guessing but the time between me shouting "hello darling" and my wife arriving home would have been about 8 to 10 minutes.

The very next day another incident made me raise my eyebrows. My 15 year old son was working in my study, allegedly doing his homework. I heard him call out to me, "What?" as teenagers do. I went to the bottom of the stairs to see him standing at the top. I must have had a stupid expression on my face. "What is it?" he said.

"What's what?" I replied rather lamely.

"What do you want?"

This was turning into a farce. Before this exchange gets too boring I'd better skip a few lines.

"You called me," he said.

"Actually, I didn't," I replied.

"Yeah, you did. I heard you clearly."

Well, I had called him some twenty minutes earlier but hadn't received a response. What was going on here? Clive explained that the energies in the house might easily have been upset by the floods and the huge damage our home sustained. Well, maybe so and that would certainly explain another odd series of events, although I don't see that they were linked to *timeslip*. The flood had ravaged the back garden, a garden on which much time, expense and love had been expended. Many trees and shrubs were dead and dying, weeds were growing and it looked a mess. Thankfully the shrubs in the many pots had all survived the wretched inundation. One such potted plant was a Japanese acer. Around the base of the tree was a layer of fossils, the kind you pick up on the limestone paths and hills of the Cotswolds; the mulch with a difference. The lip of this pot stood some 20 inches (51cms) off the ground. For several mornings in a row some of the pebbles and fossils were removed from the pot and sprinkled around on the ground.

I puzzled over what might be the culprit or cause. Too heavy for birds, too high and heavy for hedgehogs, cats didn't seem likely since I'd never seen cats picking up stones. No way dogs could get into the garden, nor foxes or badgers. I was bemused. Only one thing for it; I phoned Clive. For a moment there was silence as he digested my weird story. To my considerable surprise he proposed a solution to the mystery.

"I think you're being nudged by the garden devas. They're telling you that they're not happy that you're neglecting the garden. Tidy it up, Pete. I think you'll find that the fossils will stay in the pot then."

I hung up and thought for a moment or two. Checking there wasn't anyone in earshot I said aloud, "OK, OK, I'll sort the garden out." I confess to having felt a little foolish.

Sure enough, next morning none of the fossils had been disturbed; nor the morning after, nor again the morning after that. However, on the next morning there was one fossil on the ground. The following morning there were several, and then there were piles all over the place. Could Clive be right? Saturday arrived and I vowed to devote the whole day to a garden tidy up. From dawn to dusk I toiled without a break for lunch. Short breaks for tea and cigarettes I did allow myself. Before it was too dark to see anything, I decided I was done. I looked around with a sense of satisfaction and a mild backache.

Would next morning see fossils and pebbles displaced from their pot or would they remain in place? It was with a certain anticipation I hurried into the back garden early next morning. Not one out of place. All was just as it had been left the previous evening and to this day that is the way it has remained. Never once has a single fossil left the pot since my Saturday exertions. So, was Clive right? I leave that to you.

A delicious event marked the writing of the few paragraphs above. It was around half past midnight. Something hit the back of my head, rolled to the front of my head, landed on my chest and fell to the floor. I turned all the lights on trying to see what it was. Lying on the carpet was a tiny L-shaped piece of ancient leather, just 2cms (0.79 inches) at its longest. No amount of searching gave me any indication from whence it had come. Clive and I wondered if this was a sign of approval as we continue to write this book? We wondered at the significance of its L-shape. It wasn't until my wife came home that light was shone on the possible relevance. "It's L for Lily," she said. For several years now I have been advised that my own spirit guide is a young teenager called Lily. And maybe it was Lily who was removing the pebbles and fossils to motivate me to tidy up her garden?

Now back to timeslip. My experiences possibly brought about by the unsettling of the energies in my home reminded Clive of this gem. He thinks that this story originally came from Carl Jung who had come across it in a local newspaper. Jung subsequently investigated it as far as he could. It happened somewhere in Central Europe.

A man went to visit an address, replying to a newspaper advertisement for the sale of an item. His destination was an old building several stories high. He rapped with the very old fashioned door knocker. After a pause an upstairs window was flung open and an old woman poked her head out asking him whom he wanted. She was dressed in a rather old fashioned way with a shawl round her shoulders. The man gave her the name of the person that he was visiting. There was a pause while the woman seemed to take some time to absorb his request. Eventually she said, "The whole family is out. You may enter and wait if you wish."

Not having anything better to do, the man said that he would. After a pause the beshawled woman opened the door and led the man to a room where he was left to himself. He was charmed by the room. It was very old fashioned with a big oak table in the centre, a pendulum clock with roman numerals ticked loudly on the wall. Heavily embossed Victorian wallpaper hung on the walls and other large and dark Victorian furniture was arranged around the room. The man sat and waited. The only entertainment that he could think of was to play with his pocket watch to relieve the boredom. After over an hour with no arrivals and with the apparent disappearance of the elderly woman, he gave up his wait and let himself out of the house, closing the door behind him.

After a few minutes and having walked a little away from the house, the man realised that he had left his watch behind. He retraced his steps. Upon reaching the building again, he stopped in shock and his mouth dropped open. In the few minutes since his leaving, the appearance of the house had completely changed. The front of the building was now very dirty, windows were broken, paint was peeling from the previously well maintained door.

The man mounted the steps to the door and raised the now rusty knocker. The noise of the knocks now thundered as though the interior of the hallway was empty of furniture and carpet. No aged crone came to now peeling window and no-one opened the door. The man stepped back down the steps scratching his head in disbelief and puzzlement. Confused thoughts were whizzing round his head. He had no idea what was going on. After a few minutes he managed to contact a neighbour and on asking about the occupants of the near derelict house was told, "No-one has lived in this house for sixty years, all the occupants are dead."

The man was absolutely flabbergasted. He was so out of sorts by this 'double reality' experience that he left. After a day or so wrestling with the events, he went to the police and with their assistance was able to regain entry to the house. In the room that he had sat in on his first visit, he found his watch. It was rusted, tarnished and covered in dust as though it had been there for decades. No-one could ever provide an adequate explanation for the man's experience.

According to Jung this really happened and was reported as an event rather than as a fictional story. *Timeslip*; fact or fiction?

Before leaving *timeslips*, the Philadelphia Experiment deserves a mention. It is difficult to really accept it as a fact; nevertheless rumours persist leaving us to wonder. Briefly the story goes something like this. In October 1943, the destroyer USS Eldridge was the subject of a dramatic experiment. It is claimed that while the warship was in the Philadelphia Naval Shipyard it became invisible.

Naturally, and reasonably enough, it was claimed to be a hoax. The US Navy certainly denies any such experiment took place. Employing the Unified Field Theory some argue that the combination of electromagnetic radiation and gravity bent light around the ship rendering it invisible to observers. In an earlier experiment observers claimed that the ship almost disappeared and was surrounded by a green fog. In another we are told that while it nearly disappeared, it left an indentation in the water where the keel should have been. However, in the October experiment the observers stated that the ship disappeared completely in a blue flash.

The Navy admits that the Eldridge was engaged on a degaussing experiment at the time. Degaussing was employed by the Royal Navy and the US Navy to demagnetise their ships making them less vulnerable to magnetic mines. The process required that a wire was wrapped around the whole ship.

Another story suggests that in an attempt to render the ship invisible, the surrounding air and sea water was heated sufficiently to cause a mirage. It seems this was thought might confuse observers. There does seem to be little doubt and crew members experienced a range of ailments whatever the cause. Some of the ship's company became disorientated, others mentally ill and some disappeared entirely. One report even said that crewmen were discovered fused to the hull. Reports tell that Einstein and Tesla were just two of a whole army of scientists working on the Philadelphia Experiment. (To add to the confusion, Tesla was dead at the time.)

But just a moment's rational thought is bound to deliver the verdict that this story is nothing more that an intriguing hoax. However, there is a problem. Within minutes of the Eldridge being seen in Philadelphia it was also seen 375 miles (604 kilometres) away in Norfolk, Virginia.

Could this be an example of *timeslip* on a large scale? This event, or non event as the case may be, is well documented and may be researched under its correct name of Project Rainbow.

Theos Energy

*Introduction to an enhanced form
of animal consciousness.*

In 1997 Birch watched helplessly as a cat was torn apart. A pleasant afternoon walk in the country with a friend turned into disagreeable violence. Visiting a picturesque church, they parked the car at the roadside. As they alighted they were greeted by an elderly cat coming out of the shrubbery. They spent a couple of minutes stroking and talking to it. As they moved on to the abbey, two men arrived with a couple of wolfhounds. For some reason Birch and friend turned back to look at the cat. What met their eyes left them cold. The wolfhounds were ripping the gentle animal apart.

Birch was incandescent with rage, shouting and swearing at the uncaring owners of the wolfhounds. They behaved as though this was a common occurrence. One man hurled the carcass of the unfortunate animal into a black plastic bag, threw the bag over his shoulder and sauntered off along an adjacent path. Birch felt traumatised, angry, and powerless in the situation. It stayed with him for ages.

In a mystical sense, perhaps the cat sacrificed itself as a gift to Birch's unfolding consciousness. Maybe it helped him to wake up to the potential of his subsequent work. Whether this act was key or not, Birch cannot be sure.

It was years later that the information impulses concerning the rise of animal consciousness, started to arrive. He enlisted the help of his good friends, Mary and Joan Fitzgerald. They have such great compassion and a real connection to the spirit of animals. They are also powerful healers and mystics.

In a recent visit to Greece Joan visited the ancient site of Delphi. There she was contacted by the Oracle which told her that their group of three, Joan, Mary and Birch should continue their work. This feedback was welcomed. The group meets most weeks to work on healing along with various other tasks that present themselves in meditation. Perhaps more importantly they have recently started to link into, and project, the Theos wave; the ascending vibration for increasing the conscious awareness of the animal kingdom.

The Oracle at Delphi was so important to ancient Greek culture that the centre was functioning for a thousand years. The priestesses would enter a trance and give answers to questions put by supplicants. The Oracle was so valued a present was always given in payment. Special depositories were built to hold the often valuable gifts. Science now tells us that there is a release of gases from below the ground in the area. Could the gases create expanded states of awareness? The priestesses chewed bay leaves to give themselves a hallucinogenic 'power boost'. Unfortunately many of the gifts over the centuries consisted of animal sacrifices which in many people's view would pollute the area energetically.

Now we move to the rise of animal consciousness. Birch received information impulses from his intuition concerning Theos energy. He makes no claims for what is now described, other than this is the information that presented itself to his consciousness. That's why he calls it information impulse. So, what was this *information impulse?*

The energy of the Theos energy comes to the Earth in tight spirals from the cosmic realms. It is a very strong and powerful energy vibration, empowering the animal kingdom to free itself from the domination of humanity. You three, Mary, Joan and Clive, are one of the conduits along with certain aware animals and helpers from other realms.

This energy is a wake up call for animals to take responsibility for their futures, to develop themselves on the Earth, individually and as groups. It will give them the conscious awareness to protect themselves from the abuses and controls of those elements of uncaring humanity. There will come a time when animals will no longer merely be a resource to be farmed and used as humanity wishes. They will have the opportunity to take responsibility for themselves. These are the most propitious times for this to be done. They will be assisted, not only by the Theos energy, but also by animals of higher consciousness in this and other realms.

In cases of abuse, real or potential, animals will be able to protect themselves against issues that they see as against their interests. This protection will take a number of forms, subtle and overt. Humanity, or those humans with sufficient consciousness, will need to develop an alternative relationship built on co-operation and mutual respect. Nothing else will work.

There will be radical changes to animal organisations. Some will collapse as they fail to respond to changed situations. Others will grow stronger. There is a possibility that a war will break out between animal and human kingdoms unless humanity adapts.

Birch wonders if MRSA is one skirmish in this war.

Animals will make their presence known to you. The three of you will have the opportunity to support and contribute to the animal kingdom in different ways and in co-operation with the Theos energy.

Birch says he knows very little about the animal kingdom. He asked why should he be involved? An answer was forthcoming.

That is precisely the reason for your involvement. You have few preconceived ideas. You and your friends are open to receive communication from non physical sources. We see your 'team' as well prepared. The two cats in Joan's home, Star and Willow, are guardians, and well aware of this work. This is part of their development. They are beings skilled in protection and healing. It will be helpful for you to watch for changes in social relationships in animals, in information in the media, through many of your friends, as well as psychically.

On a slightly different note, it is no accident that you three are in Cheltenham doing this work. This town is to the south of the Heart of England. In Chinese thought, the psychic heart of a human is just underneath the physical heart. Do you understand the analogy? Do you think that it is an accident that the government's communication centre is in this town? We can assure you that it is no accident. On this level you are working with the battle for the psychic heart of this Sacred Isle. It is indeed sacred that you three, along with many others in the conflict, will tip the balance in favour of the forces of light.

The outcome of this conflict will be a significant contributor in the final level or 'shape' of consciousness at 'crossover' time, you understand? (This refers to the winter equinox of 2012.)

The upsurge in animal consciousness generated through the Theos wave weaves a path through this tricky scenario. All is connected. Dance and play with the magic. Enjoy, stay calm, remain connected. The ride may become bumpy. However, you have decided to be here to do this work. We are here for you. Listen to your intuition on many subjects, check out your promptings. If you feel that they have validity, go with them. Avoid being deflected. Be careful of false prophets and false energies. There are those that seek to deflect you. As one of your human contacts has said, many of the lower negatives have been nullified by the work already completed. More powerful negative forces have lifted their heads above the parapet. And because of the work of the light forces, you have been attacked psychically. (Birch explains that this refers to the sense or feeling under attack mentally, that general malaise for no apparent reason, the inexplicable fear and vulnerability. That sense of discarnate negative energies being close.) *This is a measure of your success. Protect yourself, call on us, use the protective words, call on the energies of light.*

Much of this you have heard before many times. However, it is important to keep this issue in mind when dealing with the higher energies to which you are now exposed. Concerning Saint Anthony and Saint Christopher, these are beings named thus by your Christian religion. They and others are part of the animal consciousness work. You are in good company, yes? Be confident.

In the past your society experienced the Industrial Revolution. This will be the Animal Revolution. It will be no less traumatic for those that resist it and equally as dramatic as the earlier revolution.

All humans will need to re-evaluate their knowledge of that which they consider intelligence. In the past humans have considered themselves superior; masters over animals. It will come as a shock to discover that many animals are as intelligent and, in some case, more intelligent than them.

Some of the biggest traumas will occur in religions when they are forced to realise that their elitist view of humans, in relationship to the other creatures on the planet, has collapsed.

The old separation between wild and domestic animals will cease. This is largely a man-made division between those animals that have been useful to enslave and those that are useful to butcher in bloodlust. The sharing of the planet between what remains of humanity and animals will be an important focus for attention.

Vegetarianism among animals and humans will become a necessity rather than a luxury. Animals will develop the ability to flood their bodies with toxins at death in order to bring humanity and carnivores to the new awareness. This will create a crisis in protein consumption which can be dealt with. An agreement will be reached when low level organisms such as krill will be made available for food. The abuse of the food chain and gluttony will become tantamount to crimes.

Ceremonies to bless food will be seen as an essential part of eating. The spiritual element of food will move from the mystical to the practical.

Old political and social systems will be put under intolerable strain. Some human groups will shut themselves away in an attempt to continue their old lifestyle. They will slowly die as they will not be in tune with the vibration of the times.

As the Master Jesus said, "You can read the face of the heavens but you cannot read the signs of the times."

Those that have shut themselves away will be viewed with compassion by the rest of humanity.

In a recent meditation, Birch tuned into all the animals that they had contacted through the Theos wave. He saw all of them receiving the energy through their feet, into their chakras and energy bodies drawing up the energy in a way akin to osmosis. Animals of the same species were grouped together; horses, bears, elephants, mice and voles, forming a circle. The scene was very dramatic, lightening exploded across the sky, rain fell. In a second meditation the numbers of animals had grown enormously. They were grouped in a large circle as more and more became attuned to the Theos wave vibration.

This is a further information impulse. *Animals have a great potential for fast psychic development. They are not hung up on ego or the material will. They are not plagued by doubt, fear of the unknown or 'what everyone else will think' as masses of humanity are. Their psychic natures, conscious understanding, can develop at a phenomenal rate given this.*

The Theos wave has been designed to be very grounding. Its transmission through the Earth is a key to this. Because of this grounding feature the whole process can be very balanced with animals having the benefit of being in equipoise between Earth and cosmic influences. There will be much less tendency for them to 'float off' into the ethers. Many humans will wish to have their own Theos wave. Depending on developments within the human race this may become possible.

Animals can and will waken extremely quickly. Those watching the upsurge in energy and its rapid effect on the animal kingdom will be breathless because of the lack of blocks already mentioned. Coming from their current position of near powerlessness, the big question for many animals will be what to do with this enhanced awareness?

There are animals gathering in other realms, members of the amphitheatre of beings, ready to guide in these matters.

In recent projections Birch said that he had seen a fish very still in calm waters. It sported exotic serrated, curtain-like fins. There has also been a strange dog with a very square head.

There will be time lags for many of the manifestations to appear to humanity, firstly because the animals will fear a violent backlash, and secondly so that resolution strategies can be worked through. What will happen quickly will be self-defence and avoidance; avoidance of abuse and imprisonment as well as reaction by animals to abusive, insensitive humans.

Concerning the animal rights movement, this was initiated by conscious vibrations from the cosmic much as the Theos wave is now. It has successfully raised the profile and the awareness of animal consciousness in humanity in the Western World, particularly in urban centres.

We all live in a free will universe, a world of duality, therefore all is allowable. Inevitably darker forces have sought to invade this movement and push forward their agenda. This can be seen in the extreme violence, threats, and abuse employed by certain sections of the animal rights movement. The dark forces find willing accomplices in those individuals who are ego driven; overwhelmed by their own shadow, weak and underdeveloped mentally and spiritually. These forces, and their human accomplices, have had a certain amount of success in slowing down the success of the animal rights movement in order to further their agenda. This approach again drives the opposition into a mental bunker, creating strife and slowing down co-operative change. Again we urge you to progress the work by making ever stronger the Theos energy. Tune in daily. This will make the work stronger and stronger, and limit the damage done by the negative elements. Be sure to protect yourself.

We do not condone any of your so-called sports using animals as a pawn in the ego games of humanity. In a recent TV clip on the Cheltenham Gold Cup winner, much was made in the report of the jockey and owner. There was scarcely a look at the horse which had done virtually all the work to win.

We do accept that in many cases, an evolutionary approach will be the best way forward in many of the changes to come. We were interested to see through the eyes of Clive, a new approach in the training and racing of horses being undertaken by a trainer near Marlborough. This person is removing the metal shoes from his horses and allowing them to race on their natural hooves. He claims to be making winners out of 'also rans' using this natural approach. It also considerably reduces the injuries to hooves and legs, according to the trainer. In addition he is allowing his horses to congregate as a herd at his headquarters. This gives them the opportunity to live a more natural existence. As we have said before, we do not accept that horse racing is beneficial to the animals. However, any steps along the path to freedom and self-determination we would encourage.

On the subject of horse racing we see the abuse of breeding enormous numbers of potential racehorses. Most of them will be cast aside in order to produce a very small minority of fast race winning horses. In turn they too will be disposed of at the end of their racing career, or at their time of standing at stud. (Retirement from racing and being used for stud.) These abuses must and will be terminated. This so called 'sport' designed for the monetary enrichment of a few already rich individuals, and the greed of others who wish to join them on the rich list must, and will, cease. Again we ask that you assist the process in your meditations to influence humanity. Already there are intelligent horses within the sport which have consciously been born for the very purpose of which we speak. They need your help.

We ask that you tune into the insect kingdom; a rich source of information. They are always 'buzzing around' seeing much and are capable, with the help of the new vibration, of working intelligently as well as co-operatively. By this we mean that the whole of the mosquito kingdom, for example, could marshal its resources to attack humanity. Ants also have the potentiality to function in the same way. You will recall that we previously mentioned the possibility of warfare between the animal and human kingdom.

If this became reality, and we are all working to prevent this, then there is no certainty that humanity would win such a war. In fact we believe that a conscious animal kingdom would, most likely, win. Sheer weight of numbers would ensure victory.

It would be extremely useful for humans of sufficient sensitivity and interest in the kingdom to work assiduously to build bridges between the two. Clive, remember your healing from insect bites was achieved in Guatemala? These persons would truly be the *ambassadors of the future. Perhaps such ambassadorial contacts could communicate with the mosquito family to find some other way of feeding, and to refrain from passing on dreadful diseases.*

Now the world of cats is very interesting. They spend much time in healing and communicating with other realities. The higher cat beings will channel much conscious raising energy for the cats of the third dimension through the Theos wave energy. They are certainly as intelligent as bears or horses, but their attention span in large co-operative ventures tends to be small. They easily become bored with such pursuits and will simply switch off, go to sleep, or move their consciousness to other realities. Because they are so individually independent, this trait, when accentuated, can become arrogance in the negative. With the vast increase of energy now becoming available to them, they will need to watch this.

Your meditations and 'tunings in' are of great assistance. We urge you to plan healing and energising rituals in rural or sacred environments. This will greatly encourage the animal kingdom, particularly attuned to such places, to make great use of the new energies available to them. The period around the summer solstice would be particularly beneficial. On such occasions a larger group including sensitive and empathetic friends would help increase the manifesting of such energies.

Consider the animal dances conducted by indigenous peoples. These bring the consciousness of both kingdoms into closer union, even though it might mean the sacrifice of an animal life for the benefit of the tribe. This is a pure form of sacrifice; the animal honoured by those who cause its death. In such activity is recognised the interrelationship of both kingdoms.

Now the interrelationship has a need to be revived on a higher level of the spiral, not for sacrifice this time, but for higher communication and co-operative purposes. In such rituals, allow space for animal energies to enter your consciousness and to inspire you in thought and deed.

An interesting feature of the new energy from an increased consciousness perspective, is the development of 'character' in individual animals. Before Theos, animals merely aped, for the most part, the characteristics of the humans with whom they came into contact. This is no longer the case.

For thousands of years, humans have developed and wrestled with an entity in their beings known as the ego. This ego has been both the protector and policeman of the personality. This has been a peculiarly human function from which the higher forces and beings have learned much. However those in charge of this 'project' believe that such an entity, as part of the animal consciousness, would not serve the individual or group animal consciousness. Neither would it assist in the development of the communications between the two kingdoms. Furthermore, it would not serve the Earth Mother.

The development of the ego is too slow in these enhanced energetic times. Therefore a different system of individual animal development will be made available. This will exclude the worst excesses of the human experiences with the ego and give greater flexibility for action and social development. It will also inhibit the development of negative karma. This newly developed facility will be tied to intuition. It is important that you don't get too hung up on this material. It is provided for your information and interest. Realise that the work is your meditations, rituals, and your communication with animals. Be aware of contacts both incarnate and discarnate. This is important work that you are playing your part in.

From a higher consciousness point of view humanity can be viewed as one energetic centre of the Earth consciousness. The animal kingdom is another. Thus as humanity and animals, individually and in the mass consciously evolve, this assists in the raising of consciousness of the Earth Mother. The animal consciousness, and that of the vegetable kingdom, is already under way. It is most important that humanity realises its part in this unfolding, and doesn't get left behind.

It will be much more difficult to catch up after 'crossover' for the reasons already mentioned. Reality and opportunity are much more plastic now.

In the recent past there have been books and articles claiming that the human population of the Earth will decline rapidly in the enhanced energy times. We say that there is no certainty that this will happen. Individuals will make the decision to stay or go depending on whether they have completed their mission in this particular lifetime. Alternatively they may find the enhanced energetic conditions too uncomfortable to stay. Where that leaves the ultimate population level no-one knows, not even those with higher awareness.

The recent legislation on hunting was an attempt to influence public opinion initiated by the beings of light. It could also be viewed as an attempt to isolate those that conduct this activity and direct the blood lust. The impact of such isolation would generate a bunker mentality. This is regrettable but also a sign that their battle is lost. This form of perverted consciousness can be squeezed towards extinction. We see it as another pressure acting in tune with your work.

Both dark and light forces work through your legislators in order to further their agendas. You are well aware of this dance of light and dark consciousness. Both ends of the spectrum have their champions in your parliaments, police, civil service and judiciary. 'By their actions ye shall know them.'

The regular 'tuning-in' to the Theos wave will have the benefit of assisting in keeping you balanced within your various bodies, physical, mental, emotional and psychic/spiritual. It is also of general benefit to your health and contains great protective properties. The wave contains all the strength and power of the beings that are responsible for its transmission in other realms.

From our point of view humanity is such a wonderfully talented race. But it is also one of the most frustrating to deal with. Working with you is definitely an art form rather than a science. We are not denigrating you. We honour and respect the work that you are doing. This is also a growth opportunity for us in many sectors of the universe.

We wish to point out that this communication process is a co-operative approach with Clive. His eyes and communication skills are linked to our knowledge.

From Birch's point of view in an altered state, he looks at something or reads something with the mental equipment switched off and a connection to the Theos energies and beings switched on. He is in control. For him, the difference with other forms of creativity is that advice and words to say or write 'pop' into consciousness that would not normally be his form of expression. Sometimes a large amount of information will arrive that he could not possibly have developed alone. The above suggests this to be true.

Enhanced animal consciousness has been addressed elsewhere. 'The Prophets Way' by Thom Hartmann is one such book.

Muller created the Salem Research Institute, hired a bio-chemist and a few other scientists, and compiled a two-inch thick hardcover book published in English. It chronicles tens of thousand of experiments in which human tissue was cultured (in a Petri dish). This method proved more effective (and cheaper) than research using animals. One of the best examples hits home the case with some force. Human tissue sample tests showed that *Thalidomide* had the potential to cause mutations. Studies on rabbits required by the British equivalent of the FDA, showed no such potential risk. So the product went to market as a 'proven, safe cure' for morning sickness, even as some scientists working with human tissues were worrying out loud that it might cause birth defects.

'Animal Speak' by Ted Andrews tells of how early priests, priestesses and magicians would adopt the guise of animals. They wore skins and masks to symbolise a re-awakening of energies within themselves. They performed rituals in accordance with the natural rhythms of the seasons to awaken greater fertility and life. To them every species and every aspect of their environment had the power to remind them of what they could manifest within their own lives. It was an aid to bridge the natural world to the supernatural, awakening the realities of both within the environs of their own lives.

Though these rituals and behaviours may seem primitive, even silly to the rational minds of modern society, they are even more powerful today, and the law which governs the physical and spiritual are no less viable.

The following two quotes are from 'The Sense of Being Stared At' by Rupert Sheldrake.

The sixth sense has already been claimed by biologists working on the electrical and magnetic senses of animals. Some species of eels, for example, generate electrical fields around themselves through which they sense objects in their environment, even in the dark. Sharks and rays detect with astonishing sensitivity the body electricity of potential prey. Various species of migratory fish and birds have a magnetic sense, a biological compass that enables them to respond to the Earth's magnetic field.

There are also a variety of other senses that could lay claim to being a sixth sense, including the heat sensing organs of rattlesnakes and related species, which enable them to focus heat and track down prey by a kind of thermographic technique. And there is the vibration sense of web weaving spiders, through which they can detect what is happening in their web, and even communicate with one another through a kind of vibratory telegraph.

This second quote claims that ... *some horses anticipate their people's arrivals, either when they come to feed them or to visit them in their paddocks, or when they return from absences of weeks or months. In one case this occurred under clinical observation.*

We had a mare and her foal in the intensive care unit at the university of California Veterinary hospital at Davis. One day when we came to visit, the doctor in charge came to us and said, "I have never seen a horse more connected to its owners than yours." He went on to explain that the horse's whole attitude would change about ten minutes before we would walk through the door. The entire staff knew when we were coming by seeing the horse change her attitude. Because the unit was specially isolated, had four inch thick concrete walls, steel doors and heavy padding on the walls, this is not a case of super sensitive hearing. Somehow the horse knew when we were there by a sense that had yet to be explained.

Birch talks of the biologist, Rupert Sheldrake, who has proposed the theory of morphic resonance. This suggests that there are 'fields of understanding' whereby animals, individually and in groups, can pass learned behaviour to other groups of the same species although they are not in physical proximity. Various studies have shown evidence to support this theory. For example, a group of monkeys on an uninhabited island were shown by humans how to wash coconuts in the sea. The whole group learned this behaviour from a lone female monkey. Within weeks, disparate groups of monkeys on another remote island started washing coconuts in the sea despite having no physical contact with others.

The 'fields of understanding' phenomenon works in the same way as the Theos wave energy, although a little slower. Some morphic learned behaviour can take generations to manifest and encompasses a far wider span of the energetic spectrum. It is not related to purely physical learned behaviour, but to the development and utilisation of consciousness in many forms.

Morphic resonance was available to the animal kingdom before the karmic split with humanity, although it will continue to function and is thus evolutionary. Theos energy is revolutionary, creating the conditions where the split could manifest and making available developmental consciousness conditions.

In a newspaper article in the US, a duck was shot by a hunter in Tallahassee, Florida. It was hit in the legs and wing. Assuming it to be dead the hunter put the duck in his fridge, (presumably so it could be cooked and eaten later). Two days later the fridge door was opened and the amazed hunter saw the duck raising his head. This tough bird was subsequently being cared for in an animal sanctuary and had a good chance of survival. This story is included as an example of another admirable quality of one of the members of the animal kingdom. What the world needs now is an enhanced perception of the animal kingdom, to paraphrase the Burt Bacharach song.

Joan received a vision of a pig on a lead. It was a particularly bright and intelligent pig. The other end of the lead was held by a man. However in this situation, it was the pig leading the man. Subsequent to this vision Mary and Joan were led to visit a friend who lived near a pig farm. The animals were kept cooped up and chained; they could hear the chains rattling. The smell was indescribable and they felt the animals were badly housed and treated. The two ladies knew that they had been led there to do some healing for the pigs. They drove close to the farm and left a quartz crystal as a physical sign of their healing.

It was also Joan who saw this amazing scene in the Cotswold Farm Park. A shire horse, the 'boss' of the show, was grooming a highland longhorn cow which was in an adjoining paddock. The latter was clearly enjoying the experience. After a while a donkey in another adjacent paddock wanted to be part of the grooming. When it didn't happen the animal started to bray in a fit of frustrated temper. Could this be an example of the Theos wave/ timeline development of conscious connection between animals across species which they had been working on?

On the other side of the world a flock of seagulls attacked a horse race, causing minor injuries to the jockeys but none to the horses. The race track was also having problems with ibis birds wandering across the course and disrupting races.

So, you may say, "This is all very fine and dandy, Birchy, but what does it have to do with the Theos work?" The above stories outline some of the incredible qualities possessed by our fellow inhabitants of this living planet. The Theos energy will take their abilities much, much further. It's time for us humans to wake up to this, otherwise we will have big shock coming later as the realisation dawns that animals no longer need us and are certainly no longer inferior.

Mary also had a fascinating insight during the meditation with Birch on 7th April 2007 concerning birds. The three, Mary, Joan and Clive, had previously wondered about their role concerning the Theos wave vibration. Mary perceived them in an all-seeing role as they fly above.

She also saw the beat and rhythm of their wings as having a vibrational impact on the Earth, certainly in a psychic sense. The rhythm and movement of this reminded Birch of certain movements conducted in *chi gong* which are working with our energy bodies, physical, mental, emotional and psychic/spiritual as we perform these exercises. So says Birch, this beating of the wings has three purposes. First, the psychic and physical vibrational impact on the energy bodies of Gaia (and on the birds at a physical and non-physical level). Second, it provides an element of blissful play as they swoop and soar in the sky. Third, it's a group activity as they beat their wings in unison communicating their divine intention.

Birch recalls the Chaos Theory which tells of the butterfly in China flapping its wings causing a hurricane in Florida. This is very profound mystically as well as scientifically; a subject for much profound meditation for Birch.

As Birch rested during the night after the meditation, he tuned into the beating of birds' wings and to the Theos energy. As a result he considered himself fortunate to enter an almost blissful state. There was some important connection between the world of birds and the Theos wave. Despite effort, he couldn't quite bring the impression into his conscious awareness.

It was Barbara Marciniak who said that birdsong was a connection between the third dimension reality and higher dimensions. She added that this connection was for our benefit in our movement between the dimensions. Recently Birch feels he has been honoured by a single blackbird which has sung outside Joan's house during meditations. At the end of each meditation, the song ceases. Marciniak also stated that she believes that birds have free rein to move between the dimensions at will. This was the reason for the sudden changes both in growth and decline of bird populations in the third dimension.

Birch tells that those animals living in 'relative' comfort, performing their age old routines without great suffering, are less likely, in the first instance, to make the consciousness shift. Intelligent creatures driven to frustration and desperation by their circumstances, will be more able to move quickly. These latter animals will more quickly break from the group consciousness of the past. This pain and discomfort route will break the mould and offer a fast route to the new consciousness, free of the ego pathways of humanity.

Once in the new consciousness, animals will perceive humanity in a changed light. Their old perception of all powerful gods, abusers, or merely background, will change to one of fellow beings, to be adjusted to.

During a meditation, an elephant presented itself to Birch's consciousness. It was anxious to make its presence felt and did so by demonstrating enormous ears and a very large trunk. It communicated to Birch that the elephant consciousness is already attuned to Theos energy, certainly those in discarnate state. One advantage these animals have is that a large proportion of the population is living in protected environments. Birch refers to game parks which enable them, quietly and without fuss, to develop themselves psychically. Their high intelligence is well known to humans. They will have a strong psychic relationship with receptive humans. One drawback is their relatively small numbers. This being the case, every animal and contact should be highly prized and cherished.

A friend of Birch tells the story of sitting with their mutual friend and co-ordinator of the Temple Study Group, Jacques Rangasamy. It was summer and they were sitting in his garden. A wasp arrived and started buzzing around Jacques who, unconcernedly, ignored it.

"Doesn't it worry you?" the friend asked.

"Not at all," Jacques replied "Wasps feed on fear."

And the stories keep coming. Hazel tells of a crow attacking a pigeon. Two other pigeons attacked the crow, pecking it and driving it off. There was a item reported on TV of a stray dog in Nigeria that found an abandoned baby in the forest. It picked the baby up by its clothes, carried it across a busy road, and deposited it among its pups where it was found by humans. There are other stories throughout history of a similar nature.

Birch doesn't attribute any of the above stories to the impact of Theos wave energy except perhaps, the attack by seagulls on the horse race. He reckons it might be close to the Theos energy, if not influenced by it.

Birch was given an insight into the death of a wild life expert. He was killed in a very rare incident when stung in the centre of the chest by a manta ray which stopped his heart. His death was obviously a great tragedy for his family, friends and a loss to the world of media and those that enjoyed his wildlife programmes. It is not Birch's intention to upset anyone and he doesn't wish to criticise, however there is another aspect to the death of this man. Birch was told by his guidance that the wildlife expert's death was an effect created by the man's acts after his manhandling of wild creatures, for example catching and tying up crocodiles. These events were shown as great televisual events but were terrifying for the creatures involved. Snakes were also caught and played with almost inviting them to strike. That was a key point of these scenes, the prodding and stimulation of these animals so that the viewer was in a state of excitement over the outcome of the contest. The end result was always the upset and frustration in the animal for the sake of entertainment. Eventually nature fought back.

This slant is bound to cause offence to some for this television personality had enthusiastic audiences all over the world. However, this was the message that was received from the spiritual guidance.

Most recently Joan, Mary and Birch created a *timeline*. (See previous chapter for explanation.) They called it Earth+1. In Earth+1 they asked that the DNA of all people connected with animals be healed so that the accumulated baggage be disposed of. It was hoped this would facilitate the clearing of human and animal relationships. Birch saw the *timeline* suffused with the colour blue. Joan sensed the presence of Francis of Assisi. With a prompting from Mary, they called on the guardians of the Theos wave to protect the *timeline*. Birch sensed four horsemen here.

A development in the Theos work occurred when Mary started to channel the presence of beings responsible for differing groups of animals, their intention was to work with us on the project. The first one to make their presence felt was one which looked, to Mary's eyes, much like Yoda in the *Star Wars* films. When she pointed the bizarre similarity out to him he was happy to be viewed as such. He told Mary that he was the contact for elephants and made the point by flapping his 'Yoda' ears. Later it came to Birch that this being was the contact being for other animals that sensed largely with their ears, Giraffe, buffalo, water buffalo also horses had a connection to this being.

He told the little group of three to be very vigilant and very discerning about every aspect of our lives. Every thought has an energetic charge affecting the universe. Birch saw 'Yoda' leading his group of animals along the *timeline*. This connection between this *timeline* and Theos energy would increase self awareness and communication between animals individually and group consciousness.

The next one to arrive in Mary's consciousness was a cat-like being which said, "We are working with cats already. You know how difficult that is, they are such contrary beings?" Birch saw a butterfly with an aura of light around its edges. This was symbolic as Mary felt that there was no responsible being for the insects that could be detected. This was confirmed when Birch received the message from the insect kingdom, "I don't think that we can do this." Birch responded, "We can't leave it there." He felt that the group must try to help insect involvement.

In the past Mary has received healing from a tiny insect that landed on her palm. Despite the miniscule size of the insect she felt the healing energies move all the way up her arm. On a second occasion she picked a beautiful yellow moth from her window sill, held it in her hand and felt healing energy coming from the body of the insect despite the fact that it was dead.

A beaver appeared to Clive in meditation. It represented both that animal and the duckbilled platypus each coming from the same planetary source, he was told.

A calm pale being said "Work with me, this is what you are doing." He held rats and mice in his hands; dead by poisoning. Mary said that poisoning was due to infestation and that they could be moved to other places. The being said that his animals were mainly killed in experiments. Later in another meditation, the being re-appeared holding live animals. He was clearly much happier.

In a later meditation Birch tuned into this being and felt a mutual working of energy, rather than 'one way traffic' which he had perceived to be the case previously. On this occasion the being showed Birch how to mutually work with the Theos energy creating a greater effect then before. In this model in which both contributed, as the Theos energy passed through Birch and on to the being, the latter metamorphosed it through his consciousness. He then returned it to Birch who did likewise so this ball of energy was ever increasing in strength as Theos energy was added to it. This went on for some while. It was the creation of something like a sun which was having energy ever added to it and then thrown off, in this case for the benefit of the animals working with the calm being.

Mary saw the being responsible for domestic animals as a goddess/ shepherdess figure with hair of light. She was a golden colour. Later this being became Brigid; or Saint Brigid to Christians. Donkeys are under the guardianship of Brigid, as are pigs. Later Birch had a deep experience after tuning in to this being/ saint/ goddess. This story is told later in the text.

A primate being very warm and rounded came into consciousness to say, "We are being used and abused in animal experimentation."

When linking with the bird kingdom Birch saw a bird sitting on a branch as a symbol and contact for this group of animals. This bird was hawk like with a curved beak and large owl like eyes. The plumage around the head was black with a purple streak.

This spell of input stopped and the group started to work through the intermediaries presented. Almost immediately another input was added. One morning Birch, in his morning meditation, upon tuning into Brigid; the being for domestic animals, was informed that fields of resonance had been set up for each animal grouping. In this mode when an animal of whatever species reached the stage of individuals consciousness then that individual would be automatically 'plugged in' to the field of resonance appropriate to his group. Each field is a source of enhanced learning and development within which the being responsible is connected as well as those beings that set the fields up in the first place.

It was a significant input to the way that they had been working; it took them out of their comfort zone. They had slipped into a mode of control of the meditation and visualisation rhythm. It brought home that other beings in the cosmos were at the heart of it all. In reality they were responding to their promptings and requests. This was an enhanced way of assisting the Theos energy, by focussing it on those that were ready. It is faster and more effective than the other method of transmission through water, air and then in to the body of the creature.

Beryl Sevior channelled this message from St Francis.

There are many forms of confirmation being given to you all at this time to bring the swifter lifting of the Earth and of everybody in whatever role. Within the skies you might see various cloud formations depicting sacred geometry patterns similar to your crop circles, or patterns made by the birds. The insects will likewise be working upon the Earth creating their symbols and maybe the animals in the fields will at times walk in certain formation to again create designs. You may also observe that some flowers are flowering profusely at various times. This would be to help the people, for colour is also a very good healer and therefore some of the plants will be blossoming at times that you might think unusual. Every single form of life is taking part in this grand finale of earthly life and the moving from one portrayal into the next. Oh is it not of the most exciting?

To complete this section, the media has given many column inches to the story of Oscar. Oscar is a cat in a Rhode Island nursing home, and not an especially friendly cat at that. However, he has a remarkable gift. Shortly before a patient dies he goes to them and curls up close to them on the bed. There he purrs providing a comforting sound. Thus far he has predicted the demise of some 25 patients to each of which he has provided his singular form of comfort.

It is significant that he never enters the rooms of patients unless they are soon to die. It is reported that on one occasion the medical team thought a patient was soon to die. They placed Oscar in the room which he quickly left. Oscar knew best. The patient did not die imminently as expected. However, shortly before the patient died the following day, Oscar had returned and was there on the bed.

One doctor has suggested it might be possible to train a cat to predict death. The same medic also wondered what was in it for the cat.

Birch believes that Oscar came into this world with his senses already attuned to the onset of imminent death. He certainly didn't need a clinician who, despite much scientific training, has minimal sensitivity to the onset of a patient's death, but does possess training and experience of course. Anyone who knows cats will tell you that a person cannot train a cat, cats train people. There is a saying 'Dogs became civilised on man's terms. Cats became civilised on their own terms.' This is another example of an arrogant attitude that humanity is superior in nearly every respect to animals.

The question of what does a cat get out of it would be hard to answer by a scientist who would not have the sense and sensitivity of cat owners and lovers who know the ability, intelligence, sensitivity and psychic ability of these much underrated animals which are beings in their own right. From a mystics point of view Oscar has come into life with a mission to aid the passing of those who may find it difficult to accept the separation of body and soul and the true state of affairs when leaving the physical body as well as the reality that awaits them.

A comment was made about Oscar being an omen with the subtle inference that he could be a bad omen. This is a hangover from the Middle Ages when the prevailing religion in the West was burning so called 'witches' as part of the denigration of the female and the pursuit of power over the populace.

There is no such thing as an omen, good or bad, if you follow the idea that we can create our reality minute by minute. We are not storm tossed beings powerless in the sea of reality, although there are people that would wish us to think like that and not be in our power.

This is a vast subject and ongoing. Birch is anxious to talk to anyone who has evidence of the changes in animal consciousness.

Chi Gong

A powerful Oriental system of fitness and health.

In the early 1990s Birch spent three years learning and working with a form of *tai chi* called *tai chi yang* style. He found the experience enjoyable and fulfilling. It helped his body in as much as his natural movements changed. Gradually it boosted his confidence. He still struggles today to find objective reasons why this should have happened. At the end of the three years, the teacher moved the *tai chi* towards a martial art and away from the purely energetic dance outcomes. This change took all the energy out of the classes and he lost interest. At around this time, life changed for him and he left the class. As time passed, he forgot this form of *tai chi*.

That was the end of oriental movement systems for Birch until his return from the Americas in 1999. He returned with amazing memories, and a widened horizon concerning the world. Rather less positively, he also brought back with him a really bad knee problem. This injury was the result of abusing his body with long distance running years before. It was brought to a head by backpacking a heavy load through the Americas, plus climbing steep pyramid steps.

He returned to work in the UK, however his knee problem continued to deteriorate. Eventually he was limping and in constant pain when walking. An injection and various proddings from doctors caused no improvement. The attitude was one of, "Well you're 56 years old; let's hope that it doesn't get any worse. Come back in six months."

Unfortunately it did get worse; and worse and worse. Refusing to give up he went to a chiropractor where he found some alleviation of the pain. It improved the knee by 50%. At the end of the series of treatments he was told that no more could be done. Birch asked the chiropractor what he should do now.

He was advised to try *tai chi*. His mind flashed back to the practice he had done in years past. His mind also returned to another contact that he'd made a few months before. He had been to Chartres with the Temple Study Group the previous summer. There he'd practiced a little *chi gong* led by another person, Martin Kelly.

As a result of the advice of the chiropractor, Birch rang Kelly. He discovered that Kelly taught *chi gong* as a healing method. Just the thing he needed. They arranged for Birch to visit Kelly for one-to-one classes in his home. At that time Birch had no idea how fortunate he was to be working with this very skilled and wise man. And as if that wasn't enough, he had Kelly's undivided attention.

Birch was encouraged when he discovered Kelly had Oriental students. There were Chinese practitioners in Birch's home town. But the very fact that Orientals had chosen to work with Kelly seemed highly significant to him. They obviously knew something important about Kelly and his teaching.

Kelly interested Birch. He appeared to be in his mid sixties, yet Birch knew him to be around twenty years older than that. He moved with a grace and fluidity difficult to match by people in their thirties. He was a marvellous ambassador for his chosen art. And even better, Birch enjoyed working with him not least for his great sense of humour.

For two and a half years Kelly taught Birch the graceful and healing movements of *chi gong*; an art very similar to *tai chi*. Entering his flat was like entering a temple. The world outside could be shut out temporarily as magic was weaved inside. After each session Birch would resume outer world activity and go to his place of work.

One day, they were working with a routine called 'dragons gate'. This is a series of movements which have the health benefit of building the immune system. At one point, they were in a stance called 'meditation' within the dragons gate routine. Suddenly Kelly's face and body changed in front of Birch. Instead of Kelly there was a strong faced Chinese gentleman; very different from Martin. Gradually the vision faded and they completed the routine.

Afterwards Birch quizzed Kelly. Birch was told that he had just seen one of Kelly's guides and that that part of the routine had the potential for magic. This happened on another occasion at the same point in the routine. So there is magic in *chi gong* as well as healing!

Birch had been working with Kelly for two and a half years as a student, and was perfectly happy to continue with this arrangement. On some occasions he had persuaded Kelly to teach him twice a week as he was learning a form of *tai chi* called *tai chi chuan* as well as the *chi gong*. One day towards the end of the lesson, Kelly stepped back and looked at Birch.

"Time for you to get on with it, now."

The chick was being kicked out of the nest.

Unsure of his next step Birch wondered what he was going to do with all this *chi gong* and *tai chi* knowledge. He was soon to find out.

OK, let's take a break from the story and learn a little more about *chi gong*. There are many uses and explanations. The following are those relevant to Birch. It is the working of energy in order to harness the power of the universe, and make it user friendly for the benefit of humanity. It empowers individuals to heal themselves of illness and self-destructive behaviour. And it allows individuals to take personal responsibility and to amplify personal powers.

In traditional Chinese thought, the three powers of Heaven, Earth, and Humanity represent the total of all the forces within the universe. (Or at least the universe as we know it.) By virtue of the balance and harmony of these powers, we enjoy health and vitality, attain power and longevity, and enhance our awareness.

In today's stressful world *chi gong's* versatility assists us in preventing disease, balancing emotions, and calming the mind. It is a healthcare system, simple to learn and use, can be practised at any part of the day, at home or at work, indoors or outdoors, requires no special equipment, expensive facilities or athletic skill. Simple as it may seem, so potent are the healing powers and benefits of *chi gong* that some of the cures it achieves are discounted as 'miracles' by some critics.

Birch can testify personally to the healing potency. After being dismissed by conventional medical opinion over his knee injury, within two years of working with Kelly his knee was completely healed. If he had left himself in the hands of conventional medicine, Birch would be limping painfully, and perhaps even suffering further deterioration.

One translation of *chi* is 'air' and thus, by extension, denotes energy and vitality. *Gong* can be a general term meaning 'work'. *Chi gong* could be translated as 'energy work'. *Chi* is the basic building block of all matter, the immaterial energy that constitutes all material form. Quantum physics verifies a fact that was evident to ancient Taoist science. The essential nature of atoms and molecules is an array of various energies in particular patterns. *Chi* is the basic energy that comprises all matter and animates all living things. It is the life force of the three levels of human existence; body, energy, and mind, from the molecular level of metabolism and cellular division to organic functions of digestion, excretion, respiration, reproduction and circulation. It is the primary factor responsible for human health, physical and mental; the main gauge of vitality and longevity.

The following extract is from 'Qigong for Health and Martial Arts' by Dr Yang, Jwing-Ming. (Spelling varies!)

According to the experience of Qigong practitioners, Qi can best be explained as a type of energy very much like electricity, which flows through the human or animal body. When this circulation becomes stagnant or stops, the person or animal will become ill or die.

Although there is no precise Western definition of Qi, it is often referred to as bioelectricity. In fact, it was recognised in the last decade that Qi is actually the bioelectricity circulating in all living things.

Qi can also be explained as a medium of sensing or feeling. For example, when a person's arm is hurt, the Qi flow in the nerves of the arm is disturbed and stimulated to a higher energy state. This higher energy state causes a sensational feeling that is interpreted as pain by the brain. In addition, the difference in energy potential causes an increased flow of Qi and blood to that area to begin repairing damage. Therefore Qi, the nervous system, the Qi channels, and the brain are intimately related to each other.

The second concept you should know is that of Qi channels, which circulate Qi throughout the body. For the most part the main Qi channels are found with the arteries and nerves. A glance at any anatomy book shows that large sheaths of nerve fibers accompany the arteries throughout the body. The Qi channels do also. Like arteries and nerves, the Qi channels are protected by the body's musculature, so that they are hard to affect directly...

The third concept you should understand is that of acupuncture points, which are called cavities. Along each of the channels (as well as elsewhere on the body) are points where the electrical conductivity is higher than surrounding areas. These points which are called cavities, because they can often be felt as small depressions or concavities, are more sensitive than other parts of the body. These are the locations used for acupuncture.

Chi Gong blends soft, gentle movements of the body with a calm contemplative state of mind. The energy generated is distributes throughout the body via a network of major and minor channels and meridians which form a complex grid. The grid serves both the circulatory and nervous systems.

There are several points to consider during practice. First, silence the human mind by turning off the internal dialogue. Let the stream of consciousness flow naturally in the background of your mind. Next, set all worries and problems of daily life aside prior to practice. Stay calm throughout practice sessions and finally, enjoy and have fun with the technique. The latter has been one of the most endearing aspects of the techniques. It has helped to make the whole practice such a great pleasure for Birch and many other exponents of the art.

It is important to realise that *chi gong* movements have very little in common with aerobics, body building, strength training or any of the other exercise systems of the West. *Chi gong* is not concerned with building muscle or sculpting the perfect body. The real objective of these powerful techniques is to build mental and physical well being by encouraging the circulation of chi. Traditional Chinese thought says that each person is made up of three essential parts; mind, body and spirit. By performing *chi gong* routines, humans can nourish all three elements at the same time. Practiced properly, these exercises can build self-confidence, boost the immune system, and give a new sense of balance in every day life. The latter is considered very important in Chinese medicine.

Chi gong, as Birch discovered, can help to relieve the symptoms of certain specific conditions. Principles of balance, energy, and self-awareness are born in mind. The roots of *chi gong* lie lost in the mists of time. It has been practiced for at least five thousand years. Early forms developed, it is thought, when men saw that animals did not develop the degenerative diseases to which humans were prone. They started to mimic the movements of animals and lo and behold, improved health resulted. Thus early forms bore the name of animals; the crane and the bear among others. In China and the East there are 200 million practitioners. In hospitals in China there are *chi gong* healing departments, particularly the military hospitals.

Regarding claims for longevity for *chi gong*, the evidence is in stark contrast to the West. The approach and accepted process for the ageing process in the West is that we all go through a slow decline lasting thirty years or more. In this process if we survive at all, there is a gradual increase of infirmity, more and more pain, more reliance on others, mental deterioration until we are mercifully released from our bodies.

This is not the way for the 200 million practitioners of *chi gong*. Evidence suggests that *chi gong* prolongs life while reducing the debilitating effects of aging. Recently a *chi gong* master in China died at age 104. A key factor was not that she had managed to survive degenerative diseases that long, but just as importantly she was working to within weeks of her death. In *chi gong* the degenerative diseases of the West can be avoided with regular practice.

There is gathering scientific evidence that there is a genetic 'cut off' point in humanity. At this point cell reproduction and death will ensue. Birch's view is that those probably variable 'cut off' points are at a greater age than we commonly accept. So with sensible living and regular *chi gong* practice, a ripe old age can become a reality rather than a matter of good fortune.

Birch jokes with those that he has been working with in *chi gong* practice, that they can live creatively to 120 years old, much to the chagrin of their families, perhaps? In all seriousness he doesn't believe this to be merely a joke.

More *chi gong* later but for now, back to the story and chicks being ejected from nests.

Around the same time that Birch was having the conversation with Kelly, one of his friends who was learning *tai chi chaun*, asked him to help her with some of the form with which she was having difficulty. He was able to help her and here opened another chapter in his dance with *chi gong*. He realised that he had the skill and the teaching ability to pass the art onto others. After all, he had benefited first hand from the potency. He did a little advertising to test the water. He realised that there was no point in offering *chi gong* teaching in the same way as Kelly and others. What was the point of learning such techniques with him, an inexperienced teacher, when people could go to more experienced and able instructors? He decided that one area that wasn't being covered locally was that of a teacher going out to the community and into people's homes.

So it was that a new chapter in the Birch story began. One of his first students was a mature lady whom he taught in her home. She was a feisty lady, great character, great fun, who had previously done yoga and was open to 'alternative' movement systems. The other students were a young 19 years old couple who he taught in the home of the girl's parents. He had blue, punk style hair and she had pins and metal studs all over her face; not the most obvious candidates for such an alternative activity, but they were also open and enthusiastic students. All three were great students for someone starting to teach.

So there he was, now a teacher. He had taken the plunge, given up his full time job, and taken three day week employment to give himself time to develop *chi gong* teaching. Having dipped his toe in the water he found himself enjoying the teaching. Seeing the enthusiasm of his first three students he went another step and started an evening class in a local hall. It struggled for numbers at first but kept going, and was still going two years later. But further expansion proved difficult. He had his three students and one small class, and that might have been how it remained, had it not been for a series of events which changed the whole rhythm of his teaching.

One morning at breakfast he opened the local newspaper to find Kelly's familiar face staring back at him. Kelly was in a classic *chi gong* stance. Next to the photo was an article which wrote of Kelly and the benefits of *chi gong* for health and fitness interesting stuff. At the bottom of the article was the name and telephone number of a woman who was starting some classes in *chi gong*. She was looking for tutors to lead these classes. Birch called, left his details, put the phone down and forgot it. There was silence. As weeks passed into months Birch continued with his three little classes and part time work.

One morning the phone rang. On the other end of the line was Barbara Piranti, the person who had been looking for tutors in the long forgotten article. She offered him two classes of six weeks duration. The students were to be mature with classes in rural areas. He gladly accepted. Barbara was an employee of an organisation called Gloucestershire Rural Community Council; a charity which promoted activities in rural areas.

Barbara was a real live wire and fortunately for the beneficiaries of *chi gong* classes, had become committed to the idea of providing these classes for people that couldn't get into the larger towns in the area. They might have had difficulties with communication, be infirm, or both. She had seen the benefits of *chi gong* through her mother who was a student of Kelly's. Barbara had the vision of spreading these techniques, giving the benefit to those who would not ordinarily have had the opportunities to experience these health giving techniques.

So he started the classes. The six week sessions turned into permanent, on-going classes as students became hooked on the health benefits. The other two tutors who had taken up Barbara's call dropped out for different reasons. More work came Birch's way. Suddenly he was working full-time as the work rolled in. He dropped his part time employment.

He was being pushed to be more creative with the techniques as many of the students either couldn't stand at all, or could only stand for limited periods. This creative element developed into a major feature of his work. He was teaching between eight and ten classes each week, so the energies of *chi gong* and the creativity necessary carried him along on a wave. The only element that tired him during this period was the large amount of driving between the classes. They were rural and distributed throughout the county of Gloucestershire.

One day the manager of the Elderly Persons Centre, one of the class venues, told Birch that there would be a visit from the president of the centre during one of their regular classes.

"Fine," said Birch. "The president can join us in the class."

"Oh no, that would not be appropriate in this circumstance," replied the manager.

Normally he encouraged bystanders to join in. The movements are quite simple in many cases, and are much better done rather than watched.

The day of the visit arrived and there they were doing their thing; fourteen mature ladies and gentlemen. As the class progressed a man entered the room, hard faced and intense. He looked around and disappeared. Birch thought he looked like a secret policeman. Within a couple of minutes of 'hard face' disappearing, an entourage swept into the room. At the head was an elegantly dressed woman. Birch recognised her; he'd seen her on TV. It was one of the Royal Family. So that was what all the fuss was about, and that was the president!

Following on behind was the manager, someone whom he presumed to be a lady-in-waiting, 'hard face', and various other people he didn't recognise. The manager signalled Birch to stop talking and they waited briefly while HRH, followed by her entourage, moved to the opening in the circle of chairs. Birch assumed there would then be a short conversation with each of the students. Now this group comprised people of character, aged though many of them were. The majority were well over 80, and some approached 100. Being impressed by things around them or being overawed by a VIP, was clearly not part of their agenda on the day. HRH moved into the circle, the group stared back as though to say "go on then, impress us."

HRH stopped at the first man; Ronald.

She bowed her head slightly and said in gracious tones, "Do you like the *tai chi*?" Ronald was a somewhat irascible character. As a much younger man he had been head of the Trustee Savings Bank. He had been a man of some clout in the business world. He looked back at her, eyeball to eyeball.

"No I hate it, it's horrible!"

At this point there was a slight pause and silence. Perhaps a little twitching from management ranks in the entourage. Birch felt calm. He knew the group to be very self-determined. Switching off hearing aids or stomping out if they didn't like what he was teaching was par for the course. HRH maintaining calmness and dignity, moved around the group speaking to each person in turn. Birch was impressed with her as a person. He is not a royalist. He believes it is past its sell by date, and long ago should have been consigned to the history in which it is steeped. However this person was fine and treated each person with the respect each deserved. Whether the members of the group were going to treat her with the same respect, well, that was still open to debate.

Halfway around the circle HRH stopped at a woman who had attended all the classes. She always did the exercises, never missing one. There was the graceful bow as the standing president spoke.

"Have you been doing the *tai chi* long?"

"I have never done it before in my life," came back the reply.

Birch makes no claim that this was deliberate, but he did get the impression that the group was now starting to enjoy itself. The bizarre procession went on. Unfortunately he couldn't hear anything else that was said. However he could see that the centre manager had developed a slight tick in one cheek.

Finally the head of the entourage reached Birch's chair. He was asked if he did this class as a charitable act.

"Certainly not. This is my livelihood." One wonders if Birch had a smile on his face at this point. With that HRH and the entourage swept back out of the door.

The group and teacher sat quietly for a minute or so. Then Ethel, who was 102 and as deaf as a post, but still living on her own spoke.

"Wasn't it nice for her to visit the poor old folks?" It was impossible for her to keep the glint out of her eye and the slight smile on her face as she arose from her chair, grabbed her walking stick and walked away to a well earned lunch.

This is another Ethel story. At the end of one class Birch was standing in front of her. Suddenly she looked him up and down and said, "Mmmm... You are nice and slim aren't you?" At this, the rest of the class collapsed with laughter. 102 years old and still the sap is rising!

So *chi gong* was his employment and source of living for three years until one day his intuition whispered to him. It was time to release the teaching and create space for something else to enter his life. He was even given an end point to continue running the classes. That time came and he felt comfortable to gradually run the classes down, handing over to other teachers those groups that wished to continue. Other things started to present themselves for his attention and action. Perhaps the time will come when it will be right to publish them. We shall see.

Before we move on, there are two more stories worth mentioning, and then a simple exercise. It is interesting that *chi gong*, the alleged root of all *tai chi* and martial art systems, came to the West and has started to make its presence felt here. It is really only in the past decade that it has become, and is still becoming, popular. Bruce Frantzis, an American who lived in the East for twenty years, became a lineage master after working with the previous lineage holder in China and tells the following story.

Prior to the end of the Chinese Civil War in 1949, most of the knowledge concerning *chi gong* was held in secret by certain families in China. In this way they could maintain their power and authority, particularly healing power, over others. At the end of the Civil War when the communists came to power, the health system in the country collapsed. Many doctors and nurses were dead, hospitals had been destroyed. Mao Tse Tung, the new leader of China, went to the families who held the *chi gong* knowledge and asked them to release it for the benefit of the masses. The families refused. Mao then went back to the families with an ultimatum.

"Unless you release the knowledge that you hold concerning the healing properties of *chi gong*, I will kill everyone in your family, men, women, children, relatives near and far; everyone."

The families caved in and the knowledge was released; so much so that *chi gong* departments were started in the hospitals. Some Chinese emigrated to the West, particularly USA, where techniques were taught and of particular significance for Birch, books were written. This literature enabled him to supplement the knowledge gained from Kelly and to develop his own, specialist programmes.

Lineage was mentioned above. This was the system by which the knowledge had been passed down through generations. As we have seen it was not until the revolution of 1949 that *chi gong* was accessible to others. The émigrés and the new freedom to communicate these systems ensured that this ancient and powerful knowledge would find its way into other Western countries.

There is a warning from Birch however. Teachers should exercise care when passing techniques to students. The processes are so strong that it is possible to unbalance the unwary and insufficiently untutored. So there is a place still for lineage, perhaps in a more flexible and responsive way to the needs of students.

For those who wish to explore *chi gong* further, Birch advises first to learn with a respected and experienced teacher with whom the potential student feels comfortable. Take it slowly.

Two of his students were talking with another *chi gong* teacher, telling her that they were working with Birch. This other teacher snorted with a certain amount of indignation, waving her hand dismissively and saying, "Oh, he's of a different lineage."

Well, yes, he certainly is. This is his lineage, developed from the skill and knowledge of Kelly and others, and has a life span of all of seven years. In these enhanced, energetic times, time span is not fundamental. Neither is the secrecy of the past. Now is the time for this ancient and powerful knowledge to be used by all who wish to benefit from it.

And now, a final story. Mel Robson was a martial arts expert and bodybuilder. He was diagnosed with cancer in 1984, and given just weeks to live. He found *chi gong* and slowed the disease down so much so that he was still alive in 1990, leading a creative life teaching *chi gong* techniques. He felt the need to share his *chi gong* knowledge with others and as an almost final creative act, produced a video of 'the eighteen', a very powerful *chi gong* healing routine. Shortly after finishing the video, he died. He had given his last gift and had completed his mission. His video is one of Birch's most treasured. When he watches it he sees triumph of the human spirit. If there is anyone that he would dedicate this book to, it would be him. So it is that I am glad to defer to Clive's wishes. This book is so dedicated.

The following is a simple exercise; it is the stance that Birch teaches first to all his students who are able to stand. It was also the first exercise he was taught.

THE STANCE Stand with feet shoulder width apart, feet pointing straight forward, knees relaxed and slightly bent, shoulders, arms and hands relaxed, back straight, tailbone tucked in, head up, eyes looking forward, gaze relaxed.

This is an energetic posture in its own right despite the appearance that nothing is happening. Energy will flow around the body. The weight of the body will drop through the body to the floor through the feet, relieving pressure on shoulders and lower back.

At first your thighs, knees, ankles and feet will ache. This is because they are not strong enough. Continue with the exercises slowly building up the time that you can stand in this position. This will greatly improve posture and lower body strength.

So, whenever you have a couple of minutes, drop into the stance and relax. You might be in the supermarket queue, waiting for a bus or train, or simply waiting. Gradually over time, if this is done regularly, muscles and joints will get stronger. Stamina will improve.

In the West we stand, sit and move within the 'flight or fright reflex'. Stress seems to have taken over our bodies. Standing with tight shoulders and hips up straight puts great pressure on lower backs and shoulders. When we get a little older we start to have shoulder and lower back problems. The 200 million adherents that practice the stance do not get bad backs or shoulders, at least not from the way that they stand.

So if you see anyone standing in an odd way, but looking totally relaxed, you know where they got it from.

Denouement

As scientists tell us, all material manifestation is vibration. From a mystic's point of view the difference between energy bodies in humans, (physical, mental, emotional and psychic/spiritual,) is the rate of vibration. The higher the rate of vibration, the more difficult it is to be aware of it. Thus all reality outside of our awareness is unobserved because of its rate of vibration.

There is no point in predicting future events. All humans are creative beings living in a free will universe, creating their future, moment by moment. All are involved with creating their futures.

There are sensitive souls who can predict trends rather than concrete futures. Even these sensitives only perceive a part of the future. The good ones are like gold dust. Check them out. Don't take the word of people who make claims. We can all be fooled. There are at least as many charlatans as genuine examples.

The whole potential panoply is so vast it is impossible for our third dimensional consciousness to perceive more than a small segment. It is important to be as positively focussed as we can. In this way, we can create a better future for ourselves and contribute to the futures of those around us.

If Birch feels he has an intuitive insight for a possible future, then he follows it with as much courage as he can muster. It was a series of these insights that took him to the U.S.A, Mexico and other countries. He allows his 'higher self' or 'higher consciousness' or 'soul consciousness', whatever we might call it, to guide him in these matters. It is thus important, in Birch's view, to be discerning in the messages received.

If humanity, singly or in the mass, can transcend perceived weaknesses and traits of character, there are hidden sets of laws or universal governing factors to which we are subject. For in his present understanding, everything within mankind's understanding is subject to universal law. Free will functions within that framework. We move from one set of laws to other higher forms as our understanding unfolds. Coupled with this is the idea that we are learning nothing in this lifetime, but merely tearing aside the veils of our forgetfulness to access the truths that we already know at a deeper level of consciousness.

Gradually Birch has realised that those possessing abilities in the psychic and spiritual realms, does not necessarily mean that they were not balanced in other fields of their being. By that he means physical, mental or psychological balance.

In short then, sectors of society consider those with claimed psychic abilities are crazy. They suggest that there can be no place for those with psychic abilities in the conventional Western world. This is not so in Birch's view.

There is no luck, good or bad, and no chance happenings in this life. Equally there are no victims of cruel or beneficial fate. We come into this life with a 'menu' of opportunities and experiences we have chosen to explore. We are free to choose either to explore them, or not, in this lifetime. We take our pick.

Is Birch content? The answer is an empathic 'Yes!' Is he happy with his life? Again we hear the cry, 'Yes!' He is not a recipient of one of the 31 million prescriptions handed out by doctors for depression in 2006 in England. His life sustains and fulfils him. He aims to pay attention to the lessons and gifts that he has received along the way.

Well, do you believe he's mad, deluded or egocentric? We are left to make up our own minds. For Birch, his reality makes perfect sense. With years of work on the different elements of his being, he feels great; physically well, psychologically and creatively well. Looking at him now, he looks nowhere even close to his 64 years. It puts me to shame. (Or at least makes me feel I'm missing out on something.)

He looks around at the stress, chaos, anger, unhappiness, war and discord and ponders that maybe the 'lunatics' should have more say in the running of the 'asylum'. By that he means that the old paradigm of material being, has totally failed. There are alternative ways of developing as people and as a society.

We each have our truths and beliefs. Remember the admonition over the lintels of the entrances to the monasteries of Tibet prior to the Chinese invasion, 'A thousand monks, a thousand religions'. For him this is a central truth. Even those adhering to a particular faith have their personal vision of it. Followers of mystical paradigms have for too long kept their truths to themselves. They have too often held the same view as the cynical ones of education; that the process of speaking their truth would be akin to 'casting imaginary pearls before real swine.'

This is not his view, but it is for each of us to make up our own minds.

Finally, it is not necessary to study spiritual matters in order to enhance our souls. Everything is already known to us. It is simply a matter of removing the curtains that be-fog our memories and our soul memories.

The penultimate words come from John Wesley (1703-1791).

Do all the good you can,
    by all the means that you can

In all the ways you can,
    in all the places you can

At all the times you can,
    to all the people you can

As long as ever you can.

And finally, finally Mark Twain

Twenty years from now you will be more disappointed by the things you didn't do. So throw off the bowlines. Sail away from the safe harbour. Catch the trade winds in your sails. Explore. Dream. Discover.

Enjoy the ride. That is why you are here!

www.ingramcontent.com/pod-product-compliance
Lightning Source LLC
LaVergne TN
LVHW011323080426
835513LV00006B/172